When I consider the greatest minds and hearts that have impacted my life and learning, Reuven Feuerstein's genius and caring stand out above all others.

—Jim Bellanca, executive director,
Illinois Consortium for 21st Century Skills

I have been unabashedly dedicated to Reuven Feuerstein for his impact on transforming the learning trajectory of students of color. His ability to revitalize their intellectual capacity was seemingly miraculous. He has provided us with his tools, not only for their benefit, but also for the benefit their potential can provide to our society.

—Yvette Jackson, CEO, National Urban Alliance

Professor Reuven Feuerstein was an extraordinary architect of the intellect. My personal memory of him is of this smallish man, leaning slightly forward, with shocking white hair framing an ever-present black beret and always with a sparkle in his eyes. In his work, Feuerstein is a giant in his field of cognitive science. His passion for life and learning is legend. Feuerstein's Theory of Cognitive Modifiability changed the intellectual landscape forever, as others replicated his belief and understanding of a changing brain, rather than a static one. I realize Professor Feuerstein is a figure from my professional past I shall never forget. I know he changed my teaching forever.

—Robin Fogarty, Fogarty and Associates

Reuven Feuerstein was one of a handful of thinkers and practitioners in the 20th century who made a significant, lasting contribution to our understanding of human learning and human potential. Educators, parents, and others involved with human development will continue to draw on his path-breaking body of work.

—Howard Gardner,
Hobbs Professor of Cognition and Education,
Harvard Graduate School of Education

Reuven Feuerstein was a great man who fought to give every human being the chance to learn to their greatest potential even when they were considered to be unteachable. His methods of teaching and learning have made a most powerful and impactful contribution to the fields of education and psychology.

—Kathleen J. Bellanca, CEO,
International Renewal Institute

I first encountered Feuerstein's notion of dynamic assessment in collegial conversations with Ann Brown and Joe Campione at the Center for the Study of Reading in the late 1970s. The idea resonated with me immediately—so simple and yet so revolutionary! The assessment question is not, How well can you do X? *but instead,* Under what conditions of scaffolding can you do X well? *It means that responsibility for doing well is always shared by the individual and community in which learning occurs. That's powerful!*

—P. David Pearson, professor,
Graduate School of Education,
University of California, Berkeley

Reuven Feuerstein is one of the great pioneers in the application of an understanding of the modifiability of the brain to improving learning. Rather than bow to the dictates of orthodoxy, he grasped what was possible, and helped teachers help students to achieve it. One can never summarize the work of an individual whose passion and dedication has impacted so many lives.

—Renate and Geoffrey Caine, Caine Learning

Reuven Feuerstein's work, over many years, was groundbreaking, with important implications for educators both in the United States and around the globe. He helped us understand the development of children's thinking and their acquisition of cognitive structures.

—Charlotte Danielson, The Danielson Group

Changing Minds and Brains— The Legacy of Reuven Feuerstein

Higher Thinking and Cognition Through Mediated Learning

Reuven Feuerstein
Louis H. Falik
Refael S. Feuerstein

additional contribution by
Shmuel Feuerstein

foreword by
H. Carl Haywood

TEACHERS COLLEGE PRESS

Teachers College
Columbia University
New York and London

Published by Teachers College Press, 1234 Amsterdam Avenue, New York, NY 10027

Library of Congress Cataloging-in-Publication Data can be obtained at www.loc.gov

ISBN 978-0-8077-5620-1 (paperback)
ISBN 978-0-8077-5621-8 (hardcover)
ISBN 978-0-8077-7353-6 (ebook)

Printed on acid-free paper
Manufactured in the United States of America

22 21 20 19 18 17 16 15   8 7 6 5 4 3 2 1

This book is dedicated to
Rav Aharon and Batia Feuerstein z"l

Parents of Professor Reuven Feuerstein

of blessed memory

"Hear, my son, the instruction of your father and don't forsake the teaching of your mother" (Mishlei 1:8).

It is through their transmission to their children of the Jewish tradition between the two world wars in Botosani, Romania, and the creation of a warm and strong family, in those hard times. Mediated learning experience was generated, experienced, and flourished in their home. .

Reuven Feuerstein was deeply influenced by these multiple influences, and enabled to bring their values and meaning to millions of people in the world who need them. It was for him a source of constant reflection and attribution.

This book reflects as much their legacy as it does his!

Contents

Foreword

The contributions of Reuven Feuerstein to the field of cognitive development, cognitive assessment, and education are many and important. Although somewhat varied within these general domains, they have been focused primarily on one central theme: *mediated learning*.[1] His two major applied programs, now referred to as the *Feuerstein Instrumental Enrichment* (FIE or just IE) programs (Feuerstein, Rand, Hoffman, & Miller, 1980; Feuerstein, Rand, Falik, & Feuerstein, 2006) and the *Learning Propensity Assessment Device* (LPAD) (Feuerstein, Feuerstein, Falik, & Rand, 2002; Feuerstein, Rand, & Hoffman, 1979), are in use in many countries, across cultures, languages, ages, and settings. The conceptual scheme that underlies, enriches, and embraces these applications, *Structural Cognitive Modifiability*, reaches beyond FIE and LPAD to extend intellectual lines of supply to cognitive and educational habilitation and rehabilitation with culturally different and culturally deprived children, youth, and adults; persons who have suffered both traumatic and endogenous encephalopathy; young adults of poor educational attainment who seek military service, further education, and employment; persons with psychiatric disorders; displaced families; chronically unemployed adults; and especially children and youth with intellectual and developmental disabilities. LPAD and IE are now important diagnostic and therapeutic instruments in the hands of educators, special educators, psychologists, speech and language therapists, social workers, psychotherapists, caretakers of persons with disabilities, and many others. In spite of their popularity and widespread application, these programs do not constitute Feuerstein's principal legacy. Each of them will undergo revision, updating, cultural adjustment, and even improvement at the hands of his many students and followers—which is exactly as it should be. He has, however, left an enduring gift: the concept and practice of mediated learning.

Both L. S. Vygotsky (c.f., Karpov, 2005; Vygotsky, 1978, 1986) and André Rey (1934; Haywood, 2012) recognized that standardized psychological tests often miss important aspects of the abilities, especially the learning aptitudes, of the persons who are tested. Both observed that the collaboration and intervention of an adult or other more cognitively competent person led to the uncovering of hidden abilities, abilities that had been masked by individual differences in prior learning opportunities and challenges. Neither Vygotsky nor Rey actually specified, in any detail, the nature of the interaction between test-givers and test-takers that could facilitate such unmasking of abilities. Vygotsky focused on a didactic method in which he presented models to the test-takers (and learners) and guided them to apply the models for new learning (Karpov, 2005, in press; Karpov & Haywood, 1998). Rey focused on error curves and the nature of the learning process rather than on the nature of the interaction that promoted learning (Haywood, 2012; Rey, 1934). Jean Piaget had been one of Feuerstein's professors at the University of Geneva (as had Rey), but Piaget was far more interested in describing what he considered to be the typical course of cognitive development than in any kind of intervention designed to alter that course. It was the landmark paper by Reuven Feuerstein and Ya'acov Rand (1974) that called attention to the critical nature of the learner–adult interaction. That paper launched 40 years (and counting) of elaboration of the concept of mediated learning (Feuerstein, 1977) as well as research on the nature, practices, effects, and correlates of mediated learning in action (see, e.g., Klein, 1991, 1992; Tzuriel, 2001, 2013; Tzuriel & Shamir, 2010). Feuerstein's ideas of mediated learning have been detailed and conceptually integrated into his framework of structural cognitive modifiability. Those concepts form the core of the "mediational teaching style" (Feuerstein & Hoffman, 1990; Feuerstein & Feuerstein, 1991; Feuerstein, Mintzker, Feuerstein, Ben Shachar, Cohen, & Rathner, 2001; Feuerstein, Rand, Jensen, Tzuriel, & Hoffman, 1986; Haywood, 1987/1993) that constitutes the "how to do it" component of *Instrumental Enrichment* as well as of some conceptually related programs of cognitive education. Programs in which a mediational teaching style is a principal component include *Instrumental Enrichment* (Feuerstein et al., 1980, 2006), *MindLadder* (Jensen, 2000; Jensen & Jensen, 1996), *Bright Start* (Haywood, Brooks, & Burns, 1992), *Cognitive Enrichment Advantage* (Greenberg, 2000a, 2000b), *Peer Mediation with Young Children* (Tzuriel & Shamir, 2007, 2010), and *Mediational Intervention for Sensitizing Caregivers* (Klein, 1996, 2003).

   Although the central aspect of this book is the work of Professor Feuerstein, the book also contains original chapters by colleagues, collaborators, family members, and students of Feuerstein. Those chapters emphasize the breadth of the concepts and applications that are derivative of the notion of mediated learning experience. The highly personal approach to the recording of history, especially the elusive history of thought that is exemplified in this work, has been chosen deliberately to reveal the evolution of Feuerstein's thinking about mediated learning. It would be fair to say that his thinking on that subject, as on so many others, was divergent indeed. Many years ago I was privileged to attend a lecture given by Feuerstein in Washington, DC. Although I was by that time well acquainted with both Feuerstein himself and his earlier elaboration of the concept of mediated learning, I was astonished to hear him lecturing about visits by children to museums and libraries as opportunities to promote learning by way of mediation. As the lecture unfolded, this application seemed more and more natural and logical. Every exposure to the concept of mediated learning experience (MLE) seemed to reveal new applications and new dimensions. That process continued throughout Feuerstein's life. In Chapter 3, "Applications of Mediated Learning Experience," readers get a sample of the ways in which MLE has been applied by Feuerstein himself, examples drawn from his personal experience. The only surprise is that the subject of MLE applications could actually be treated in a single chapter!

Much of Feuerstein's professional life was spent working with children and youth who were culturally different or culturally deprived—in Feuerstein's own terms. These clinical experiences led him to focus on the developmental consequences of sociocultural disadvantage and atypical development, which in turn promoted an emphasis on "deficient cognitive functions" as well as on the various life circumstances that could—and often do—result in cognitive deficiencies. Thus, Feuerstein's concepts have both developmental and social-historical components, and these are reflected throughout the book, often in ways that reveal the interdependence of those dimensions.

For at least the last quarter century of his life, Feuerstein was increasingly interested in the neurophysiological bases (or at least correlates) of cognitive and affective life. His efforts to relate structural cognitive modifiability and mediated learning to observable nervous system activity are also reported in this book. They constitute a basis for much discussion, research, and elaboration.

The obvious goal of mediated learning is change, primarily change in the ways in which individuals approach learning and problem-solving situations. It is, therefore, reasonable to expect some discussion of what changes and how the change process takes place within the framework of mediated learning. That expectation has not been neglected; rather, it is thoroughly explored in Chapter 4, "Mediated Learning Experience and the Nature of Change," and in Chapter 7, "How Mediated Learning Experience Produces Structural Cognitive Modifiability."

Theorists and other thinkers usually hope that their work will help change the world for the better, and sometimes it does, as Feuerstein's work has done. Of greater importance is the effect of new concepts and theories on the cumulative scientific and intellectual enterprise. Thus, one is successful as a thinker to the extent that others who follow will continue and extend one's concepts through research and application. That goal is certainly being reached by thinkers and researchers who have continued to explore Feuerstein's work. One can be sure that the future will bring many more such explorations and that Reuven Feuerstein's concepts will continue to enrich cognitive developmental thinking and research and bring a richer, fuller cognitive development to children, youth, and adults around the world.

—H. Carl Haywood, Vanderbilt University

NOTE

1. Feuerstein typically used the term *mediated learning experience*. Inclusion of *experience* originally was intended to emphasize the developmental aspect of his concepts: The experience of mediated learning was seen as a necessary condition for adequate cognitive development. I use the more general term *mediated learning* here to refer to any adult–child interaction that meets Feuerstein's criteria for mediational interactions.

REFERENCES

Feuerstein, R. (1977). Mediated learning experience (MLE): A theoretical basis for cognitive modifiability during adolescence. In P. Mittler (Ed.), *Research to practice in mental retardation: Vol. 2, education and training*. Baltimore, MD: University Park Press.

Feuerstein, R., Feuerstein, R. S., Falik, L., & Rand, Y. (2002). *The dynamic assessment of cognitive modifiability: The Learning Propensity Assessment Device: Theory, instruments, and techniques*. Jerusalem, Israel: ICELP Press.

Feuerstein, R., & Feuerstein. S. (1991). Mediated learning experience: A theoretical review. In R. Feuerstein, P. Klein, & A. Tannenbaum (Eds.), *Mediated learning experience: Theoretical, psychosocial, and learning implications*. Tel Aviv, Israel, and London, England: Freund.

Feuerstein, R., & Hoffman, M. B. (1990). Mediating cognitive processes to the retarded performer: Rationale, goals and nature of intervention. In M. Schwebel,

C. Maher, & N. Fagley (Eds.), *Promoting cognitive growth over the life span* (pp. 115–136). Hillsdale, NJ: Erlbaum.

Feuerstein, R., Mintzker, Y., Feuerstein, R. S., Ben Shachar, N., Cohen, M., & Rathner, A. (2001). *Mediated learning experience: Guidelines for parents.* Jerusalem, Israel: ICELP Press.

Feuerstein, R., & Rand, Y. (1974). Mediated learning experiences: An outline of the proximal etiology for differential development of cognitive functions. *Journal of International Council of Psychology, 9/10*, 7–37.

Feuerstein, R., Rand, Y., Falik, L., & Feuerstein, R. S. (2006). *Creating and enhancing cognitive modifiability: The Feuerstein Instrumental Enrichment program.* Jerusalem, Israel: ICELP Press.

Feuerstein, Rand, Y., & Hoffman, M. B. (1979).*The dynamic assessment of retarded performers. The Learning Potential Assessment Device: Theory, instruments, and techniques.* Glenview, IL: Scott Foresman & Co.

Feuerstein, R., Rand, Y., Hoffman, M. B., & Miller, R. (1980). *Instrumental Enrichment.* Baltimore, MD: University Park Press.

Feuerstein, R., Rand, Y., Jensen, M., Tzuriel, D., & Hoffman, M. B. (1986). Learning to learn: Mediated learning experience and Instrumental Enrichment. *Special Services in the Schools, 3*, 49–82.

Greenberg, K. H. (2000a). *Cognitive Enrichment Advantage teacher handbook.* Arlington Heights, IL: IRI/Skylight Training and Publishing, Inc.

Greenberg, K. H. (2000b). Attending to hidden needs: The Cognitive Enrichment Advantage perspective. *Educational and Child Psychology: Psychological Influences upon Educational Intervention, 17* (3), 51–69.

Haywood, H. C. (1987). A mediational teaching style. *The Thinking Teacher, 4*(1), 1–6. Subsequently published in *International Journal of Cognitive Education and Mediated Learning, 1993, 3* (1), 27–38.

Haywood, H. C. (2012). French-to-English translation of Rey, A. (1934). Un procédé pour évaluer l'éducabilité: Quelques applications en psychopathologie. (*Archives de Psychologie, XXIV, 96*). *Journal of Cognitive Education and Psychology, 11*, 274–300.

Haywood, H. C., Brooks, P. H., & Burns, M. S. (1992). *Bright start: Cognitive curriculum for young children.* Watertown, MA: Charlesbridge Publishers.

Jensen, M. L., & Jensen, M. R. (1996). *The MindLadder parent-as-mediator parent education program.* Roswell, GA: Cognitive Education Systems.

Jensen, M. R. (2000). The MindLadder model: Using dynamic assessment to help students learn how to assemble and use knowledge. In C. S. Lidz & J. G. Elliott (Eds.), *Dynamic assessment: Prevailing models and applications* (pp. 187–227). London, England: JAI/Elsevier.

Karpov, Y. V. (2005). *The neo-Vygotskian approach to child development*. New York, NY: Cambridge University Press.

Karpov, Y. V. (in press). *Vygotsky for educators*. New York, NY: Cambridge University Press.

Karpov, Y. V., & Haywood, H. C. (1998). Two ways to elaborate Vygotsky's concept of mediation: Implications for education. *American Psychologist, 53* (1), 27–36.

Klein, P. (1991). Improving the quality of parental interaction with very low birth weight children: A longitudinal study using a mediated learning experience model. *Infant Mental Health Journal, 12,* 321–327.

Klein, P. S. (1992). Assessing cognitive modifiability of infants and toddlers: Observations based on mediated learning experience. In H. C. Haywood & D. Tzuriel (Eds.), *Interactive assessment* (pp. 233–250). New York, NY: Springer.

Klein, P. S. (1996). *Early intervention: Cross-cultural implications of a mediational approach*. New York, NY: Garland Publishing.

Klein, P. S. (2003). A mediational approach to early intervention in Israel: Mediational Intervention for Sensitizing Caregivers (MISC) of typically developing and hard to reach children. In S. Odom, M. Hanson, & J. Blackman (Eds.), *International perspectives on early intervention* (pp. 69–90). Baltimore, MD: Brookes.

Rey, A. (1934). Un procédé pour évaluer l'éducabilité: Quelques applications en psychopathologie [A method for assessing educability: Some applications in psychopathology]. *Archives de Psychologie, XXIV*, 96.

Tzuriel, D. (2001). *Dynamic assessment of young children*. New York, NY: Kluwer/ Plenum Press.

Tzuriel, D. (2013). Mediated learning experience and cognitive modifiability. *Journal of Cognitive Education and Psychology, 12* (1), 59–80.

Tzuriel, D., & Shamir, A. (2007). The effects of Peer Mediation with Young Children (PMYC) on children's cognitive modifiability. *British Journal of Educational Psychology, 77,* 143–165.

Tzuriel, D., & Shamir, A. (2010). Mediation strategies and cognitive modifiability in young children as a function of Peer Mediation with Young Children program and training in analogies versus math tasks. *Journal of Cognitive Education and Psychology, 9* (1), 48–72.

Vygotsky, L. S. (1978). *Mind in society: The development of higher psychological processes*. M. Cole, V. John-Steiner, S. Scribner, & E. Souberman (Eds.). Cambridge, MA: Harvard University Press.

Vygotsky, L. S. (1986). *Thought and language*. Cambridge, MA: MIT Press. (Original work published 1934)

Prologue

Much of what we have learned about mediated learning experience (MLE) and the potential for cognitive modifiability has come to us through our working with children and adults. The relationship is reciprocal . . . as we help them, we constantly learn about and adapt our theories and techniques. Here, we offer two somewhat contrasting experiences of mediated learning with children, families, and students that will frame our discussion and reflections in this book—one from the classroom and one from our clinical experience.

MEDIATED LEARNING EXPERIENCE IN THE CLASSROOM

Students in the 4th grade of an inner-city American school district were learning *Instrumental Enrichment* (IE) as part of their curriculum. The program brings mediated learning experience into the developing and strengthening of cognitive functions. These were students from minority groups and low-income families. They were students who were functioning below their expected grade placements, and for whom the general society does not hold out much hope with respect to advanced educational achievement. This was the reason why the school district had brought *Instrumental Enrichment* into their curriculum: to overcome their deficits and enhance their learning experience. They had one period each day of Instrumental Enrichment, that the teacher then bridged into the larger curriculum, integrating the concepts, vocabulary, and learning strategies acquired into their learning of reading, writing, mathematics, and other content—geography, science, literature, history, and so on.

One morning, a substitute teacher came to the classroom. It was announced that their regular teacher was ill, and would be out for an extended period of time. The students then asked: "Will you teach us IE?" When the new teacher responded "What is IE?" the students conferred among themselves, and sent a delegation to the office of the principal. To the principal they said: "We don't want this teacher. Send this teacher away. We need a teacher who will teach us IE. Send us a teacher who will teach us IE. It is very important to us. It helps us with our learning of all other subjects!"

This from 4th grade, low-functioning learners! We offer a number of observations: The IE teacher had mediated them well, so they understood how their learning of strategies and concepts would help all their other learning; they had a sense of their power and potential to learn; they had a conscious awareness of both the importance and potential of their learning; and they were able to make relationships between the cognitive processes involved in learning and academic proficiency. We will leave the reader to consider the nature of the relationships that these young learners appeared to have incorporated, and speculate about the effect on their current and later learning as well as their future cognitive potential.

We believe that reflects the essence of mediated learning experience, which we address throughout this book, that answers these speculations and responds to these observations and others!

MEDIATING THE SPECIAL NEEDS OF A CHILD

David was adopted by parents who were very busy, very high-functioning international business executives. They traveled constantly, sometimes taking David with them and sometimes leaving him for extended periods of time with caregivers. Some of the caregivers were either inadequate or harmful. At the time David was brought to me, he was 10 years old and extremely low-functioning. He had almost no language and very limited interactional skills. His parents' travel schedule precluded extended placement in any educational or day care settings, and those who had assessed and observed him previously concluded that he was severely retarded, and they made recommendations accordingly.

I spent part of 2 weeks observing him, literally getting down on the floor with him as he ran a small toy car back and forth making *zoom, zoom, zoom* noises, seemingly endlessly. One had to be very observant for the small signs of recognition and relating—watching his eyes slowly focus on me, orienting himself very so slightly to my body posture, following my actions as I emitted sounds, and the like.

On the basis of these observations, I overruled the recommendations of the specialists and pushed David's parents not to place him in an institution for severely retarded children. Rather, I found a foster home for him, with foster parents who were prepared to accept him, place him in, and fight for the most normalized environment possible, and who would be amenable to consultation from myself and others whom I sent to them to maintain David in a family and school environment. Over the next 5 to 6 years, we monitored and adapted his program. It was a struggle, with much need to renew energy and reinforce both signs of progress and make adjustments to get him back on track. We taught the foster parents both how to work with and how to make demands on the teachers. Sometimes we had to "backtrack" and place David in a classroom of younger peers, or provide short-term, intensive "pull-out" exposure—for example, when he was not making adequate progress in reading, or when he acted antisocially due to language limitations or frustration with tasks that were too demanding.

Fortunately, the school placements and the teachers with whom we worked were open to making adjustments and became supportive mediators, taking cues from the foster parents whom we trained and the consultants we brought into the environment. Slowly, his parents began to see the progress, began to spend more time with him (interrupting their business travel schedules), and both experience his changes (and potential) and get gratification from spending time with him. This reveals an important "truth" about being parents: Once we see ourselves as "good parents" and our children respond to us positively, we experience the natural pleasure that being parents entails.

Eventually, David completed high school in an almost fully normalized environment, and joined the army after his school completion with his peer group. In the army, he became quite proficient, continued his learning, and eventually became a noncommissioned officer with great responsibility. Many years later, when David was the commander of an honor guard at the funeral of one of my nephews, it gave me added comfort as we looked into each other's faces and recognized our relationship, but he maintained his duty and confirmed his sense of purpose, control, and mastery of his life.

The destiny of this seemingly severely retarded individual, who would have been relegated to an institutional life and would have had no hope for fulfilling his family's expectations and joining his community as a contributing member, was modified by the application of mediated learning experience. Over time, with much energy and engagement and the involvement of many educators, professionals, and members of the larger community, his human potential was realized.

Preface

On April 29, 2014, as we were beginning the final editorial work for this book, Professor Reuven Feuerstein passed away. He was in his 93rd year. He was deeply involved in this project, and felt that this book would be a good testament for his life's work. He came to care deeply about it as the transcription, conceptualization, and eventual editing occurred. He lived long enough to see his visionary theories and innovative methodologies accepted and confirmed by educators and psychologists, and by the burgeoning field of the neurosciences and what can be called the "brain revolution." But he did not feel that his work was finished. He remained mentally energetic, continuing to refine and develop his concepts, in spite of his weakening physical condition. Many of these "new" formulations are expressed in this volume. To the very end, his orienting response to every day was "What do we have on our plate? Let's get to work!"

This book had its origins in a series of leisurely "conversations" that Professor Feuerstein was encouraged to have in front of a video camera in the fall of 2010. They occurred over a period of several months, in the quiet and comfort of his home, in his own words, at his own pace, in a sequence of his own choosing. His son, Rabbi Rafi Feuerstein, the deputy chairman of the Feuerstein Institute, initiated this activity and helped prepare the content, collaborating with Professor Feuerstein on areas that should be included in the discussion. Rafi felt that a comprehensive and personal presentation of Professor Feuerstein's theories and practices, after more than 6 decades of significant activity affecting the lives of thousands of children and families, should be recorded for history.

Reuven Feuerstein's lifework has been to develop and disseminate theories and practices that have stimulated new thinking in psychology and education, and have generated a rich and detailed descriptive literature, both directly and through scholars and researchers around the world who recognized its impact and potential. Most would agree that Professor Feuerstein has been a seminal thinker and has influenced both academic and practical applications in cognitive and developmental psychology. With such creative thinkers and contributors, being able to access the products of their generativity and gain insight into the process and sequence of their thinking is a meaningful experience. It offers the potential for deepening and broadening our understanding of the theories and the approaches developed from them. So it is and was with Professor Reuven Feuerstein.

The motivation for transforming parts of Professor Feuerstein's discourse into this book comes from the fact that the concept (and practice) of mediated learning experience is the central pillar of the theory of structural cognitive modifiability (SCM) that Professor Feuerstein formulated, and has been one of the most used and quoted aspects of the theory, even by those who do not use our more formal programs such as the LPAD and Feuerstein Instrumental Enrichment (FIE). This book presents MLE in its own light, from the perspective that he struggled to keep clearly focused and applied in a variety of ways to diverse populations, with illustrations and examples from his long years of experience and deeply insightful perspective.

We want the reader to have a picture of how the process of producing this volume occurred. Professor Feuerstein wanted us to be present at as many of the filming sessions as possible. He wanted someone to talk to, someone with whom he had collaborated on a variety of conceptual and writing projects, someone who would listen, engage with him encouragingly though nonverbally through eye contact and facial expressions and even sometimes conveying that something was unclear or confusing. After each taping session, we "debriefed" the experience: Was it clear, meaningful? Should other things be added? This was not a new role for us, as in recent years he liked for us to help him consider other dimensions of content to be included in his presentations, and to be in the audience, within his eyesight, often as though he was talking to us in spite of an audience of numerous listeners. So for many of the sessions either or both of us sat next to the camera, and it was as though we were in a dialogue—he speaking and we listening and reacting, albeit nonverbally.

Much later, a transcript of the lectures was prepared. As he read it he began to wonder whether it should be transformed into a book. As we thought about it, it seemed to us that although most of the ideas and case examples had been written about previously, this was a unique opportunity. One could see the evolving tapestry of theory and concept, and could obtain a feeling for how he made meaning from the development and how he gained and elaborated upon his thinking from the many individuals whom he had studied, interacted with, and helped. As a dynamic process, there were two directions clearly evident: the ways in which the theory developed (and continues to be elaborated) and the contributions of those children and families he assisted that contributed to the further refining of his theory.

In fact, as we began to work with the material that served as the basis for this book, new ideas and frameworks occurred to him. And as they occurred, the energy, excitement, and pleasure of discovery was rekindled—in the 9th decade of his life, after more than a half century of passionate and dedicated activity, continuing into the time of this writing! We were, and continued to be, in awe! Thus, a rather remarkable, but not unanticipated thing happened. Even though we were editing an existing text, new aspects emerged and were incorporated. *Dynamic* to the end!

As a consequence of this ongoing creative process, he wanted some additional perspectives reflected. Thus, he asked two longtime colleagues and significant contributors to his work to add their perspectives: his brother, Shmuel Feuerstein, lecturer at Ashkelon Academic College/Bar Ilan University (Israel) and author of several works relating mediated learning experience to cultural transmission and Judaic studies; and his son and overall collaborator in this project, Rabbi Rafi Feuerstein. These contributions add a significant depth and applicational significance to the book.

We are pleased that Professor Carl Haywood consented to write the Foreword to this book. He was instrumental in bringing Professor Feuerstein to the United States in the 1960s, to George Peabody College of Vanderbilt University, to introduce his theories and practices to the United States, and has remained a valued friend and colleague throughout the years. His Foreword will set the tone for the special qualities of this book. Professor Haywood became an early collaborator of Professor Feuerstein's, participating in the development and dissemination of both the instrumental enrichment program and the dynamic assessment (LPAD) methodology. He has, over the years, continued to advocate for the theory and applications, both innovating and elaborating through extensive writing, training, and consultation. He can truly be considered a major scholar in cognitive psychology, mediated learning, and dynamic assessment, and his observations regarding this volume are very meaningful for us.

We had several objectives guiding the preparation of this book—to preserve Professor Feuerstein's somewhat informal, conversational style, so that the reader can have the experience of a personal encounter, learning from the *teacher* who is passionate and committed to our understanding. A second objective is to convey the organic nature of the theory and its deep and abiding implications for humankind. And lastly, to give voice to the influence of Judaic culture in the formation and development of Professor Feuerstein's lifework. He was deeply religious, has throughout his life brought his knowledge and familiarity with the philosophy and practice of his Judaism into his educational and psychological theories and practices, and devoted his life to the transmission of his culture, again to the benefit of humankind.

In Chapter 1 of this volume, Professor Feuerstein distinguishes development from modifiability, and differentiates his point of view from that of his mentor Piaget. In Chapter 2 he defines and describes the universal parameters of MLE and addresses the reasons for those who do not receive adequate mediation. He also discusses what for him was a lifelong issue—differentiating "cultural difference" and "cultural deprivation." In Chapter 3 he takes this discourse further as he considers issues of application of MLE to life events and demands. The nature of change, behavioral and structural, is the focus of Chapter 4. In Chapter 5 he reviews the sources of support that have emerged to validate his theory and practices, both behavioral and scientific. Chapter 6 brings him to a topic that concerned him deeply in the later years of his life—the search for the genesis and development of spirituality (morality, ethics, religious belief) in the material and structural aspects of our neurodevelopment. Chapters 7 and 8 discuss applications of how MLE relates to cognitive modifiability and how it can and should be applied. Chapter 9 addresses a critical aspect in the understanding and application of MLE, that of "mediational questioning." Chapter 10 brings MLE (or the lack thereof) into the modern context of digital communication and rapidly available information through technology. Professor Feuerstein felt that these two additional chapters would meaningfully elaborate his discourse and add depth to the reader's understanding.

Much of what is in this book has appeared in other places. For those who have not had previous exposure or deep access to the literature, the book *Beyond Smarter* is a good starting place, summarizing the scope of the work and relating it to recent developments in the field of cognitive modifiability and neural plasticity (Feuerstein, Feuerstein, & Falik, 2010). This volume takes much of what is in that book and presents it from the deeper perspective of Professor Feuerstein's own personal recollections, adding many new and insightful elaborations. One of his motivations for doing this book is his conviction that mediated learning experience has not been fully explicated, and that we must continue to expand our horizons of understanding. With all of the previous writing and dissemination of the theory and practice, he felt that there is still so much more to know and understand. Two examples of his concern will suffice: To many in the world, his theory of structural cognitive modifiability and the application of mediated learning experience as the motive force of achieving modifiability have been generalized to a wide range of learning activities, at times losing the focus on the special and necessary qualities of "experience." This concerned him, and he saw this book as an opportunity to address this concern. Second, a number of years ago he formulated 50 different mediational interactions, and felt that they had not been sufficiently elaborated. Although this book does not directly or systematically address these 50 interactions, by implication and elaboration he reflects on many of them. In this, we see his need to continue to probe and more deeply understand the mechanisms, processes, and outcomes of mediated learning experience. We hope and believe that this volume addresses this need. If successful, this volume will contribute to the deepening of both the understanding of MLE and its application.

It is our hope, as it was Reuven's, that this book—which has now turned out to be his last—will weave together theory; applications; stories of MLE at work in changing lives, minds, and brains; reflections on new findings from neuroscience; and expectations for where research may take us next. We further hope that this synthesis and the suggestions for implementation will be of help to parents, teachers, therapists, and graduate and undergraduate students of education and educational psychology.

The editing that we have done (from the original full transcript) has brought the language from the spoken to the written format, overcoming some of the natural awkwardness of one who is not speaking in his native language, and occasionally we have moved examples and material into closer and more integrated places to produce a clearer narrative. We have also taken the liberty, in full consonance with Professor Feuerstein, to add occasional bridging and elaborative material, as we have done in collaborative writing projects over more than 25 years. In this regard, we must acknowledge the contribution of our editor from Teachers College Press, Jean Ward. Jean has been our advocate from the publication of our first book with TCP, and we know her to be passionate in her belief in Professor Feuerstein's theories and practices. Thus, as our editor for this publication, she has offered many observations and suggestions, both in relation to the theory, but also relating to implications for teachers and the educational context. We have been grateful for this input, and have incorporated the vast majority of her suggestions into the text.

Thus, this book represents a collaborative effort, in which we hope to achieve a meaningful and noteworthy experience for the reader, access to a unique personal dialogue, with the objective being to draw the reader into Reuven Feuerstein's thinking process—as though as we read the pages of this book we are sitting with him.

L.H.F
R.S.F
July/August 2014

Changing Minds and Brains—
The Legacy of Reuven Feuerstein

Mediated Learning Experience and the Theory of Structural Cognitive Modifiability

Much about mediated learning experience (MLE) and the role it plays in creating the structural cognitive modifiability that is possible for all human beings has been well described elsewhere, by myself and by my colleagues and students. In this book, I take the opportunity to think and recollect with you, the reader, about the development of MLE and SCM, their implications and applications, and about my personal journey with MLE since its inception.

The theory of structural cognitive modifiability presents an optimistic view about the human being and the propensity to be modified. It occurs naturally through mediated learning experiences in parental and educational contexts, as we have the need to nurture and educate our children. This is the source and motivation of MLE. But not all MLE is positive. Modifiability itself is possible and actually happens both positively and negatively through other experiences.

Many of the elements that make human beings flexible, plastic, and able to be modified in the structure of their mental processes and ways of behaving have their source in MLE. And yet we emphasize that not every development is accompanied by positive change!

As we proceed through this book, we will confront a variety of questions that can be posed to enable a better understanding of the way by which human beings develop, the most drastic changes that can happen in the course of development, and the possibilities to modify certain deficiencies. These questions have developed organically, as I and my colleagues continue to think about and elaborate the theoretical and practical implications of the work, and as a consequence of the revolution occurring in the brain sciences, challenging and confirming much of what I have thought about and acted upon over a span of more than 60 years. Two examples suffice to express this ongoing process—one conceptual and the other practical. Conceptually, I have been increasingly considering the role of consciousness in the conduct of MLE. I address this further in Chapter 3. Practically, I ask why, for instance, children born with Down syndrome are considered not able to benefit from direct exposure to stimuli, meaning they are unable to benefit by themselves from what they see, what they experience, and the way by which they are confronted with realities. Why are they not able to learn by themselves, while through mediation they are able to succeed? The application of our approach to cognitive modifiability, as I will describe from several perspectives in the text that follows, will provide some of my thoughts about this question.

DISTINGUISHING DEVELOPMENT FROM MODIFIABILITY

Modifiability is an active departure from a given pattern of growth. It opposes the expectations of exact stages of development. In this sense, it must be differentiated from the concept of development that proceeds according to natural, biological, organically programmed sequences. Development is linear, from one point to another. Modifiability changes the course of development—it is multitracked and multifaceted. Changeability is a fact of life—life produces changes. Modifiability is the opposite. It intensifies and eventually goes counter to the expected and predicted development. This contrasts with Piaget, who was a constructivist. For example, he held that analogies were not available to children before the age of 11, or approximately when they enter the stage of formal operations as described in Piaget's stages of mental development. We have had numerous experiences where younger children could solve analogy problems if they were presented with the stimuli in a systematic way, and helped to organize the information.

Exposure to Stimuli

In this regard, we have seen some very interesting differences between human beings who are exposed directly to stimuli. Some learn from the first experience they encounter. Once they have seen something, it becomes familiar to them; they learn the functions of the particular object that they have encountered. If presented with a container of liquid, they know what can happen if the object is thrown away or inclined. A glass of water that the child encounters for the first time may teach the child that if you incline the glass of water, the water will be spread all over and will be lost. Other children will not learn this even though they experience it many times. Many years ago I adapted an experiment from Piaget that we called the bottles that demonstrates this principle; we will return to this later. It is described in our book *Beyond Smarter* (Feuerstein, Feuerstein, & Falik, 2010).

Proximal and Distal Determinants of Development

So an important question is, "What makes one individual able to learn from the exposure to stimuli whereas others don't learn at all, or in order to learn require a great deal of exposure to something?" These differences have always been explained by differences in intelligence, by differences in the inborn capacity of the individual, determined by either heredity or other factors that were supposed to affect the individual. Heredity, genetic disorders, chromosomal disorders, organic dysfunctions, or other factors *within* the individual (endogenous factors) as well as those in the environment (exogenous factors), such as cultural and social deprivation, were used in order to explain differences between individuals' capacities and propensities to learn and to become modified through direct exposure to stimuli.

These various hypotheses represent *fixist* views about intelligence (a subject we will return to later): intelligence determined by the nature of the brain, by the genes inherited, and other conditions affecting the individual's activity. The concept of SCM considers these various determinants the *distal factors*: determinants of certain behaviors and certain functions of the individual. From the perspective of SCM, they are not considered those that ultimately determine individual's capacities and propensities, and their skill formation. They by themselves will not produce such differences between individuals. The factors that must be considered as determining the potential of the learner are the *proximal factors*, addressed by the provision of MLE. If there is a lack of mediation, then the distal factors will predominate, as described in Figure 1.1. There are two reasons for the lack of MLE: (1) Mediation is not given (for a variety of reasons), and (2) the individual is not able to benefit from the mediation offered, again, for a variety of reasons. I will return to this differentiation in more detail later.

If an individual who has been affected genetically, chromosomally, or by other elements that create deficiencies in functioning is given mediated learning experience, the distal determinants will not obstruct the development of functioning. Effective provision of MLE will result in individuals who—despite the fact that they have experienced distal determinants—turn out to be able to benefit from and become modified by the experiences to which they were exposed.

**Figure 1.1. Distal and Proximal Determinants of
Differential Cognitive Development**

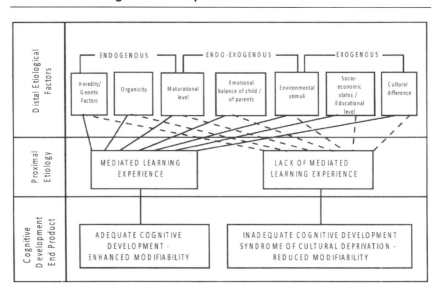

Cultural Factors

Individuals with potentially quite normal cognitive structure who were not
affected by distal determinants but were not exposed to mediated learning experience may act deficiently as if they were affected by other distal
factors—for example, as though they had an organic hereditary endogenic
condition.

I made this observation from studying thousands of children in different
settings over many years, in clinics, classrooms, and family interactions. We
have seen a number of people who, despite the fact that they didn't show
any signs of inappropriate internal, organic factors, and had apparently normal brains and apparently normal genes, lived in an environment that did
not mediate the world to them. These people showed great difficulties in
becoming modified by learning processes, in becoming adapted to new situations, and this became a source of deficiencies, the reason being that they
were not exposed to MLE.

Before I define the nature of MLE, I want to share an interesting example of the effects of a lack of mediation:

I describe a young man who came from an important and high-functioning family that enabled him to experience, to be exposed to the world. He met with very important stars in the film world. He visited many countries together with his father and mother. And he had no serious, observable physical or mental factors to explain the fact that he was not able to learn either reading or writing or adapt to certain experiences. When we tried to figure out where this deficiency came from, why he was not able to benefit from all of these opportunities, it turned out that although the parents were really concerned with the child, and took him with them everywhere they went, they never took care to transmit to him what they saw, what they experienced, where they were, what they were there for, and in what way should they react to conditions they experienced. He was just not offered any kind of mediation. And this turned this child into a very seriously deficient boy who—because of this condition—was actually suspected of having some internal (distal) determinants for his deficiency. The only explanation for his deficiency was lack of MLE.

MLE AS A PROXIMAL DETERMINANT OF MODIFIABILITY

We have two ways of learning; one is through being exposed to stimuli. There is no doubt that being exposed to stimuli is a source of learning, a source of amplifying not only our knowledge, but even our structure of mind. Being able to benefit from our exposure to stimuli, however, is strongly dependent upon whether or not the individual has been exposed to MLE. I will say here, and perhaps elsewhere in this book, that "all teaching is not mediation; but all mediation is teaching."

Differentiating MLE from Direct Exposure Learning

MLE is defined as the interposition of initiated, intelligent, goal-oriented individuals who interpose themselves between the world of stimuli impinging on the child and interpret what one is supposed to see; not only this, but the mediator must be interested in and concerned with certain elements that the child has to learn. The mediator will make things available to the learner in a way that she or he will be able to learn from them, understand them—not only to learn from them in order to know the particular object, but learn how to approach reality and the stimuli being exposed—to learn from them, to experience them, and eventually to use this to transfer structures of knowledge acquired to a variety of conditions, including to those areas of functioning that are progressively less familiar and more complex. So, for example, the parents who took their son on their travels never described their experiences to him, either before they happened, while they occurred, or afterward. As a result, he never learned from the experience or anticipated future experiences. In the same vein, classroom teachers who take students "out into the world" to have direct experiences with its stimuli enhance the likelihood of infusing MLE into the learning process if they prepare students for the experience, mediate the experience while it is happening, and reflect with students afterward about the meaning of their experience.

MLE is a way of interaction that differs greatly from direct exposure to stimuli inasmuch as the exposure to stimuli may or may not affect the individual. The individual may observe the stimuli and learn from it, but at certain other opportunities may not even be aware of the stimuli. So, in direct learning experience, there is a very large degree of probability regarding whether the individual will register the exposure, either because of an inability to receive the stimuli, understand it, experience it, or because the stimuli doesn't appear at the appropriate time. MLE ensures that the stimuli will be available to the individual. The mediator does everything to make sure that the encounter will be focused and that both the receiver and the provider of the stimuli will be in some way in a state of consonance.

I have seen children, and even adults, who pass by stimuli without observing them. This is very clear and easy to observe in children who are asked to observe certain pictures, and they are unable to follow those elements that they need in order to understand what it's all about. There are many examples that illustrate this. Consider children who do not see that a part of a certain object is missing. They are not able to say what is missing. I've seen children who pass by streets and never know their names. They don't turn to the right source of information they need in order to learn something about it, because no one has mediated by showing that streets have names and that the names appear on signs. The same is true for other characteristics of the world that they are exposed to. It takes a mediator to make the child focus on a particular source of information that was passed by; only through the focus of the mediator does the stimulus become a center of interest and the child then becomes ready to interpret it, learn it, and become informed about it.

Here is another example that shows the relationship between cognitively active modalities of thinking, mediating optimistic views and the gathering of relevant information.

I was with a group of children in a museum in Los Angeles, and there was a wonderful painting of a desert scene in which the horses were pulling a wagon that was about to fall down a ravine—the wagon was hanging on the edge. In the picture a number of people were trying to bring the wagon back because it was a matter of life and death to have this wagon. They still had some horses but they didn't have a wagon, and to stay without a wagon would have meant very great danger to their existence. So they had to bring back this wagon by all means. We were standing in front of this picture and I was explaining how important this wagon was for the life of these people, and I asked the children, "How do you feel? Will they succeed and bring back the wagon with the ropes they have attached to the wagon and which they are dragging, or will it not be possible?" One of the children listening to me ask my questions, approached the picture, looked very carefully, and then screamed out loudly "Yes! Yes, they will be able to do it!" "Why?" I asked. "Because they found a rope (he observed that a rope was attached to a pulley) and it is attached to a pulley, and this increases the power of their dragging." Because he was optimistic, because of his *need* to act in an optimistic way, and his *knowledge* of the pulley as a device, he came up with a very important finding. But he didn't initially see it; he had to look carefully before he found it, because the pulley and part of the rope was covered by the sand.

Another example: the special education teacher who "confessed" that he was not following the "curriculum" because it bored his students and they were not learning. Instead he took them for walks in the neighborhood around the school, they observed various objects and events, and then returned to the classroom to record their experiences, develop vocabulary, make stories, and consider the various implications of what they had experienced. Part of his "confession" was "These kids can learn!"

So the individual who is alerted by MLE (my questions emphasizing both the danger and the need) can be oriented (made alert) to an optimistic way and can make a cognitive perceptual effort. In the museum, my intention was to mediate the importance of the need to search for ways to resolve the conflict. In the example above, the child was focused by the mediation and perceived something that was not easily seen by the naked eye. He had to approach the picture (the stimulus—physically and mentally) himself in order to see it and then come up with the cognitive idea that a pulley will help those people drag back this very heavy wagon.

Mediation and Orientation to Stimuli

The lack of availability of stimuli and the need to re-evoke in our memory the stimuli that we have seen before is something to which the individual will require orientation. Thus, one of the important differences between MLE and the exposure to stimuli directly, without mediation, is that the mediator—knowing and having the intention that the child will have an opportunity to be exposed to the stimuli—doesn't expect that the stimuli will be sufficiently salient for the child, or that the child will be attentive enough to see them. Instead, the mediator places the stimuli in front of the child, modifies the stimuli in such a way that they will have certain characteristics that will affect the individual in the most appropriate ways, and *creates a need*.

DIFFERENTIATING PIAGET'S VIEW FROM OURS

This is the great difference between direct exposure to stimuli and MLE. Piaget laid major emphasis on the relationship between the stage of the development of the individual and the readiness, capacity, and propensity to see the things that are exposed directly. Piaget considered the development of intelligence as being the outcome of the interaction between the stage of development and the stage of maturation of the brain, and the experience that this maturation permits the child. If the child is mature enough to see certain things and to experience and to interact with them, then it's fine. But Piaget's view was that this does not occur unless a certain developmental stage is reached.

Diagramming Direct and Mediated Learning

In order to depict the relationship of direct to mediated learning, we created a diagram that differentiates them in the process of learning, and is presented in Figure 1.2. In this schema, there are three major theoretical aspects portrayed, including that of Piaget. I would actually say only two because the first one, the limited behavioristic Stimulus-Response relationship, doesn't consider itself a theory. The behaviorists have, in a very intentional way, avoided using the term *theory*. They describe certain behaviors, and they claim that the development of intelligence is the direct outcome of

Figure 1.2. S-O-R Model for Direct and Mediated Learning

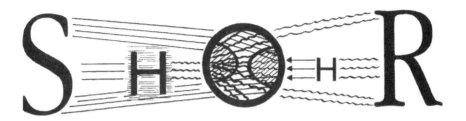

the person being exposed to such stimuli and the kind of response produced to the stimuli—hence, the "stimulus/response" reaction. The chain of reaction/response creates the types of changes, of development of knowledge, of modalities of response, skills, and so on that the behaviorists refer to as intelligence. This is depicted by showing the "O" as the organism, and interposing the "H" as the human mediator that interacts with the "S" the "O" and the "R."

The Behaviorist's View

The behaviorists were reacting to theories of intelligence and learning as attempting to consider the individual learner by looking into "the black box of our thinking processes." They denied the possibility to do it. They were much more interested and oriented toward producing certain types of behaviors by using a great variety of modalities, conditioning processes, and the direct relationship between the stimuli and the outcome that could be controlled and measured "objectively." So behaviorists used only the S and the R. They did not really look for (or want to know) what is occurring in the organism in which all this is happening and what kind of processes undergo this response, or how the perception of the stimuli (experience) is reflected in the learner's perception and performance. MLE is thus intimately related to the reactions and responses that individuals give and experience in their interactions with their worlds.

　　Piaget denied the validity of such an approach. He did not believe the associationistic and behavioristic theories were able to understand human development and the ways by which intelligence developed. He felt that in order to understand development, you have to look to the organism in which this process takes place (in our model, adding the "O" to the diagram—"S-O-R"). And he introduced the term *the stages of development*, which were marked by the stages of the maturation of the brain, as a way to explain the types of interactions through which the individual develops progressively through encounters with stimuli.

Piaget's View of Development, and Ours

According to Piaget, children below the stage of "formal operations" are not supposed to compare, don't see sizes, don't react to certain qualities of the stimuli as compared to children of more advanced stages. Children prior to the stage of formal operations (in Piaget's view usually not before the age of 7 or 8) were not considered able to turn a stimulus into a symbol, even though we know the very beautiful ways by which children develop symbolic thinking as they engage in symbolic play. Very early, at ages of 3 and 4, they may turn brooms into airplanes or a horse and ride on them on imaginary journeys. They show a readiness to assimilate the object to their particular needs at the moment as if saying, "I would like to have a horse and I take the broomstick for the horse, and I experience it the way I want." So the stick is assimilated with their desires and needs.

This kind of symbolic play starts at a different point in the child's development and relates, as Piaget points out, to the child's maturation level. Symbolic play then leads the individual to understand the symbols and the signs as a replacement of the reality. A symbol is in some way a representation of the reality. The broom represents a horse. And the child rides on it and represents it in a symbolic way, doing the particular activity that a rider does with a horse.

So Piaget actually considered the development of intelligence. I'm not speaking now about development of knowledge (knowledge is clearly made possible by interaction with knowledgeable adults or peers, the conveying of what adults or peers know something about, transferring their knowledge to the child). Rather, I am thinking about intelligence as the operational knowledge and functions that permit the individual to modify and organize things, and learn in an inferential way about elements that are not known otherwise than by logical inference.

This part of development, from the point of view of Piaget, refers to and actually originated through his observations of the interaction of the child with the world and its objects. For Piaget there is only an objective world. He does not need the human being as a mediator. The human being is one of the objects with which the child interacts, and the object is a source of knowledge, but it is also a source of changes. The adult represents to the child variations of the views the child has, and the child is able to assimilate and then accommodate the particular elements that the adult has proposed, presented, and taught.

But the human mediator who appears there is like any other object that becomes a source of operations, of thinking, of comparisons, and so forth. In Piaget's view, the child doesn't see the human being in any way other than as one more of the objects that the child interacts with.

From my point of view, this is very problematic: We cannot explain the great variations and differences between individuals as to the degree of changes produced by them during the encounter with stimuli. There are people who are exposed to stimuli and benefit from them in a very meaningful way. Others can pass by stimuli many times and not be affected by their encounter or by their interactions with the particular stimuli, as my example below regarding the structural nature of plants will illustrate.

How to Explain Differences in Human Behavior

In what way can we explain these differences? Of course, the easiest way is to say that the individual who does not react is *stupid*. But what does this mean? Why isn't the individual affected by the stimulus? What is the element that makes this interaction useless and ineffective so that the child is not affected by it? We came to the conclusion that direct exposure to stimuli may not be effective in individuals *even if* they have been exposed to them, if there has been no experience of the kind of interaction and learning that we came to describe as mediated learning experience (MLE).

The Piagetian concept of interaction is, as I have pointed out, an interaction with an objective world. Even when there is a human being involved who is one of the sources of information (is one of the "stimuli"—in certain cases, a provocative stimuli) to which the child interacts in a way requiring learning something that is at variance with previous ways of thinking, even then—from the point of view of Piaget—the effect is not the subjectivity of the human being. It is the human being representing a certain point of view, a certain knowledge that the child receives. According to Piaget, this develops a "separational" type of thinking. But again, Piaget considered this an object.

In contradistinction to this approach, we have found that individuals are very different in the way they react to the object. Some of them do not really benefit from their exposure to objects, not even from objects that are in some way represented by the mediator. And we have considered, together with Vygotsky, that the development of intelligence is the product of an interaction with the social world, with a world that is interacted with in a way that is shaped by the intentions of the mediators in a child's life (parents, teachers, other concerned humans).

What Makes the Interaction "Mediation?"

It is important to point out that when human beings act as an object, as simply a source of information, they are not mediators. Teaching children what has happened, where it has happened, what dates are, what figures are, and so on, even skills, is not necessarily mediation. They are sources of information that may eventually be replaced by books or by television or by other sources of information generating knowledge.

Mediated learning experience occurs as the outcome of an interaction with an intentioned mediator. The mediator is a human being who interposes between the "S" and the "O," between the stimuli and the organism to which mediation is addressed, and who interposes between the "O" (the organism) and its responses (the "R"), on both input and output levels. The mediator produces in the learner a number of changes because of the power of the intention that is mostly carried out by a state of awareness, and also creates awareness and consciousness: the teacher who has an objective in mind for the learning experience—"This is what we will learn, this is what is important, this is why it is important"—and conveys it in an explicit way to the student.

I emphasize this because those who deal with quantum theories, quantum physics, lay great emphasis on consciousness (see elsewhere in this book, and particularly Chapter 6). It is the consciousness and the awareness of the individual, and in certain cases also the willful orientation of the individual to certain phenomena, that produces the changes. From our point of view, awareness is the most important element in the interaction that leads to meaningful change, creating a different structure in the individual.

In our diagram, the mediator—the "H"—is not of an overwhelming size. It means the "H" covers only a small part of the interaction between the individual and the stimuli. It's only for a selection of stimuli in which the mediator interposes himself. And although direct exposure represents the greatest part of the activity of the individual, MLE only affects a narrow band of interactions. The effect is that the stimulus impinging on the individual, rather than affecting directly the organism, goes through the mediator. And the mediator who receives the stimulus observes its effect and meaning, changes it—its nature, its power, its strength, its color—and does this in order to affect the organism in the way that the mediator wants it to become different for the learner—more powerful and salient. That is the "intentionality" of the mediator.

> For example, the child sees an object, sees a glass, but doesn't know what this glass contains. He also doesn't know what is going to happen with this glass when it falls down, what will happen to the liquid that it contains. And he may manipulate it on his own, do all kinds of things with the glass, and may find out by himself what is happening when this glass is inclined in a way that the liquid is spread out or what is happening when the individual throws it to the ground.

The mediator who observes this process (and the learner's response) interacts with the child in a very different way. The mediator has an intention to make the child able to understand what is characteristic of this particular container and the way it has to be handled. The interposition between the child and the glass makes the child not only aware of the nature of the object but also increases awareness of how to look at objects in order to become able to extract from them their nature, their characteristics, and their way of being handled or the way they serve us in their characteristics.

> I want to give you an example that is a very strong point of evidence. How many times do people go through gardens and see all kinds of plants? How many of these people who are exposed constantly to these objects see all the differences between the objects and are able to define the differences between (if we are speaking of plants) monocotyledon and dicotyledon plants? Very few people! Will they see the grass as a certain structure of the leaf, with the leaf constantly following parallel lines? Will they see that grass never creates a trunk? They see, for instance, a palm tree, very high, and yet will they know that you cannot extract from this palm tree any piece of wood? They never ask why, what is the difference between a palm tree and other trees. So you can go by trees and plants in your own life, observe differences between them, but if you are not offered an interpretation as to the structure—in this instance, the morphological nature of these two sets of plants, the monocotyledon and the dicotyledon—you can go by these phenomena over years and years and never know what they are.
> The minute I explain this to a large class of intelligent adults, even students of history, teachers, and so on, they come back and tell me that now they cannot go by a tree and not compare

them, and beyond trees, everything they are seeing now they are comparing and searching for the differences and trying to understand in what way they are different. What does it mean that if I mediated to you how to look at these two categories of plants, giving you specific information (for example, the monocotyledon has a very different morphology in terms of the leaf, the roots; the monocotyledon plant doesn't have a root; there are a series of small rootlets, whereas the dicotyledon has a central root out of which grow roots and not directly from the plant itself)?

But it is not simply the information. I mediate the information in a way that encourages an interaction by which the learner constantly compares the objects being exposed, whereas the individual who is just exposed to the stimulus will have a very limited repertoire in order to become acquainted with the world. My goal as a mediator is to produce parameters to develop comparative behaviors that are then used in a variety of other encounters with stimuli.

Affective Dimensions

The same is true for feelings. People may feel something and not know what it is. If they are given some kind of mediation, if they are given some kind of awareness about what they feel, they change in a very meaningful way. Learning experiences can be considered in the same way, as a series of mediated interactions in which the teacher explores with students their feelings and thoughts about the content, and makes relevant and meaningful what is being learned—for example, how geography and climate affect how people think, react, and learn: being on a desert compared to being on an ice floe in the Arctic.

In the realm of psychotherapy, this is well illustrated in the work of Jeffrey Schwartz, a psychiatrist who deals with people suffering from obsessive-compulsive disorders. In his book *The Mind and the Brain* (2002), he describes the resistance that his affected clients have to any attempt to dissuade them from engaging in ritual behaviors (don't wash your hands a hundred times). He found that through a mediational process (our term) that is accompanied by consciousness and awareness, the client can substitute normal behavior for the pathological tendency to do something in an obsessive way. Schwartz identifies four steps (reattributing, refocusing, relabeling, and revaluing) to help the individual develop an alternative, more realistic adaptive response for the reframing of the individual's thinking and responding.

So the mediator endows the mediatee not only with modalities of seeing things, but with modalities of thinking. Awareness is created that in order to better understand the relationships between two objects one can compare what is different, what they have in common, and if this relationship that has been created of commonality and difference applies to a variety of other things. Using superordinate concepts that are more advanced and more abstract (for instance, instead of saying "yellow" and "black," say "color"; instead of saying "big" and "small," say "size"). The concepts conceptualized (size, color) are characteristics of the interrelationship between two things, and are applicable to many other types of stimuli. Thus, the mediator endows the mediatee with modalities of perceiving and experiencing in ways that direct exposure to stimuli may not provide.

THE PROCESS OF MEDIATION

The mediational process starts very early with an important activity of the child. It starts by offering the child the possibility to focus visually, to create a relationship by making eye contact with the mediational figure. Children who are deprived of this experience are often diagnosed as being on the autistic spectrum and are considered developmentally delayed (see Carbone, O'Brian, Sweeney-Kerwin, & Albert, 2013; see also Feuerstein, Falik, Feuerstein, & Bohacs, 2013, Chapter 10). These children may not be able to focus and create a kind of attention, willfully orienting their eyes and holding their attention for a meaningful period of time. In such instances, things seen by chance (randomly) are selected out and concentrated on, with the child focusing upon objects that are of relevance and interest. I will elaborate on this in much greater detail in the next chapter.

Developmental Factors

There are many studies (including the classic work of Skodak, 1942; Skodak & Skeels, 1949) in the area of early childhood showing that children in orphanages who are devoid of stable figures, who are always being cared for by different people, have very little opportunity to create stable, affective, emotional relationships and are often not able to focus and develop attention.

This is a phenomenon that we observe today in many children who don't create eye contact because of early deprivation of this type of relationship. The mother who wants to be in contact with her child approaches her child and looks at the child in a way to capture interest and focus. But then if she goes too far away, out of contact, and the child doesn't see her the potential for the child's focusing is diminished. At a given stage in physical development, the child sees only about 40 to 50 centimeters away. If the mother adjusts her position so that the child will be seen by her, this enables the child not only to create a contact, but because the mother is a very familiar figure, well known to the child, each change in the expression of the mother will be immediately recognized and registered and will become a source of learning. "Now my mother is happy with me; what did I do?" And you can see children at very early stages in their development, as early as 3 months, learning to do what will make their mother laugh. They do all kinds of mimicking, they prefer certain sounds, and they really interact with their mediating mother in a way that shows that they have learned from this familiar figure who is known to them that each change can be related to some kind of behavior.

This provides a primary form of a cause-and-effect relationship. The child learns that responding in one way will make the mother sad and responding in another way will cause the mother to be happy. The result is that the child learns to orient behavior according to what the child would like to see in the mother's face.

Today we have an epidemic of ADHD, of attentional deficit disorders that may well be the product of lack of or insufficient mediated learning experience in early childhood (Herz-Piccioto & Delwiche, 2009; Newshaffer, Croen, Daniels, et al., 2007). What we did with my grandson Elchanan is a perfect example of how to respond to this phenomenon—to foster learning and development where it is vitally needed, and where spontaneous learning would not likely occur:

> Elchanan, a child with Down syndrome, had difficulties in raising his head and holding it in ways that would enable him to make eye contact. We felt that this weakness would deprive him of certain types of interactions. So we took Elchanan's head in our hands, and looked at him to establish eye contact. As his eyes moved away, we reoriented his head to reestablish and maintain his eye contact. And by doing this, we taught him to give a more differential attention to our faces than he gave to the various other stimuli that attracted him.
>
> Furthermore, we knew that as a Down syndrome child the weaknesses in the peribuccal area and his protruding tongue would not allow him to become vocally adequate or able to use his voice and make sounds properly. So in order for him to have a better

capacity to dominate his peribuccal muscles, we made him imitate three movements, related to associated sounds. He didn't imitate the protrusion of the tongue, because he had a long tongue, but we repeatedly made sounds as we formed our mouths, well within his visual focusing field—*bah, bah, bah* (with widely stretched lips); *boo, boo, boo* (with mouth shaped circularly); and so on. Not only did he start to anticipate and imitate us within the first few weeks of his life, but today he has a clear voice and clear articulation, much more so than many other children with Down syndrome. They may be clever children, but they are mumbling.

Responding to Mediation (in Early Language Development)

When we speak about mediation, we do not speak only about the input; we speak also about the way the child reacts to the input and responds to it. As the mediator, I interpose myself between the stimuli and the learner's response. In the situation of linguistic stimulation I described above, we interposed ourselves between the observation of certain things, we structured the imitation of our behavior, and from this we interposed ourselves in order to encourage the child to articulate sounds, vowels, and consonants. Compare this to the experience of other children who for some reason are not given this kind of mediation. It is either not offered, or for a variety of reasons the child is unable to benefit from it (see Figure 1.1, Proximal and Distal Determinants).This is why mediation needs to start at a very early stage in life. As the exposure to an object becomes very familiar, and the child observes all the differences between the way the mediator (for the young child—usually the mother) was before, and learns to observe the mother's reactions and changes. But whether she changes and she starts to cry or laugh, for example, these are changes of a normative perception of this phase, and the child learns very rapidly to interpret this and relate it to certain types of experiences with the mother that have become familiar, expected, and meaningful. In this way, the mediator has the opportunity to provoke in the child the desired change.

Protruding the Tongue—An Early Intervention

Here is an example that is taken from the very early stages in development of the child where we were able to teach children how to protrude the tongue. This was a very problematic issue because, according to Piaget, children cannot imitate unless they know the object of imitation and the imitative part of the body. According to Piaget, imitation can happen only after the child can represent and observe experience. We have shown—and I've not been the only one to do it—that children are able to imitate the protrusion of the tongue at the age of 3 days. I kept the child's face well fixed in my hand and I repeatedly protruded my tongue, repeating it about 100 times. Then all of a sudden the child began to make movements, an effort that is understood as a construction of a movement—not a movement that comes out by itself, but the child literally constructs the movement that imitates my movement. Sticking out the tongue is a construction, and we mediated this construction—we made the child able to imitate me.

We have done some research where we have offered a number of children three movements (protruding the tongue, protruding the lips, and widening the lips), and we wanted to see which one of these three would affect the efficiency of the imitative process. We had 30 children where we started with protruding the tongue, 30 children where we started with protruding the lips, and 30 children where we started with enlarging the mouth area, the lips, and we wanted to see which one of them will affect the capacity of imitation. There was a clear difference whether we started with protruding the tongue or whether we started with protruding the lips. If we mediated the protrusion of the tongue, which is probably the more complex type of behavior, then the other movements are much more easily done. After the child learned to protrude the tongue (and with about 100 repetitions), the protrusion of the lips took only 30 to 50 repetitions. We had a mean of about 45 that was a great difference with the protrusion of the tongue. And then we started by rotation of the order, and there was a difference in the means. And by this we learned that if you mediate to children something complex and they learn to imitate it, the capacity to imitate will become meaningfully facilitated and much greater efficiency will be observed in those children.

> I remember teaching Yudah, when he was 30 days old, to protrude his tongue. Then I went away, and when I came back 8 months later Yudah was in his mother's arms standing in the entrance, and when he recognized me he expressed great excitement. The mediational experience that I had given him many months earlier made him able to remember a complex behavior. Because he could not call me by my name, but he clearly recognized me, he protruded his tongue as a sign of recognition! This kind of behavior was not considered possible by Piaget, Zazzo, and many others in the field.

SUMMARIZING THE MEANING OF THESE
DIFFERENCES AND ACCOMPLISHMENTS

By way of summary, there are two modalities by which individuals learn and develop; one is through direct exposure, primarily emphasized by behaviorists where no awareness and no consciousness is needed, and a second, reflected by Piaget, who conceived learning as a sole product of the maturational process making the interaction with other stimuli possible, according to the age and the maturational level of the brain.

These two perspectives do not really do justice to the way human intelligence develops. We have proposed a third way, the provision of the human mediator. Here I point out that in our schematic of the mediated learning process (see Figure 1.2), the mediator is designated as an H and not an M. I did not want people to say, "Oh, the mediator can also be a computer, the mediator can also be a book, the mediation can be offered by a tool (after the Vygotsky conception)." I wanted to clearly emphasize that the mediator can only be a human being, which is why we have inscribed here the letter "H" for the word *human*. The mediator has a very important characteristic that neither a computer, book, nor tools have: The mediator has an intention. Where this intention comes from will be discussed later, but it is clear that when the mediator interposes between the child and reality, when the mediator wants the child to learn to imitate, the mediator makes sure that the child will be able to look at the stimuli (perhaps the mediator's face) in a constant way and be affected by it.

This intentionality gives the interaction a very different quality and a power that will then affect the capacity and propensity of the individual to be affected by direct exposure. But this means that whatever I have learned through a mediational process will then become a source of learning in a vicarious way. It means I will start to mediate to myself once I have been meaningfully affected by the mediational process. I have *interiorized* the mediational process.

From this point of view, mediated learning experience has to be considered the most important determinant in human development and in the development of cognitive processes. Not only this, but also to a very large extent it shapes the emotional affective feelings that mark the individual.

A final allegorical example: A child is bitten by a scorpion as he was lifting a stone. After assuring himself that the child is not significantly injured by the bite and does not need medical care, the father interposes himself between the child and the child's act: "Before you lift a stone, you better be careful about what may be under the stone." Here, the father (mediator) creates in his child the awareness of what he has to do and in what way he should do things, what he has to look for before he does certain things, and what he has to learn from the experience. The mediator is here affected and empowered by a certain intention: I want my child to learn how to be changed, be modified by all experiences, by all perceptions that he will be exposed to.

CHAPTER 2

Defining and Describing Mediated Learning Experience

In this chapter I will describe and elaborate the three major conditions for mediated learning experience:

1. intentionality/reciprocity
2. transcendence
3. the mediation of meaning

Without these three, there is interaction but it is not mediation. To be mediation the interaction must be accompanied by these three parameters in a systematic, conscious, and intentional way. Ultimately, as I will describe below, this is experienced by both the mediator and the mediatee as important qualities of the shared experience.

INTENTIONALITY/RECIPROCITY

The first thing that characterizes the quality of the MLE interaction, in contradistinction to what occurs in direct exposure learning, is that the mediator brings an explicit intention to the experience. This example will show what I mean:

> There is an *object* to my intention: When children see the wind blowing through the trees, and are asked (as did Piaget in one of his classical and repeated interactions with children), "What makes the wind?" they would often respond "The tree!" In this instance, the mediator might respond by showing the child that it is not the tree that makes the wind, but that the wind moves the leaves and branches of the tree. The mediator might ask the child to blow against the leaves to experience and understand the movement, and observe other situations of similar causality. The mediational

intention is to have the child distinguish between proximity and generation, as a concept that will have far-reaching effects (see my discussion of *transcendence* that follows).

The Intention of the Mediator

In the classroom, intentionality begins when what is to be learned is clearly described to the students, in terms of "what, when, how, and ultimately why" (introducing transcendence—see below). My intention as the mediator is that I want the child to be affected in certain ways, and I will interpret the stimuli in terms of my observations and the meaning that has been transmitted to me by my previous experience and my cultural heritage. I convey my intention, and expose the child to certain things that might not be seen, or might not be the focus of initial or spontaneous interest. I will take the stimuli that I want the child to perceive and be enticed by and I will change them. I will give meaning and focus attention on their appearance, size, function, and so forth, so that the child will say, "Oh, that's very interesting, this is what I would like to see, this is what I like to do, and so on." I will do everything I can (creatively, innovatively, with embellishment) so that the child will see in the stimuli all types of dimensions, and will be interested in them in many new and interesting ways. My intention as the mediator shapes the stimuli; I don't just let the stimuli come in the way they are.

For instance, for younger learners, if I know children like a given color, I will select stimuli that present the color (for example, a large red balloon) that they will attend to and then perhaps compare them to other stimuli of a similar color. If I know that children like certain modalities of expression, such as singing a song or tapping on a drum, I will use these preferences to give the particular stimuli that I want the child to attend this quality, to enhance its meaning. If children like to imitate certain behaviors, like making noises of favorite animals, I will offer my mediation in a way that will respond to the readiness of the child to become affected by it. This is the role of the mediator. I do not wait until the stimuli arrive; I go and find them and bring them into the interaction. My intention is not passive but rather highly active and initiatory.

Intentionality manifests itself in a great variety of ways. When teachers mediate to children, rather than just teaching and transmitting information, they shape their way of talking to children, their way of presenting the information that they want to transmit in a way that makes the child alert ("Oh, yes!"), excited ("Oh, I couldn't believe it!"), and they receive from the child the types of responses that make interaction with a particular stimulus experience a very meaningful one.

I have been asked the question, "When is a behavioral intervention not mediation?" Let me relate an example where mediation doesn't appear. You don't have the time to mediate to a child who is reaching out to touch the flame of a fire. So you do scream from afar. You are too far away to take away the child's hand, but you can scream, "No!" Saying "No!" makes the child bring back the hand from the fire. You succeeded in saving the child from having a burned finger. But what will be learned? Will the child learn not to put fingers into fire or electricity? Not necessarily. You have made the child retrieve the hand from the fire by your scream, but you did not mediate anything, and the child may continue to do this thing in other places that are no less dangerous.

Mediation Modifies Our Approach

So mediation involves modifying the way you approach explaining the experience to the child. It's a very different way of handling exposure to objects and events. After the danger has passed, the mediator explains, "You know that you must be careful when striking a match, to keep the flame away from your fingers so you do not burn yourself, and to be careful not to let the flame touch the cloth on the table. But we will light some matches together so you can learn how to do it and how to be careful. Then, when you are older, you can help your family when they need to light a fire." In this way, I can mediate to children after I've demonstrated the dangerous act, helped them control it, and protected them from the kind of experience where I had to act in a nonmediating way.

The most interesting thing is to see children react to this kind of mediation. They react in a kind of reciprocal way. That is, when I make children aware of why I intervene in the way that I do, when I create an understanding of why I held the hand with the match, why I help them hold the lighted match in a particular way, and I explain my intentions, children can internalize my intentions and turn these intentions into determinants of their own behavior, and then become their own mediator. Reciprocity is further observed when the child is affected by certain stimuli, and needs (for example, contact with the mother), and tries to repeat the stimuli by doing what occasioned the initial response, even for potentially dangerous behaviors—like reaching into the fire! It also depends on the reactions of the mother: Are they pleasant or not? Do they bring the mother closer in the interaction? In some seemingly perverse ways, some children will continue to behave badly to get responses from their parents even if the parental responses are unpleasant or even abusive. This is true in classrooms as well, where students may challenge rules or create disturbances in order to gain the teacher's attention. Children who drop pencils on the floor, or bother classmates by sitting too close or trying to copy another's work are engaging in the learning situation in a seemingly negative way in order to create a response in the teacher.

Thus, mediation is, first of all, characterized by the intentionality of the mediator: I mean to make you see something that the experience by itself will not tell you; I bring my knowledge, my experience; by interposing myself between you and the fire, I make you feel and understand that there are things you don't touch before you see and understand them, there are things you don't move before you know what is behind them, and there are things about which you must think before you do them. This is the concept that we have developed over the years, reflected in the motto of the Instrumental Enrichment programs: *Just a Moment, Let Me Think*. This is the product of a mediational interaction.

In the example above, the mediational interaction produces control over the impulsivity of the individual: Unmediated, whatever I see, I go and do! If the mediator interposes between the perception of the stimuli and the mediatee's behavior, the mediational experience becomes: "Wait, look, listen, let us think . . . can we do this, shall we do this, shall we act differently? What will happen if we do, or don't do . . ." And through this interaction, the whole behavior is meaningfully affected.

One of the characteristics of conventional teaching, as differentiated from MLE, is to conceal the reasons for the mediated intervention (for example, when a teacher simply produces an interaction without indicating the reasons why, the anticipated outcomes, and/or the ways in which the activity will contribute to further actions). In such situations, when the teacher does not explain why and how the newly perceived stimulus has been presented, for the students "it just is!" However, when teachers are explicit about their intention and articulate to their students that the learning activity has the qualities described above, they are incorporating mediation into their teaching. Why do students dissect frogs in biology, or write poetry? Why classify plants and animals, or relate them to geographical climate zones? In MLE, the mediator makes the reasons explicit, by word and deed. Ultimately, we want mediatees, in the classroom or in any aspect of life experience, to become so aware of what and why the response is happening that they become their own mediators—building reciprocity.

However, intentionality is only one of the three characteristics of MLE. Please note that I'm not speaking of mediation in the sense of Vygotsky. He spoke about mediation, proposing what he described as tools for mediation—verbal tools and other working instruments. For Vygotsky, mediation meant a social interaction that turned stimuli into "psychological tools" that could then be used to enhance the processes of learning. Instead, I'm speaking of MLE as a more differentiated interaction, as a *process of the learning* that brings cognitive functions to support the main objective of my intervention. I mediate to the child how to learn from experience, from my interaction, and for everything that will be done (acted upon), how to organize and plan various acts according to the intentionality of the MLE.

THE MEDIATION OF TRANSCENDENCE

But this is not enough. Mediation can focus upon one particular object or event that may not necessarily affect the behavior of individuals and their learning experiences in a variety of other areas. The mediator must think in what way they will give their interaction with the child the nature of transcendence—the second of the three core MLE parameters. For example, in our description of the stone and the scorpion, asking, "What have you learned by being careful not to turn over the stone?" mediates the quality of transcendence, of going beyond the immediate experience. You may extend this by learning not to touch certain money that doesn't belong to you; you may learn not to take the liberty to insult somebody who might become angry and physically attack you; you may learn a variety of other areas that are derived from your early experience with the mediation of intentionality.

Thus, I must make sure that my mediation will be a learning experience that affects a great variety of behaviors, and also a great variety of needs systems. The transcendence with which I am shaping an individual by my intentionality and the reciprocity that is generated may then increase or widen the system of needs that the learner has. For example, I may use the money that I need in order to eat to buy a ticket to hear a musical instead, or to go to a bookstore and buy a book because my need system may undergo many changes. I may feel the same need for music as I feel for food and I may give up certain areas of activities in favor of other areas of value. This implies that the choices one makes are indicative of "transcendent" thinking.

The Mediator's Goal

Transcendence can inculcate a need to plan, to organize, not to act impulsively, and to help control behavior, knowing that an impulsive action is like the stone that may have a scorpion under it.

Once one has experienced the intentionality of mediation, one becomes able to widen their need system and apply experience in a variety of ways. Transcendence is thus the most *humanizing* factor because what makes us human is mediation that enables transcending our needs and our experiences. By transferring to a variety of areas in which the learning didn't take place, the experience received in a mediational interaction extends the learning to a variety of other situations, going beyond the immediate activity and developing new systems of needs, awareness, and relationships. This does not necessarily change the instinctual elements, as in the Freudian concept of sublimation. We instead believe that there are new needs that are developed for a more focused, meaningful, and systematically experienced exposure to stimuli.

In the Freudian formulation, the lowest form of behavior (instinctual sexual needs) is elevated to a higher level of experience. We do not necessarily hold that all higher activities are simply transformations (e.g., sublimations) of simple, basic instinctual needs. Rather, the origins of behavior are much more diverse.

Multiple Modalities of Mediation

Mediated learning experience uses a variety of modalities, something that I will return to later in this chapter and more fully in Chapters 3 and 4. My intention in mediating is to turn the immediate present encounter into an experience that will go much beyond and look for other meanings. I well remember explaining the concept of transcendence to a very large and distinguished audience in Pittsburgh, Pennsylvania, in the 1960s. In the audience was Professor Jerome Bruner, one of the major figures in American educational and cognitive psychology. When I described the mediator's role in the shaping of human experience, the way by which the transcending principle affects humanity, and the variations of behavior, thinking, and human need systems, he screamed out like an impatient student, "Feuerstein! Mediated learning experience is not just for retarded children or deprived children; it's for all of us! It is what makes us human!" He understood well what I was trying to convey.

Transcendence is the second element that makes an interaction a mediated learning experience. It is the concept that we speak of when we consider the transfer of training from one area to another, but it's much more than that. In classroom learning, this is the implicit intention, but students often do not get it. Their question often is, "Why are we learning this? What difference will it make in my future?" In a paper titled "Learning to Think; Thinking to Learn" (Feuerstein & Falik, 2010), we made the point that learning content (the "facts" of a discipline) without learning strategies of thinking that manipulate and integrate that content will be empty learning and subject to a "limited shelf life."

For students, the experience is often imposed upon them to learn elements that they do not need for immediate use. Transcendence creates the condition for learning something that goes beyond the immediate. It is through the experience of *going beyond the immediate* that one becomes human.

Similarly, the mother who gives a child food and also wants the child to understand that eating is done at a given time, at a given place, and in a specific atmosphere, is transcending the need for food and extending the experience to the need for a socialized way of eating. By doing this, she transcends the simple need to get food into our bodies and brings to the child culturally determined and meaningful rituals and expectations—what anthropologists might label our "tribal" behaviors.

THE MEDIATION OF MEANING

The third core parameter of mediated learning experience, without which the experience cannot be considered a mediated interaction, is the mediation of meaning. Meaning is the experience of the significance attributed to a particular experience: What does it mean to you? What is the value of this experience? Why do I want you to experience it? What do I want you to learn from it? Why should it be so important to you? And here we are speaking about feelings, values, and moral needs. We speak about meaning as an important part of our need system.

Why Are We *Imposing on the Learner*?

Now, one of the great problems is that when I mediate to the child my intentions, I do something that is not necessarily within the child and is therefore an imposition. This imposition is not on the basic needs of the individual. When I mediate transcendence, I give the mediatee the freedom to apply whatever has been experienced to a variety of situations. But the existentialist might ask:

Who gives you the right to impose on a child your meaning? Aren't meanings something that should be distinct for each individual and not necessarily imposed by somebody? Let people choose their own meanings. What right do you have to mediate meaning? This is an imposition!

And yet we are increasingly concerned about societal values that emphasize activities, implicitly and explicitly, that are hedonistic and mindless. People are at the same time connected to others and isolated—think of the people who are part of groups but absorbed with their cellphones, texting and "surfing" in a kind of passive connectivity. When one feels connected because one has numerous "friends" on a social media site, what does that mean for the experience of connectivity? I fear that drug addition, binge eating, antisocial actions, and the like are peripheral phenomena that demonstrate a lack of personal value and meaning.

What Is My Response?

When you impose on the learner the meaning of studying a particular issue, the child may not be interested. Why do you impose this meaning? You know that by learning, you may reach such and such goals. But perhaps these goals are not the child's goals. You take an adolescent who wants to go and buy a motorcycle, and you tell him, "I know that you would like to go and study medicine. Do you know that by buying this motorcycle you may not be able to reach your goal?" The meaning of doing something may be a very strong imposition on the part of the adult, on the part of one individual to the other.

But in this example the importance of mediating meaning emerges. By giving a meaning to one's activities, choices, and preferences, the child learns that there is a meaning to life. And when the child does not accept the meaning that has been imposed by parents or teachers, the child may go and look for other meanings that have not been mediated by parents or educators, or even the larger culture. In such instances, the need for meaning in life remains, but without cues or guidelines that create the capacity to find the meaning to existence.

Endowing children with a meaning that is related to chronological age, stages of development, and so on opens individuals in unique and special ways to needs that have potentially internalized meaning. And once one has needs, the person will search for meaning even where it does not readily exist. This is why we must mediate to the children the meaning of what they do, or can do. For example, we might encourage students to consider a world event such as a flood or famine from the perspective of their family or community. Then we might ask them to consider the conditions that provoked the situation, such as global warming, the resistances to it, the implications of industrial and commercial interests, and the like. The opportunities are numerous, and they come from multiple sources—science, economics, human development, and more.

Further, the question can be asked, What would happen if you did not mediate meaning and let children choose their own meanings? First of all, children will not find meaning for many of the things that they do. Meaning is a characteristic of a certain activity, of certain experiences from which you have to extract the value or purpose. What is the meaning that makes you do something? What animates you when you choose a certain thing? You may not be conscious; you may not be aware of it. You may feel that at a given point you are devoid of a meaning. Why should I suffer? You need to have a meaning for your suffering. Why do I have to offer this to another individual? Again, there has to be some way of extracting from the behavior that which has a certain meaning. Imposing on the individual a meaning is to force a search for meaning even when the meaning is not necessarily readily apparent. It is an antidote for restlessness and anomie, feelings that plague high schools where students frequently fail to find meaning in their educational tasks.

CREATING CONSCIOUSNESS: INTEGRATING THE "UNIVERSAL" PARAMETERS

One of the major elements that unites these three parameters is that each one of them is accompanied by consciousness, by awareness, and by a "mental power" that produces a feeling of will in both mediator *and* mediatee: I choose what I want to show the child; I don't just go by the existence or the presence of a certain stimulus. I (both the mediator and mediatee) know what I want to do; I choose what I want to do, with a state of awareness and consciousness that modifies the behavior. I will have more to say about this in the next chapter. And drawing from quantum physics (which we will address later, in Chapter 6), it is a consciousness that determines what kind of elements will be seen, what will be experienced, and—by this—the great power of the human mind.

THE EFFECT OF MLE ON THE MEDIATEE,
AND THE OTHER PARTNERS IN THE INTERACTION

Mediated learning experience is what I refer to as the only way to explain the great differences between individuals. There are individuals who benefit from being exposed to direct stimuli: whatever they see they learn from; whatever they interact with affects them in a very meaningful way. They are able better to remember, to understand, and so on. There are other people who are exposed daily to the same phenomena, to the same experiences, and they are not modified, they do not learn from it, do not know what to avoid and what to do. Some of these individuals repeat the same errors again and again despite the fact that they have been exposed to the results of direct experiences, even those that were not desirable ones.

In order to explain this phenomenon, we suggest that MLE affects the individuals' *capacity* to learn, their *propensity* to be modified. I generally do not like to use the words *potential* or *capacity* because they imply something that is fixed and may have limits. But the concept of "propensity" conveys a power, a readiness, and an awareness—the mental power to learn and benefit from experience and to be conscious about the fact that certain behaviors should be considered appropriate and others less so. And MLE helps the learner differentiate between what kind of behaviors and experiences are open and available, that should be responded to, and that others should be avoided and eventually eliminated from the repertoire of functioning. This contrasts with the position of the behaviorists who consider learning solely on the results of its outcomes, and do not want to look further.

The provision of mediated learning experience interposes an initiated, conscious, aware, goal-oriented adult. We want the child to become affected by exposure to stimuli. This kind of interaction, as we have defined it, is one of the direct and proximal reasons for the differences between individuals in their readiness to be affected, and to learn and be modified by their experience.

THE THREE PARTNERS IN THE
PROCESS OF MODIFIABILITY

The three parameters that we have described—intentionality, transcendence, and meaning, and in particular intentionality—modify the three partners in the interaction, the stimuli, the person being mediated, and the mediator him- or herself. If I have an intention that you should see something, learn from seeing it, and become able to use what you have learned in other situations, I will have to do something to make this happen.

Modifying the Stimulus

I must *modify the object* (the stimulus to which you are exposed). I will show very clearly how the object is affected by what you do. You incline the glass and the water spills. You throw the glass on the floor and it will break. If you keep it straight, you are unable to drink from it. If you incline it a little bit, you can sip from it. Thus, the child becomes aware of the object through the relationship between certain behaviors and certain outcomes. And the mediator organizes the world in such a way that the child will learn from each experience, because the mediator interprets, and as a consequence, *modifies* the stimuli. The mediator makes a stimulus stronger, makes it weaker, cheerful, understandable, or sad—or any number of other potentially meaningful attributes. By interpreting it to the child, the mediator modifies the world so that it becomes salient, acceptable, and meaningfully understood by the learner.

Modifying the Learner

The second "partner" to be modified by the MLE interaction is the learner, the mediatee. The mediatee may not be interested, may be sleepy, may be focusing on something else. And I, the mediator, am interested that the mediatee sees what I want to show, what I want to be seen. If the mediatee is sleepy, inattentive, I do something to render the mediatee attentive and alert; I modify him or her in order to enable acceptance, learning, and the absorbing of what I intend to mediate. The most successful classroom teachers do this when they give careful thought to how to introduce a topic or a science experiment or a learning experience in a way that will grab the attention of all their students.

This is very different from conventional teaching. In much of teaching, if the student does not learn, it's accepted as the student's problem. The best teachers, however, are aware that they need to change everything in order to make students ready to learn. Students have to know what is to be learned. Teachers are burdened by a prescribed curriculum and may say, "They have to learn the curriculum imposed on me" and not search for ways to infuse meaning and purpose in the learning. In contrast, teacher/mediators who want their students (the mediatees) to be affected by what is the focus of the learning will work hard to make the learners alert, interested, and motivated by what is presented.

Modifying the Mediator

The third partner that is changed by the mediated learning interaction, by the intention to mediate, is the mediator. This partner is very meaningfully affected and modified by the very intention to mediate. I know that if I put something in front of the child without mediation, the child may or may not use it. I have to intervene. I have to make myself accepted so that the child will be happy to follow my suggestions. I have to do something so that the child will accept me as a mediator. Some children reject mathematics because they don't like the teacher. Some children are not able to learn to read because the one who teaches them to read behaves in a way that is not acceptable to them. So teachers/mediators must first be willing to modify themselves, and they do so by the intention to mediate. This third change is a *sine qua non* in the provision of MLE. This is especially true in the area of social and emotional identification, returning to the reciprocal nature of the intentionality/reciprocity dualism. Although this centers on certain identification processes, both mediator and mediatee undergo meaningful changes. Particularly, the mediatee develops needs to identify with the mediator by a readiness to integrate the changes induced by the mediated learning interaction, in spite of (or perhaps because of) the learning challenges that can now be accepted. The mediator who creates conditions for this transformation is very meaningfully affected and modified by the very intention to mediate.

What are the qualities of the teacher who mediates learning? There are very specific qualities that make children so alert to the mediator that even things that are not interesting to them become the center of their interest, and this makes a great difference from the kind of teaching where all you want to do is to transmit to the child an order, a piece of knowledge. We often say that "all teaching is not mediating; but all mediating is teaching!" In the former, the teacher is simply a pipeline that does not transform the nature of the thing being transmitted to the child and for whom it doesn't matter if the child listens or doesn't listen or doesn't understand. If you are not sensitive to the reactions and needs of the learner, you are not a mediator. The mediator is modified by the behavior, the approach, the very intention to mediate to the child.

REASONS FOR AND CONSEQUENCES OF A LACK OF MLE

One great question is asked by every mediator and every teacher: "What are the reasons why some children have been mediated and others not?" And I must tell you something that's very important to know, that this issue of whether mediation has been experienced is *not* a function of the socioeconomic level of individuals. Just as there are master teachers who mediate learning and conventional teachers who do not, you can find individuals who come from higher-level economic and functional parents, intelligent and well-off people who are in position to offer their children anything and everything, and yet they don't mediate. As our Instrumental Enrichment learning programs have shown teachers how to mediate the processes of learning, so too have we begun to teach parents and caregivers how to mediate their interactive experiences in the family or in care-providing settings such as elder care and home health care.

When Parents Don't Mediate Their Children

Such cases exist; it means there are individuals coming from very appropriate families that do not mediate. Partly, this may be due to certain theoretical and psychological theories that do not consider mediation a necessity. It has been posited that direct exposure to stimuli suffices, and that if the child gets information from exposure to many toys and objects and other rich stimuli (such as going to the zoo and so forth), there's no need to mediate; the child sees and experiences. It is not understood that in order to really experience one's environment, it first needs to be mediated. The child must be endowed with those tools of perceiving, of elaborating, performing, in order to be able to benefit from direct exposure. So these children are given a lot of stimuli but literally "do not see" or "do not feel" the meaning in their environments, and thus are unable to benefit from their exposure. Ann Lewin-Benham and I have recently (2012) published a book, *What Learning Looks Like: Mediated Learning in Theory and Practice*, that addresses this issue and shows ways of enhancing the child's experiences in museums and other stimulating environments.

Why Do Children Not Receive Sufficient MLE?

In addition to the distal conditions I described in Chapter 1, there are other reasons. It may be due to the fact that mediation was not offered. You can have a variety of reasons why mediation is not offered; partly (as I point out above), it may be because the adult is convinced that it is enough for the child to see, to experience, and that this will do the job. This is, to a large extent, what Piaget proposed: He believed that the child who is maturing and has opportunities to interact with objects will develop capacities and will develop inborn potential.

What Is Insufficient MLE?

We have identified two general reasons for a lack of MLE: Either (1) it was not given, or (2) the recipient was not able to receive it. Here and in the next section we will offer further elaboration. MLE may not affect the individual because it was not given. Where is this lack mostly manifest? This manifests itself particularly in the case of the children of immigrant parents who don't know the language, don't know the culture, and don't feel that they are entitled to impose their culture, their language, and their way of looking at things on their children—so they stop mediating to them. They say:

> "You learn what you learn at school, not from me; you learn what you have to learn from your neighbor, not from me; I am not able to orient you; whatever I will tell you doesn't really pertain to this culture, so you will not be able to learn from me the kinds of things you need in order to adapt."

DIFFERENTIATING CULTURAL DIFFERENCE FROM CULTURAL DEPRIVATION

This has been a central theme in my work, formulating and then responding to the potential for cognitive modifiability. In the United States, this was "discovered" in the mid-1960s as educators began to think about meeting the needs of inner-city, impoverished, minority students. Nonetheless, I have had to work hard to make and explain the distinctions. There are parents who give up on their own culture; they stop mediating it to their child. We call these children "culturally deprived." It's not that their culture deprives them; they are deprived of their own culture. By being deprived of their own culture, they are often not able to reach out to their potential of plasticity, of flexibility, of sensitivity to what needs to be learned for their adaptation.

The Transmission of Culture

The great problem was (and is) that in some cases, the continuity and transmission of the immigrant culture is not encouraged, because the children have to learn the new culture of their new country. It certainly requires a lot of the child. However, one should not stop parents from acting as mediators, even by presenting to the child a culture that is different from what is being experienced. Children who have been mediated in their own culture are culturally *different*—not culturally *deprived*. If you stop transmitting the culture to children, if you stop talking to them the way you were talking before your migration, if you stop presenting the past, if you stop encouraging a representation of how it was before at home—for a variety of emotional, effective, or socioeconomic reasons—then from culturally different the children *become* culturally deprived. Schools can help with this by valuing this aspect of experience and encouraging students to draw from their own cultures for their reading and writing, and creating homework assignments that allow parents to share culture with children. Culturally different individuals have no difficulties adapting. They may even show capacities that are beyond what you would believe from existing levels of functioning.

> Let me give a general example. Yemenite children came from a culture that was centuries behind the cultures in the developed world—however, these children had a very rich reading and writing culture. This made of them the most easily modified individuals. When they arrived in the new, advanced culture (to Israel, for example), they learned: They exceeded to high levels of functioning because they had had a modality of mediation that was given to them even though they were in a very different culture. They had the skills and perspective that enabled them to learn the new culture. *So being culturally different is not being culturally deprived.*
>
> Another example is the Ethiopians in Israel. These are the most amazingly modifiable, adaptable people. I met with them about 35 years ago, before they came in masses to Israel. I was amazed by these people, who did not learn to read. They came from a preliterate society . . . actually a "no-literate" society. They never had books to learn from. Even the Bible they used was not offered to them in the written way. All that they learned came from the way people behaved, from the habits, from the culturally determined modes of interaction, and from their incredible readiness to sit for

hours and listen as the community's leader and teacher talked to them in groups, as they sat in a circle. He would move his hand with something in it, and the children were affected by it. They would look at the hand and were very attentive. This made these people who did not read or write able to reach high levels of functioning when examined and then taught in a way that was accessible to them, consistent with SCM and MLE theory and practice, using the modalities and mediation of the dynamic assessment method that is derived from them (the Learning Propensity Assessment Device—(LPAD) (see Feuerstein, Feuerstein, Falik, & Rand 2002). And because they are culturally different but had a very rich cultural behavior and an acquired repertoire that they were given in their environment, when you gave them the necessary tools—the language, the concepts—they learned rapidly.

We have a group of Ethiopians who have been given this mediation for specific cultural elements, and they learned in colleges, in the army, in other advanced settings. They rapidly became good students and in diverse areas of high-level functioning.

So, one reason for lack of mediation may be cultural—due to immigration or poverty. Students may be low-functioning, but if you approach them to show them what they know (perhaps they don't have some specific areas of knowledge), they have the tools to learn the knowledge. Give them the tools, the instruments of learning, teach them to read appropriately, and they learn well.

We examined about 3,000 Ethiopians with static assessment tests. When they were asked for certain knowledge that they had not acquired yet, they had great difficulty performing. When we gave them a modality of assessment where we evaluated not what they knew, what they could do at the moment of assessment, but rather the way they are able to learn and how to use what they learned in subsequent later (and more difficult) tasks, they showed many improvements in their functioning and responses. Following this experience, and in intensive cognitive training experience, they were accepted to the more sophisticated courses of auxiliary activities in the army, and a number of students after their army experience were accepted for studies in prestigious curricula (law, medicine, psychology) in universities (Israeli universities have very rigid psychometric test-score limits for acceptance). The difference between what they did when they were first asked to do things they didn't know and then later things that they were taught (through systematic exposure to tasks and mediation) was absolutely incredible!

Poverty as a Reason for Lack of MLE

In some cultures, "poverty" may be more than economic. The child may well be taken care of by the parents, in terms of providing food and elementary care. But the parents may not have the time, patience, mental resources, or energy to offer their children mediation. These children are exposed to a "poverty" that affects them very severely. Many such children come to school totally unprepared for what they have to learn. They are not attentive . . . very often, this inattentiveness is considered something organic and treated with medication. Ritalin becomes the magic potion to solve the "effects" of this condition. These children have not learned to become attentive because they did not have a mediator who took the time and made the effort to focus their eyes upon objects, pointing out to them, helping them treat certain stimuli differentially: "Here, stay longer; look at it better; not once, again; look at it again," and so on. This creates in the child a readiness to invest what is necessary to learn.

So, although poverty may be a reason for lack of mediation, it is a *distal* condition, as we discussed earlier. For example, we knew of families in Poland who were poor, who didn't have enough money to give their children meat or fish more than once a week. But each penny they had they put into the instruction given to their children—the parents took away from their mouths in order to pay for instruction because they wanted their children to receive the learning so important in their culture (the mediated learning experience). Poverty was present, but poverty is not necessarily an impediment to being mediated. These parents sat with their children, going over what they had learned, asking them questions and motivating them again and again. And there are many parents in today's world, without regard to socioeconomic status, who do the same thing!

There are other reasons for lack of MLE. Some children for some reasons are rejected by their mothers or by their fathers, and they are handled in such a way and at such a distance that the parent doesn't become an appropriate mediator and is therefore not accepted by the child, and this affects the child's functioning very badly. So there are a number of exogenous/external distal factors that make MLE a rarity—the child doesn't get it, or it is not enough or not appropriate, not modified to needs, and therefore the child may be intelligent and capable, but without mediation will not develop and learn.

Children with Developmental Disorders

There is another group to whom mediation is offered but something in them (an endogenous distal factor) makes them unable to benefit from mediation. An extreme example is the autistic child. If you observe an autistic child, you see that the readiness to be attentive, to accept your mediation, to accept you interposing yourself between the learner and the object is not there. When you try to teach the child how to handle the objects, you may be rejected. Such children do not want this contact, will go away, and will not be accessible to your mediation. These children live in their own bubble, have their own preferences, distancing and distracting themselves by preoccupations with small stimuli—for example, catching a piece of wool, a string, or a scrap of paper and moving it repeatedly in front of their eyes. The major interest of such a child is to see movements. Some children have other kinds of skills that they develop very early but seemingly without any external social or interpersonal meaning and interest.

Mediating Autistic Conditions

If one tries to mediate these children, they seem impenetrable to the mediation. They do not accept it or evidence interest. In young children, the normal response when they see their mothers is to make a movement and gestures that convey "take me, pick me up." The autistic child does not. When the mother is visible, there is no reaction.

> We had a very interesting case of a mother who had twin girls. The mother immediately, after the first month, recognized the great difference between the two girls. The one was responsive; the mother immediately was able to establish eye contact, and the child followed her. The other, when the mother came by, she didn't move; she didn't make any kind of anticipatory behavior to make the mother feel that she wanted to interact with her, wanted to look at her face, wanted to see her longer. She did not express happiness when the mother came and didn't cry when the mother went away. And the mother, because these were twin girls, was able to formulate the difference between these children and reacted differently toward them. She came to the point of saying, "I cannot handle this child, she doesn't respond to me, she doesn't look at me, she doesn't take what I try to give her," and she had great difficulties, and she was very upset. The mother felt she

had no way to come close to this child, to make her feel that she's in her hands.

So we tried to work with the mother and we concluded that she would not be able to overcome this difficulty because of her disappointing experience in comparison with her other child. However, we found out that the father was a very warm person, that he was very much less affected than the mother by the autistic daughter's condition. He tried to talk to his child and to laugh with her and so on. And the fact that she didn't respond didn't bother him as badly as it bothered the mother. But then we had another mother, a "resource" for this situation: the grandmother. She was an elderly lady, stout, warm, and doing all kinds of things that she had done with her own children. We suggested that she take this child (the nonresponsive twin) and give her the intense feeling of her presence, make her ready to establish eye contact and social connection. It was an attempt to correct a possibly inborn autistic condition, by creating a very strong mediating environment. There needed to be an intensity of the environment in order to go beyond this wall, this bubble of isolation in which the child lived.

In addition, we had my students at Bar-Ilan University, as an "academic project," take on the child and give her even more stimulation. This program occurred over several years. Then we were able to place the girl into a normal school. She wasn't the very best student, but she learned to talk, read, and write. She continued up to a certain year of schooling and then become an assistant to a kindergarten teacher. She learned to sing and dance. She had acquired a warmth and ways of interacting with people. I saw her every 2, 3 months at the time and could see her changes in responding. I saw her grandmother. And I observed that the child was becoming a very different personality: open, ready to make contact with people. When she got married, I was invited with my wife to stand near her, as important guests.

Mediated learning experience, in the way that it was used here, was extremely intensive. The power of the intensity of mediation is something that goes beyond the innate condition that this child brought with her at birth. It is, of course, even more meaningful when children become autistic or are within the spectrum, as one says today, because of certain environmental conditions (lacking MLE) like the ones I described when I spoke about the caregiver who did not allow the child to do anything else but be exposed to some inadequate presentations of the world and of life.

So from this point of view the autistic child can be responsive and receive the kind of mediation necessary. And further, mediation may modify even an innate condition. There is now suggestive evidence from the neurophysiological research that even the genes may be modified in this child that previously were silent, following the intensity of our mediational interaction and, in the case I describe above, the wonderful personality of this grandmother who dedicated her whole life to this child.

Mediating for Hyperactivity

Another focus for MLE is children who are, for a variety of reasons, hyperactive. When you try to mediate to them, when you try to show them something, their attention will already be somewhere else. Attempts to catch their attention may not be effective because they are not in the same spot (attentional focus) as when you tried to show it to them. There are a variety of reasons: Children with sensory deficiencies don't maintain focus for prolonged periods, or auditory difficulties interfere with their hearing for a certain time, or lack of early mediation of focusing behavior creates in an initially chaotic world (for them).

Thus, the condition of hyperactivity may not permit the individual to receive the mediation that has been offered. If we speak to such children when we try to mediate, the internal endogenous (distal) condition (running from one to another place, from one to another topic) makes them unapproachable, impenetrable, and mediation doesn't reach them. So this child ends up as one who has not received MLE. In this condition, one has not learned to focus, has not learned to treat different stimuli differentially, has not learned to sit down in order to let the perceived element become really effective. The child may not recognize what has been seen a minute before, as it has not been looked at properly.

Differentiating Distal from Proximal
Factors in Mediation

From this point of view there are conditions that are internal conditions of the individual, which we have labeled *distal*, and which make the child unable to benefit from the *proximal* MLE intervention (look again at Figure 1.1 in Chapter 1). Some children have been affected in one of their sensory input/intake functions. For instance, there are children who do not hear in the early periods of development—they are not exposed to the voice of the mother; they hear certain amplitudes of a voice but not others—and these children may suffer from a sensory deprivation or, better said, a sensorially determined deprivation. The mother attempted to talk to them, but they didn't hear. The mother attempted to show them, but they didn't see. The mother attempted to make them interact, but they were not responsive. These children may have a difficulty in being touched, and any attempt on the part of the mother to touch them may result in their rejecting the mother's attempts. And of course, this creates in the mother a certain question: "How can I approach this child?"

Mediating Genetic/Chromosomal Conditions

In this case, you have children to whom one attempts to mediate, but because of their condition, which may be organic, chromosomal, or due to postnatal accidents, the attempts will be unsuccessful. Take, for instance, the child with Down syndrome, who may be able to benefit from mediation, but needs a level of intensity in order to be penetrated by the mediational element. That is, if MLE is given the way you give it to a normal child, for the child with Down syndrome it won't make a difference. These children are not reached by it—they need a much more intensive way to be affected by the mediational interaction. If you do it only five times, showing how to imitate, it doesn't change them. Do it 100 times, do it under very special conditions, do it by a certain familiar mediator. You have to figure out what is the best way to make the child operate and be affected by the attempts at mediation. And if you succeed in going beyond this barrier and make the child benefit from mediation, you will have a very different child from the one you were used to.

> I cannot forget the amount of investment we had to do with Elchanan, our grandson, in order to make him imitate certain behaviors. We were keeping him for hours—his mother, myself, and his brothers, and looking at him and making him keep his eyes on us and see exactly the various different changes in our face. And then all of a sudden he started to imitate.

At a later point in this discourse I will address the great discovery that has been made in the last 10 years about the mirror neurons and discuss this as the way by which we have now an explanation from neuroscience for the effects of mediational interaction on the individual.

Returning to Elchanan . . . once we had done this, he learned to imitate and to use whatever stimulus was imposed on him to become more and more able to respond. He became one of the repeaters. Later in his development, when he was constantly repeating chains of words he had learned, his mother was somewhat concerned, asking, "Is this normal?" I said, "Oh, yes, he knows what he needs in order to learn what he has to learn." And, indeed, we gave him the opportunity to learn by repetition.

Elchanan today, at the age of 22, as a young man with Down syndrome, has finished two matriculation exams, one in biblical studies and another in Judaic studies, getting very high scores in both. Do you know why? Because he has learned during the period when we mediated to him to repeat, to reinforce, to crystallize the knowledge that he has been exposed to.

SUMMARIZING: APPLYING AND ADAPTING MEDIATION

MLE may not become available to children because of some endogenous condition—autism, sensorial deficits, lack of attentiveness, hyperactivity, and so forth—but all these are distal conditions, affected positively by the provision of mediated learning experience (the proximal condition), its intensity, its quality, the choice of a mediator who will make the child ready and able to function. If you do this, then MLE will become available to the child despite the barriers that are there, and with MLE there are open and optimistic prospects for development. And indeed, we have worked with many cases of individuals initially suffering from these conditions and they became very different.

Thus, MLE is a modality of interaction that is responsible for the development of tools to learn. Once the child has learned through the mediator, where mediators interpose themselves between the stimuli, the world, and the child, on what initially may be a limited range of skills and functioning, on which mediators interpret to the child, the incoming stimuli are modified in order to become better used by the individual. Once this is done, the child is able to learn from each interaction with the world through direct exposure.

Returning again to the diagram of direct and mediated learning (Figure 1.2 in Chapter 1), you will see that the "H" in the diagram is small. It may extend itself for certain children who need much more mediation. It may shrink at the time when the child needs less mediation. Mediators do not necessarily interpose themselves between the child and every reality—on the contrary. If parents "overmediate" they will become omnipotent, total universal mediators. They will make their children very dependent and with little readiness to be affected in a very direct way. But when mediation is elastic—given when necessary, reduced or withheld when not necessary—this creates the opportunity for the child to interact directly with what they are exposed to, with stimuli of the environment, with modalities of perceiving, elaborating, and responding to what has been acquired through the mediational interaction.

Now we are able to answer the question, "Why do some children who receive MLE benefit from it while other children do not?" Our answer: In order for children to benefit from MLE, it must be presented by a mediator who modifies the approach according to needs, circumstances, and sensitive observation of both stimuli input and the response capacities of the mediatee. The child's world has to be changed by the mediator following the intention to have this experience become meaningful, not only by learning this particular experience but by going beyond it through the principle of transcendence, which enables the use of one particular skill acquired at one place and time to be transferred progressively to further and more complex types of tasks that will be encountered throughout life.

Further, the mediation of meaning animates the learner and becomes the motivating energetic determinant: It makes the learner motivated to do it, interested to see it, able to repeat it. Meaning represents the energetic principle that creates the power of mind to do this thing. Intentionality and transcendence create the structure of the knowledge that is going to be learned: the cognitive elements. The meaning is the affective emotional element.

Finally, MLE is not something that I invented or created. It is a quality of human nature that insures continuity in the process of the growth of humanity. It is what makes us human! And, indeed, millennia of mediation have made us what we are today. No child is born a genius. No child is born able to do things without putting him- or herself on the shoulders of the previous generations. We are not the products of ourselves; we are the products of a culture that is transmitted to us from generation to generation. And by receiving this culture through the mediational process, we are able to go beyond ourselves and beyond previous generations.

CHAPTER 3

Applications of Mediated Learning Experience

In this chapter I consider that some of the outcomes of a lack of mediated learning experience (MLE) have consequences—behavioral, intellectual, social, and emotional. Diagnoses of various types of learning and behavioral impairments are numerous, and classrooms, treatment programs, and even advocacy groups are organized around them. Here, I offer a different point of view driven by the conception of MLE as a manifestation of my theory of structural cognitive modifiability (SCM).

LEARNING DISABLED OR TEACHING DISABLED?

First, I suggest that much of what is now designated as *learning disability* may need to be redefined as *teaching-disabled*—being exposed to teaching that disables the student. In reality, very often we are not looking at a disabled individual with disabled functions, but rather at someone who has been exposed to *disabling* teaching—exposed to a learning situation that has not been mediated, has not been offered, mobilized, or made sufficiently available.

Indeed, we can see the positive effects of certain activities, when offered to children, that require their full presence and perseverance, their need to plan and observe, and not just to deal with the familiar or easy tasks. Under conditions of mediation, they learn how to treat stimuli differentially and become much more able to benefit from the process of learning. This is a product of a conscious awareness produced by the provision of MLE. Without this consciousness one does not see or search for differences, compare what is seen and known. If this is not reinforced by a process of mediation, individuals will pass by stimuli without gathering all the data characterizing them, as we showed in our example of the monocotyledon and dicotyledon plants in Chapter 1.

This is a very difficult issue, and a challenge to the existing educational order. For example, an increasing number of children is given medication (for example, Ritalin) in order to make them more amenable to learning (to overcome hyperactive and attention deficit behavior), and eventually stimulates areas of the nervous system that (paradoxically) slows them down. But even in this condition, if they do not have an opportunity to use their "slowed-down" responses in order to be exposed to modified opportunities to learn, nothing will happen. If nobody gives these students what they need in order to use the changed status of their attention and behavior, a missed opportunity frequently seen in classrooms, then one should not expect gains. And this, in a great majority of instances, is the unfortunate situation.

THE IMPORTANCE OF CONSCIOUSNESS

One of the important characteristics of MLE is that it generates a state of consciousness, awareness, and goal orientation in the mediatee's interaction with stimuli. As I have emphasized earlier, it is the human interaction (rather than a computer, book, or any substitute for human contact), carrying out an intention and a goal ultimately shared by mediator and mediatee, that makes MLE a powerful factor in the shaping of human beings. It is this characteristic that enables mediators to choose from their repertoire of thinking and experiences those that will best fit the needs and goals toward the particular mediatee. MLE will be offered to the individual according to observed needs: to the child who is not able to name colors, who is not able to grasp the concept of numbers, who is not able to learn symbols or signs and translate them into words, sounds, or objects, and so on. The mediator chooses from a variety of stimuli that require a particular adaptation of the interactional behavior, a specialized choice of the kinds of stimuli presented and mediated.

Mediating Comparative Behavior

If I have to make a young child able to articulate words in a more appropriate way, in the classroom or family environment, I have to choose from my repertoire of interactions, in the very early stages of speech production, those that will encourage the imitation of the protrusion of my mouth so that the peribuccal muscles will become reinforced and the child will become able to articulate in a more understandable way what is being said. If I want to have a child focus on something, I do not just let the child run around with the eyes all over, but I make the object not only attractive, but something that will maintain interest and sustain perception of the object. My meditational objective is to keep the child persisting in learning what I have chosen to mediate. If I am a teacher in a classroom, I introduce and continually draw the students' attention to why we are learning what we are learning, what we will be able to do with what we learn, and how we will want and need to generalize from what we learn—having the effect of making learning a conscious process that is initiated and engaged in.

So the mediator not only interacts, interposes between the child and the stimulus, but actually makes the child aware, conscious of what the mediator's goals are and the ways by which the mediator attempts to reach these goals.

Mediated learning experience, therefore, has as its major goal the creation of an awareness of the mediator's intention, reflected by conveying to the mediatee a wide variety of perspectives:

> What do you intend by showing me; what do you mean by repeating the thing you have told me; why do you make me see similar things and teach me how to differentiate between them; what do you do in order to make me create a relationship between certain things I've seen and certain things that I have not seen yet but I can compare them and find out the differences; what do you intend to do when you make me transcend the immediate experience and wonder about the broader meaning, go beyond the particular goal, the particular issue that I've been exposed to and extend it over a variety of other situations, to go from the concrete experience to that which I can think about (the representational)?

This awareness extends deeply into the cognitive aspects of experience. The mediator helps the learner consider the commonalities with previous experience and the ways that the learner will be better able to master future encounters. This occurs through the transferring and transcending of principles that have been taught.

The three central parameters of *intentionality, transcendence,* and *the mediation of meaning* activate the mediatee's need system that becomes the energetic determinant of behavior. Intentionality and transcendence relate to the structure of the stimuli and the behaviors that I am modifying in order to transmit them to the mediatee. The mediation of meaning endows the child with the energetic dynamic determinant that will animate the individual with a will to learn, to engage, with a choice to act and experience. Here is an example from the classroom:

> Consider students whose interest in what you present to them is very limited and therefore there is very little chance that they will focus, attend to the particular objects you want them to learn, and ultimately give the necessary time, effort, and investment in order to learn.
> In such a situation, the mediator/teacher will endow the particular objects that have elicited very little interest in the students with certain characteristics that will animate their interest, and by doing so, will make sure that they will become interested, and will lend an attentive ear to the objects that have been modified by the mediator before transmitting them to the students.
>
> There are learners who show very little interest in certain objects that may be beyond their levels of functioning. For instance, a student may show very little interest in the differences between certain birds that are seen daily. They will not attentively search for the differences between two birds. The mediator interposes by making the learner aware of certain things that have not been seen, and by doing this makes the learner able not only to see characteristics that have not been observed, but enables the making of comparisons, the finding of relationships: "The two birds are the same size; however, the one has a black head and the other has a red head."

In this example, it is *comparative behavior* that makes the individual find what is common about the two objects that are seen. It can be generalized: "Size is common; color is different." The mediator does this in a way that enables the child or classroom of children to organize the world; to operate upon, extract, and adduce relationships between objects and events; and to establish relationships that contain on one hand the commonality between two objects or events, two numbers, and so forth, and on the other hand the differences between them. The mediator, through this particular mode of functioning, not only creates the structure of cognitive processes, the operations that the child learns to do following mediation, but also an interest that previously didn't exist.

Mediating Awareness in an "Autistic" Child

Here is an example of mediating awareness in an autistic child. It shows how awareness leads to engagement and breaks through the social distance. It is a very interesting example.

> An autistic girl was brought to me. She was 8 years old. Her parents described her as a child who does not really focus on anything. And indeed she ran around the room without seeing things, touched things and left them, touched other things and threw them, but did not relate either to objects or to human beings. As she ran around my office, she had to pass close by me, in a narrow space behind my desk, in order to complete the circle. She passed by without even seeing me. I tried to call her; she didn't orient herself to me. But as she passed by, she made a movement with her hands and brushed my arm, and as she did I screamed out, "I'm afraid, you touched me!" The girl stopped moving and looked back at me, surprised by my loud and exaggerated reaction. And once she did this, she understood that it was her hand movement that made me "scared." She had a *moment of awareness* of the relationship between what she had done and my reaction. She resumed moving, and on her next "pass" near me she repeated the movement and I continued to scream, "I'm afraid! I'm afraid!"
>
> We repeated this several times, and it was clear that her behavior had become purposive on her part . . . she wanted the repetition. The more I reacted with "I'm afraid!" the more she did it. She somehow discovered that her movements had some effect on somebody (me), and it became a source of real pleasure. She laughed and she continued to do it, and I continued to scream. And at a given point I even put my head down on the table and she came even closer, becoming more interested. This became a goal-oriented activity that she certainly did not have when she entered my room. But all of a sudden, having discovered the effects of her behavior, or her existence as I would call it, she wanted to have this effect prolonged. At a given point, I told her, "Now I'm tired; I can't do it anymore." She came and tried once more, and I did not respond. But she insisted that she wanted me to respond again, as I had before—another "social" connection. I began to follow her around the room and she ran away, but clearly wanted me to follow. Soon (I was becoming very fatigued) I said, "Okay, if you'll give me a kiss, then I will keep doing this." She kissed me on my cheek, the first

time this girl had given a kiss to anyone! The two parents who were sitting there started to cry because this was the first time they had observed her giving anyone a kiss. And so we continued our "game" and I became very exhausted but I felt that this "breakthrough" was so important that I continued this play. Then at a given point I stopped again, and she came back and made even more exaggerated movements, to entice me to continue. I then asked her to give a kiss to her parents. She did; they were overwhelmed with emotion, as this was the first time she had kissed them; and we continued.

In our modern environment, asking a child for a kiss in either a school or therapeutic setting would open one to criticism and possibly censure or litigation. Yet for this child, it allowed for the next step, to help her show her capacity to express affection, first to me, and then to her parents—for the first time in her life.

I mediated to this child that her existence had an effect, that her behavior related to others who will react to her. Early in the interaction she was walking around, doing nothing, aimlessly wandering around the room. All of a sudden, coming back to me she achieved a reaction. And as the "relationship" developed, she was ready to do what she had not done before: to offer me a kiss and then even to kiss the two parents in order to elicit from me behavior that she wanted, that had become socially meaningful for her. For her, this was probably a first awareness of her (social/interactive) existence—which occurred by observing the effects of her behavior on another human being.

This kind of mediation results in an expansion of awareness, of needs, and of limitations. And it can bring us, once we know our intentions, to the best choices and interactions of what to show, what to choose, what to make the child do, in order to benefit from experience. In this way, MLE is flexible, very task-oriented, and needs-oriented in order to make the mediatee not only responsive but also able to achieve strategies, understandings, and insights into what is the role of the interaction.

This girl had responded in an "autistic" manner from birth, her condition being detected at a very early stage in her development. And this caused her to become part of an autistic environment in her kindergarten and school placements (expectations and reactions) that may well have aggravated her condition. Yet the way that that she was able to react in the example above showed the possibility of finding ways that penetrated the autistic quality of her existence and made her able to benefit from a process of mediation.

This is one of the great difficulties with autistic children, and this also shows us what and how children diagnosed and observed as autistic will become—even how "normal" children will react—if they are not offered MLE. It is this quality of interaction that makes individuals able to co-vibrate, to be a part of and react appropriately to their environment. And the lack of MLE in the autistic child is a good example of how children look who have had no MLE either because it was not offered to them or because something endogenous did not permit them to benefit from mediation for their goals and development.

WHEN MLE IS NOT OFFERED OR IS INSUFFICIENT

One of our great questions is, "What is it that makes parents and teachers mediate to children?" I have mentioned this briefly earlier but I would like to focus more on this here. We see today a very great decrease in the amount, nature, and quality of parental mediation. Today, when both parents work, they may see themselves as not able or do not feel that they have to mediate to their children. They don't have the time for it . . . when they come back home, they or their children are too tired and are not available for a mediational interaction. Parents in such situations may engage caregivers, expecting them to act *in loco parentis*, instead of the parents. But neither the caregiver nor the teacher can act as a mediator and have the same interest that would animate the parents in order to mediate to their children. They are, of course, interested in the children. However, this can take the form of doing the minimum necessary, or not having the parental existential need to stimulate the child's development. However, to mediate from the perspective and need of the child is seldom fully done by those who are acting *in loco parentis*, and the other "substitutes" (books, films, the computer) are even more limited in their effect.

Thus, we are seeing today a generation of people, many of whom are growing up without this very powerful modality of interaction with the world that is empowered by the mediator. This creates a situation where so many children arrive to school with very limited strategies of thinking, modalities of focusing and awareness, and what I would call the emotional need to interact with the world in a meaningful way. Many of these children are often—actually today more than ever—considered as suffering from attention deficit disorder (ADD). There are some estimates that the incidence is growing to the point that we count approximately 20 to 30% of children who are said to be suffering from this condition.

Causes or Precipitants of This Situation

Unfortunately (and from our point of view, inappropriately), this is being considered almost a genetic inborn characteristic, and treated accordingly with types of medications that are meant to create in the individual the capacity to observe, to perceive, and to treat differentially the various types of symptoms. I say "unfortunately" because many of these children are those who have not been exposed to the differential nature of MLE. The consequence is that they come unprepared to school in terms of focusing and attentiveness; they are not ready to invest. And the medications prescribed (Ritalin, for example, among others) are in many ways actually an obstructive element. It does not affect the environment. If, on the other hand, MLE is the "prescriptive" intervention, the learner will become affected—more attentive and more able to focus—if exposed to the kind of interest that is animated by the mediator in the process of engaging in MLE.

So perhaps the great increase in the incidence of autism, ADD, and ADHD in the population can be attributed to these conditions (in the environment or in the individual's behavior). I believe and have observed that MLE has been reduced in such situations in a very meaningful way by the diagnoses (and interpretations/expectations) of the experts, by certain economic structures of our modern society, and by the fact that we live in an environment in which stimuli are very rich but if they are not mediated they are not really assimilated and thus they require and receive a very limited amount of response or accommodation by the child to what is seen and experienced.

Other Conditions Affecting Exposure to MLE

There is yet another factor to be considered: the great limitations in children's experience of MLE by the "shrinkage" of the extended nuclear family. The fact that fewer multigenerations live together in the same family environment means that grandparents are not available to mediate to children the past and bridge from the past to the future. The expression "It takes a village to raise a child" recognizes this human need for a supporting network. Many countries and cultures continue to live this way—India, China, and many aboriginal/indigenous societies (see Diamond, 2012).

MLE has to be understood as a need of the parents that makes them able to identify those elements that their children need most according to their age, condition, and interests, and according to the way by which whatever is mediated prepares their childen for levels of functioning that will be required by society, by school, and by the activities that will need to be performed.

To fully understand this, we must return to the three parameters of MLE that we described in Chapter 2—intentionality, transcendence, and the mediation of meaning—as the main conditions for an interaction that carries its power. The difference between an individual who interacts with the child but does not have the *intention* to mediate and one who has this intention is very important. The differences are very great. The individual who is exposed directly to the world, to its stimuli, may not benefit unless one has been changed and shaped by MLE. I have been able to observe a variety of conditions under which individuals, despite their direct experience with stimuli, have benefitted very little from their exposure to them because they didn't have the strategies, the meaning, or the ways to benefit from this exposure. This was true of the Ethiopian children who immigrated to Israel and children coming with their families to new and different cultures. The contrary was true for the Moroccan children I observed in their poor and isolated villages, where in spite of poverty and other environmental limitations they were well mediated by their parents and grandparents and developed adaptive responses.

UNDERSTANDING AND USING THE
SITUATIONAL PARAMETERS OF MLE

We have described—in addition to the three core or universal characteristics of MLE—a number of parameters that are the subject of mediation and that are not necessary, or the *sine qua non* of the mediational interaction. They have been described elsewhere as *situational*. I consider them the sources of the potential diversity of human experience. They are termed *situational* because they may be important for a particular individual, at a particular time and place, but may not be equally important to other individuals, depending on time, place, salient tasks or experiences, and the like. We have chosen them because of their salience for the individual's development and promotion as a contributive member of society and as an effective learner. In other writings I have further identified 50 mediational interactions that are derived from these, and I am sure that those 50 do not exhaust the possibilities! My discussion that follows addresses some but not all of the situational parameters, from which flow the potential 50 interactions.

The Regulation and Control of Behavior

This is one of the first elements that should be mediated to the individual, in an intentional, purposive, and focused way. Regulation and control of behavior is very often necessary for children and even adults who tend to act impulsively. They may not, at the moment they make a decision, check whether the data they have in their hands, the information that they have been given, and the amount of understanding they have of the situation at hand is sufficient for them to make a decision and to act appropriately upon it. I will have much more to say about impulsiveness in Chapter 7.

Impulsiveness is often observed in individuals who do not consider whether or not they are ready, or have the skills or information to take an action. They are very often animated by strong emotions, because the stimulus—the object or event to which they are exposed—appeals to their particular needs to the point that they do not resist it and act upon it, irrespective of the appropriateness of the act. In such situations, their controls and regulation of behavior does not enable them to know and tell themselves, "I am not as yet ready to make a decision; I should not do the particular thing that this encounter with the stimulus is making me do." And by this inappropriate action they may become affected deleteriously, very inadequately by their behavior, eventually leading to disastrous or unpleasant consequences.

Regulation of behavior requires that the individual gather all the data of the task when called to perform, and then once confronted with the task and understanding it, considering, "Do I have the necessary tools, do I have the necessary amount of information, do I have the skills and the effectiveness to do that kind of thing, or should I actually mobilize a variety of other functions in order to be able to fulfill the problem?" Many children hear a question in the classroom and immediately raise their hands, feeling "Yes, I would like to answer," but when called upon they discover that they have not understood the question, that they do not have the information that they need in order to answer correctly. Their readiness to answer was produced in an uncontrolled and impulsive way.

So teachers and parents must mediate to children in a very intentional way to decide whether their response will be appropriate or not. This self-regulation (awareness of why I am doing or not doing something and making appropriate adaptive responses) is not necessarily something that is acquired spontaneously or automatically. The mediator may be the one who will have to engage learners in a process of regulation, make them ask themselves the questions necessary in order to decide whether they are ready to respond. "What is missing and in what way do we find the missing part in order to do the work that is required?" Mediation here produces a kind of homeostatic function that enables the individual to respond, "Yes, I can" or "No, I cannot yet; what do I still need to know in order to respond?" or "What should I do to respond appropriately, to meet my needs and to achieve positive outcomes from my behavior?" This creates an important internal dialogue that internalizes the mediation—what I have called "vicarious" or internalized mediation.

Impulsiveness is very often the reflection of needs that are not acceptable and are not to be given satisfaction. Acting impulsively may lead individuals to very dramatic and very damaging types of behavior. Much of the violent behavior that we observe in certain people is the product of a lack of control and the capacity to regulate their behavior. The capacity to represent to oneself the effects of certain behaviors may act as an inhibiting, controlling, or regulating factor in the behavior of the individual. Mediated regulation of behavior thus is a very important determinant of adaptation of our behavior to the requirements of task and of society.

The mediator can build self-monitoring of responses into the mediatee's system, enabling mediatees to act in such a way that permits them to take into consideration all those elements that may create a situation that is not appropriate. The mediator warns the child, "Wait a minute; let's think; don't start before you are sure that it's the appropriate way of answering," and thus creates a modality and readiness on the part of the individual to control behavior. One of the reasons our Instrumental Enrichment program uses the motto "*Just a minute, let me think*" is because it tries to show the importance of regulation and control in our thinking, mediated to us by the mediator, by the environment, by our experience, and very often by our internalized (vicarious) self-mediation. Now I can mediate to myself—"Wait a minute; don't do it yet; I am not sure that I can, I am not sure that I am ready; I must check it again." And the individual who regulates self-behavior will take time to question whether the response (behavior) is appropriate—whether to act, and when to do it. A good way to describe it is to go through various representations in the mind as to how the response that will be given will affect adaptive behavior and the results obtained from it.

The process here is to represent oneself to oneself. This is a very important point. Nowadays, when our behaviors may be responsible for very meaningful and very important behaviors, it's more important than ever. The individual who lived prior to the industrial revolution may have dealt with agricultural activities during the whole day. Impulsiveness was not necessarily a potential source of great errors. But today imagine that if you simply push an inappropriate button this may create a real storm in the whole system. So you have to be able to distinguish a complex situation and ask yourself, "Do I do the right thing by pushing this button?" The results can be appropriate or may produce very difficult conditions. This is why mediating to the individual or to a group of students the need to control and regulate behavior and to be able to guarantee that what is done serves appropriate goals is more necessary than ever. The mediator will have to make the child or children aware of the importance of how to regulate behavior, both in controlling and inhibiting it as well as initiating it. Regulation contains both inhibiting and controlling, and initiating and animating the individual to do the right thing.

The Mediation of Feelings of Competence

A second element that we consider very important to mediate is the need and the capacity to feel oneself as a competent individual. Being very meaningfully competent does not always lead the individual to the *feeling* of competence. There are many people who, despite their talents and despite their capacity to perform and the fact of their performance, do not have the feeling of competence. They question constantly, "Am I really competent to do it; am I really able to perform what I'm required to; were my actions really successful?"

The feeling of incompetence is very often based on the fact that human existence has very little possibility to control its fate, its destiny, its future. Basically, our existence frequently leaves us with very little feeling of proficiency. Even though we may act and perform and may succeed in many of the things that we do, there is an existential fear that is experienced, leading us to feel incompetent, unable to predict and to control our destiny. Where does it come from? How will the individual take the need and the capacity to respond to certain tasks with the feeling, "Yes, I'm able to do it, I'm predictable in my doing, and I can develop whatever I propose to myself and feel confident and proficient in my doing it"?

Our answer is: Feeling competent is, to a very large extent, generated by the experiences of a child who has an environment of mediators who interpret the positive meaning of actions, create the feeling that the way tasks are mastered reflect competence. The feeling of competence is very often imparted to the child at a very early point in life, when the child takes the spoon and wants to eat independently. The child may bring a spoonful of milk or soup to the mouth and the soup is spilled. So the mother, sitting near the child, will hold the spoon in such a way that the liquid from it will come into the mouth without spilling. The mother does this in such a way that reinforces the feeling that the child can do it, and that despite the help the child, still the one who mastered the task.

The same is true for a great variety of actions in which the mother or the father as a mediator demonstrates and interprets to their children the effects of their behavior: "Look what you have done here; you know, for your age this is a very important act; you are able to do much more and more; don't be afraid; try it; continue to do it." And the value of this is assured by two factors: (1) that the child is offered tasks that are progressively more difficult, more complex, and less familiar, and (2) that instead of simply repeating the same task that has already been properly mastered, a new and somewhat different task is presented, encouraging the trying and doing that is necessary in order to master the task; and then the mediator provides the necessary help or the necessary tools—be they verbal, motor, thinking, and so on—that will give a feeling that indeed that tasks that have been presented can be mastered. This happens in schools when mediating teachers move students to progressively more challenging tasks.

Thus, competence is generated not only by our performance but by the reaction and the encouraging supportive behavior of an environment that makes this task not only mastered but also enables the confrontation with new types of tasks and more complex ones. This gives the feeling that it's not only what one has already learned but that there are many other things that can be learned to reach higher levels of mastery—in the task presented and others like it (but different as well).

We are working with brain-injured people who have lost functions such as talking, walking, articulating, thinking, and reading, and we are trying to restore these functions, using MLE for this end in a very meaningful way. One of the most important elements in making those who are brain-injured become able and ready to mobilize their forces in order to regain the lost functions is the possibility of showing progress—that the interventions will lead to tasks that had been lost being restored and mastered!

A young man was brought in to me with a table that he uses for communication by pointing out the letters of the words he wanted to say but couldn't. I saw this and I considered it necessary to try to make him articulate a few words. I asked him to put his hand below his chin in order to be able to articulate the word that I asked him to repeat, to imitate me. He was able to do it, and he did it in a way that showed that he made a great effort to do it. I pointed out to him that with the necessary effort he will be able to learn to speak and will not need to communicate via pointing to the letters of the word. I gave him some instructions, and showed the parents how to do it and encouraged them to make this happen again. They started to do it at home. A week later he came back with a good repertoire of words that he had learned to articulate, and 2 weeks later he began to build full sentences. The pleasure that he had and the feeling of competence that he gained through this acted as a very meaningful and powerful tool to advance his functions and use it by mobilizing himself. He will be able to gain back many of the lost functions of expressive language, and was amenable to further language therapy that we offered and he responded well to. Another young man with similar difficulties in verbal articulation, but who could write, was encouraged to do so. He began to write poetry, and when he had produced a number of poems, we had them duplicated and bound together into a "book" of his poetry that he (and we) proudly shared with others in our institute and in his family and community. Think about the transformation that occurred: from being inarticulate to such a degree that he had to learn how to make sounds, to the ability (and inner need!) to express himself through his feelings and a differentiated sense of the meaning of his world.

This is also experienced in the administration of the Learning Propensity Assessment Device (LPAD), which is a *dynamic* assessment. In the LPAD, the mediation of feelings of competency is an integral part of the process that often leads examinees to feel competence and experience changes in their abilities from the assessment process, something that does not occur in conventional, psychometric assessment.

This experience shows how individuals regain a feeling of competence and mobilize more effort and more readiness to invest themselves in order to reach the levels of functioning that were considered previously nonexistent for them. This is something that we repeatedly see happening through the mediation of a feeling of competence that both places a goal for the individual that has to be mastered and offers help to master the particular task. Then, once mastered, mediation offers the individual the interpretation of this mastery as a witness of the competence that is evidenced. It is not an exaggeration to say that the experience of success becomes a very strong and orienting need—almost an addiction that drives further actions and readiness to engage!

Today more than ever, human beings need the feeling of competence mediated to them by an environment that makes them feel and act incompetent, particularly when we are confronted with so many complex tasks that are less familiar and to which we must adapt ourselves. The feeling of competence will entice us, will enable us to go on, will mobilize all our efforts in order to achieve. Many people who are devoid of this feeling of competence drop out from the task, from their professions, and become in some way deeply passive and not ready to make the necessary effort to sustain challenge and take the risk of possible failure.

The Mediation of Sharing Behavior

This parameter addresses another very important need in today's world. We live in an environment that stresses not only the right but also the need to act as an individual, to act by and for oneself. One doesn't feel that one exists unless what is done reflects one's own needs, orientation, way, and style of life. This has very deep existential implications for human behavior and development—"Who am I, how do I relate to others, how do I accept the other's relationship to me?" One of the unfortunate consequences may be that individuals will try to free themselves from any requirements made by society. This is not necessarily related to unsocial or antisocial behavior. We want to be ourselves; we are not ready to give up our individuality. And from many points of view, this acts as a disrupting factor in our readiness to become a part of the larger society. We do not tend to share ourselves with others, but have (sometimes imposed by our environments) very limited social and interactive relationships—at best a very small circle of family or friends—and even there, our sharing behavior is not necessarily enough, satisfying, meaningful, or accepted.

This is why we choose this as a subject of mediation. We feel that the individual who shares experiences with others creates a condition of fusion with the other. It is important that we try to make the other feel like ourselves. We try to feel the way others experience us and, by this, create a kind of capacity/need to express ourselves in a very meaningful way that is comforting and encouraging of efforts to make and sustain interpersonal connections.

The need to share one's behavior exists in the individual from a very early stage in development, but it is very often obstructed by the tendency to encourage individuality. We share two lives—our own self and an awareness and connection to the lives of others—our parents, family, siblings, friends, teachers, and so on. In the family, children very often sleep in a bedroom by themselves, and in other ways parents encourage separateness, that what they have and do is not something to be shared with others: In the classroom, it is "This is your little cupboard; this is where you place your things." In the home, it is "This is your closet where *your* things are kept." In the classroom, individual spaces (lockers or "cubbies") are often created and protected, giving the student a sense of privacy and control. But another way of looking at this is that the concept of "yours" is very often stressed as a way to obstruct the penetration of others into your life—*your* feelings, *your* knowledge, *your* experience—and very little is done to encourage the individual to share existence with others.

Many philosophers have stressed the importance of the other in shaping human existence. We considered it important to mediate to the individual the need and the capacity to share experiences, feelings, and thought processes with others, and to confront the other as a way of enriching one's own repertoire and as a way of controlling oneself by better sharing and being open with the other, sharing with the other.

Sharing behavior becomes very important to mediate to the individual by creating needs and skills to identify the self with the other, with their joys and sorrows. One enriches life by not being *only* for oneself, but by acting with and experiencing the other. This to a very large extent works against a counterculture of individuation that affects in a very drastic way our readiness to share with others. In certain cases we are even expected not to show our feelings in public: "Don't show what you are; you don't have to demonstrate your ways of handling your orientation; keep certain things for yourself." This is very often conveyed not only by parents but also by teachers. We feel that this creates a very great inhibitory factor in the individual's readiness and capacity to become a part of the other.

The mediation of sharing behavior thus responds to a very important need. Teachers, as well as parents, should share with their children their concerns, talking to them and interacting in a way that shares their feelings and experiences. Sharing behavior is the way by which the individual fuses, identifying with the other, and by this sharing enriches existence. One experiences this sharing in both direct and indirect ways. An example of the latter is the process of reading. When one reads, one shares experiences with the author, vicariously identifying with the experiences being conveyed. When one reads aloud to others, one shares the experience of the text and the content it contains. When one listens to someone else reading, one has a similar sharing experience. This is closely related, and stands in some contrast, to another MLE parameter that we discuss below.

The Mediation of Individuation and Psychological Differentiation

It is no less important to recognize and promote individual identity, hence creating and reinforcing what we have labeled *individuation* and *psychological differentiation*. Although the fusion that needs to occur through the mediation of sharing behavior is important, there is also the "companion" need for individuation, to value one's uniqueness. The individual has to be given the opportunity to learn that whatever is done, the way it is done, the way one thinks or expresses oneself, is absolutely acceptable and appropriate (when it is in fact so). This does not offer a major contradiction with what we said above—rather, it is the other side of the same "coin." We want individuals to feel they don't have to mirror the other: "You are you and I am me."

> One of the granddaughters of my brother told her grandmother, "Grandmother, don't expect me to be able to do the work you do. I am me and you are you." And she enumerated a number of things by which she differed from her grandmother. This is the need to act as an individual, the right and legitimacy of expressing the self in a different way from others. She was expressing *herself*, sharing being different, and it is a legitimate, typically human need.
>
> In the classroom, students often work toward the solution of tasks using different strategies that suit their style of working and analysis of the problem. When we encourage students to share their ways of working, they often reflect their efficient individuality and gain a personal sense of their worth and integrity.

The Jewish sages say that when a king made his coins with each coin having the same figure on it, you could not distinguish one coin from the other; they were made in order to be the same. There are so many people; no one resembles the other. Differentiation and individuation are not barriers to fusion; different individualities bring special identities that offer opportunities for sharing and fusion—I bring you something that you may not have had, and by this I enrich you. But I don't enrich you by being you, by becoming you; I enrich you by being myself and sharing myself with you.

Sharing behavior, on the one hand, is an attempt to go beyond the differences, beyond individuality, and reach out to the other and make the other reach out to me. Individuation is the legitimacy and the need to be oneself. As I have said, they are two sides of the same coin of human existence.

The teacher often hears the child's answer and says, "It's not what I said; could you repeat what I said?" Teachers very often want to be a model of copying or being imitated, making the child repeat what was said rather than responding, "You are telling me something very interesting; you express it in a different way than I said it, even though it's similar; you have found a way to put this same thing into different words, with a different emphasis and it's very nice." Individuation is fostered by encouraging expression in a way that best represents identity and uniqueness.

So from this point of view, the two factors to be mediated—sharing behavior and individuation—are the ways by which the human being can be formed and made to contribute in a very meaningful way to the richness of the world. Imagine if we all would look or talk the same.

The importance of this rich diversity is beautifully expressed in the well-known biblical story of the Tower of Babel. Many interpreters claim that the great sin of the people was that they wanted to build a tower tall enough to bring them closer to God, and that God reprimanded their pride by changing their languages so that they could no longer work together. But I don't think that this is the real meaning of the story. For me, the story actually stresses the fact that the individuals wanted to fuse to the extent that there would be no differentiation among them. They didn't want to be separate. They were *afraid* that by spreading themselves over the world, they would become different from one another and that would make them uncomfortable. And God saw the danger that if they lived in the same tower and spoke the same language, their individualities would disappear, the differences between them would not exist, and this would create a poor world to live in. So the Lord mixed up their languages so that they would not understand one another, and would be unable to create the very *monotonous* world that they sought to build.

Individuation, therefore, is a very important task for the mediator. Individual difference is an important human characteristic. It needs to be valued, promoted, and for many people who present uniquely different visages, functions, and so on facilitated to enhance their welfare. To help children to bring something of their own experience, affecting the way they perceive things, becomes a very important issue of developing and enriching our world, our human universe.

The Mediation of Goal Seeking, Setting, Achieving, and Monitoring

I now come to another very important modality of mediation, the mediation of one generation to another through the need to set goals for life. Although they may change with time, there is a need to *look* for goals, *search* for goals, and *choose* among the various goals that are available. Then there is a need to *follow up* and make sure that the goal chosen will indeed be realized and brought to accomplishment.

What is a goal? A goal is, by definition, something that is distant in time from the present level of functioning, the present area of achievement; it is something that we set for ourselves that is at a given distance from us, both temporal and spatial. My current level of skills may not be achievable at the time of the seeking and setting. But they are limited by what I can do in the immediate moment. They can also be set in a time, space, and distance from my present condition. If my desire is to become a teacher or a doctor or to become a skillful handler of certain mechanical things and this is not yet present in my repertoire, then I must set my goals into the future—they are to be achieved with time.

This by itself enlarges the consciousness and awareness of the individual over time of things and models of behavior that do not exist as of yet. The small child who wants to become a pilot is very far from being a pilot, but begins to represent conditions in a way that plays out as if already there. This requires from the individual a capacity, propensity, and readiness to act upon representations that are abstract, not yet concrete. And this is by itself a very important achievement. The individual does not live only in the immediate present but also experiences a situation that is far away.

A Goal as a Temporal Experience. The widening process, the extension of the awareness of the human being to goals that are not yet there, and even if some individuals do undergo certain experiences related to the goals that they have set themselves, they even feel that they are there. This is one of the great achievements of the human mind that can experience through representation the so-called inexistent, even though the thing is not yet in its immediate present repertoire.

From this point of view, the search for a goal, the choice between goals, and the ultimate activity leading to the reaching of goals are all very enriching activities of the human mind. It is certainly one of the most important characteristics of the human being to be able to extend prior representation to such distances that enlarge the experiential world. Mediators, parents, and environments play a very important role. And children who start at an early stage in their development to turn these representations into concrete experiences by playing "as if" they are happening are readying themselves for this process at early points in their life.

Mediation of these goal-related parameters is a very humanizing activity and creates states of awareness and consciousness that are extremely important to the development of the human mind.

I am reminded of a child who had chosen to become an actor. The goal he set for himself was to be an actor. And indeed he would take the floor and perform in ways that an actor behaves. However, he was not very expressive: He had a frozen face and a flat affect. I found a coach for him, a very experienced and prominent actor, who—after working with the child for a while—came to me to say, "He should forget it; he will never be successful. . . ." I do not recall how I conveyed this information to this young man, but interestingly, as an adult he became a successful documentary filmmaker, thus fulfilling related aspects of his initial dream.

Another example of mediating goals and of mediating culture is that of the Bushmen in Africa: When the Bushman teaches his group of children how to turn a tree into a canoe, he is a powerful mediator. He does not overtly explain anything to them, but instead he places them in a position to see him as a model and he shows them that he has a goal, to turn a tree into a canoe. The sequence in which the various activities are performed will be learned by the children as steps ordered in a sequence for the goal that has been formulated and set up by the adult.

  A Goal as a Representational Act. Thus, setting a goal is the mediation of a representational act: I have to represent to myself a reality that doesn't exist except in my mind. The mediation involves keeping in mind the goal, which is an abstract element because it doesn't exist yet, and makes me able to learn that in order to achieve my goal there are a number of steps to be followed, and they have to be followed in a given order. To return to the Bushman:

First, you make the tree fall. Then you have to peel the bark of the tree from its trunk. At this point, it is not yet a canoe—it is a *representation*. The mediator creates in the children an extension of their experience from the visual, immediate, sensorial fact to a mental operation, to a representation of something that doesn't exist as yet: the canoe. Then the group of children is placed around the tree and the children see that in order to reach the particular goal you have to go step-by-step. After you make the tree fall, you have to engage in a whole set of operations and behaviors in order to avoid certain dangers that may be incurred by the falling tree. So the children stand around the fallen tree and see how the father now works step-by-step:

first, peeling the bark off the tree; then starting to hollow the trunk in order to make space for the canoe; and then performing all the other activities necessary in order to turn it into a comfortable place for people to sit.

The capacity to concretize and turn the manifest representation into a concrete and functional reality is also a very enriching and meaningful dimension in MLE and in the human experiential world in general.

The Mediation of Challenge, Novelty, and Complexity

Another element that requires mediation and that we have chosen from many others to encourage parents and teachers to mediate to children is encouraging the readiness to engage, act upon, and search for novelty and complexity of tasks. We live in a world in which we are exposed to a technology that presents such rapidity, level of change, innovation, and new elements that have to be learned in order to make appropriate use of them. There is need to help the child accept and be ready to engage in the search for and dealing with novelty, and the readiness even to go beyond the novel element to states of complexity. This does not make it easy, requiring an effort and readiness to respond. Parents do not always encourage their children to engage in something that is novel to them. Some parents say, "Well, that's not for you; you never knew it, you've never seen it, you have never tasted it, don't engage in this." The consequence is to make their children more conservative, ready to limit themselves in terms of what they have to learn and what not, what they have to follow and what not, where they have to go and where not. In this way, they become limited to the familiar, the known, the easy, the already favored: "Oh, you don't like this, don't try it; I know that you will not want to eat it later." And this limits individuals' readiness to activate themselves in a world that is not yet fully known and not totally mastered.

The challenge for the learner is often related to that which is unfamiliar. The mediator nowadays more than ever has to mediate to the child the readiness to be challenged by something new. What is new is a challenge to one's present functioning, and the new calls you to be ready to respond in a positive way to the challenge. The readiness to confront the unfamiliar may become a very important way to engage individuals in responding to the challenges of the innovative world in which we live.

However, we have to be sure that the child thusly enticed and challenged experiences a feeling of competence that enables a successful response to the challenging characteristics of new elements. I have to know that I'm competent enough to reach out and look for this novel element, and not immediately say, "No, that's not for me; that's too new for me; I'm too young for it; I'm not going to be challenged by it because I'm not able to master it." To a certain degree, competence and the *feeling* of competence have to be mediated to the child in order to respond to the challenge of the new and the complex. Without this, the child will probably either fail, or will not do or engage in what is necessary to respond appropriately.

Another element that should be considered is the readiness of the individual to control behavior and not to jump into new situations without feeling properly prepared to master them. Feeling that one has not mastered a situation or task may create a realistic caution, looking for what is needed to do, knowing the prerequisites and what are the necessary conditions to be able to respond positively to the various tasks. Parents, therefore, should not only be able to make their children ready to involve themselves in something new, in something that may be even dangerous to them; they also need to endow their children with the necessary capacity to tell themselves, "No, I'm not yet ready; it's very interesting, it's very challenging, but I do not have those tools, those characteristics, this type of knowledge that I will need in order to exceed to this particular challenge and respond to it appropriately."

So here you have a combination: on the one hand to dare and engage in new elements, but controlled by the need to know whether one is well equipped to do the particular thing—what are the prerequisites that first must be mastered before going into the particular challenging situation? MLE is not a unidimensional element where you will say, "Okay, take this situation and go up to the heights of the mountain" without knowing all the conditions required and being prepared in order to be able to master the particular task. The readiness to be challenged and to go into something more complex, more distant, and less familiar has to be mediated to the child together with the awareness and the search for the conditions that are necessary in order to master the new task, the new and unfamiliar situation.

The last parameters we address here flow directly from the conscious awareness that is promoted by exposure to the MLE experiences we have just described. To put it another way, the mediatee will not be able to move to these levels without considerable positive exposure to the earlier MLE parameters.

The Mediation of Awareness of the Human Being as a Changing Entity

The awareness of the human being as having the potential for a changing, modifying, and modifiable existence is very necessary in today's world. In the world that we live in, the needs for adaptation are greater than ever before. Imagine living 500 years ago, when you could live the same life, day by day and year by year, without having to change yourself; in fact, any change might well cause a chaos in your life. However, at this point in our existence our ever-changing environment requires a great deal of adaptation on the part of the individual. The need for adaptation in response to changing conditions and demands requires that individuals modify themselves—in behavior, aspirations, ways of approaching things. Individuals who consider themselves or are considered by the environment unmodifiable will not be given opportunities or will not be able to take advantage of them, concluding, "Oh, this is not for me; I cannot change my habits, I cannot change my tastes, I cannot change my approach; I must accept the limitations of my reality because I am unchangeable."

Can We Master Our Environments? In some situations, mediators may (hopefully inadvertently) convey the message that the world, the surrounding environment, cannot be mastered: "Listen, you know yourself; you know that this is not for you; don't try to engage into it; it is far above you or not your way of handling; leave it." This means that both the environment and the individual create a barrier between the new and the innovative and the individual's need (and potential) to adapt to it. This affects in a very deleterious way the possibilities to function and to become involved in a world that requires change and adaptation. Adaptation is a kind of change that we produce in ourselves in order to be able to respond to new and unfamiliar situations.

Self-Modifiability. MLE can convey that one can modify oneself: modify levels of functioning, intensity of experience in the world, and to a certain extent, consider the kinds of changes that happen temporary in order to respond to a particular situation experienced in the present, or even to consider them something that can be included in sustained repertoires of behavior. This leads to the understanding that one's present repertoire of needs, feelings, and aspirations should not be considered fixed, neither by our genes or heredity nor by prior experiences.

All this can be transcended. Its elements are: the readiness to consider the self as modifiable, adaptability as a conscious act, and rejection of the concept of fixity, of immutable characteristics. And as we have said elsewhere, this is now confirmed by the brain sciences!

However, awareness and consciousness of change may, under certain circumstances, represent a certain danger to the feeling of continuity of the human being. The concept of change challenges the feeling of "knowing that I am today what I was yesterday and I will be tomorrow what I am today." There is a potential threat to the integrity and the awareness of the self as having continuity. It is why it's very important that, despite the awareness and readiness to change, certain basic elements of existence should be a foundation that one can come back to and rely on, in ways that will be recognizable to self as well as to others, by having a core of elements that pertain to the self-image. In this sense, the mediation must be careful not to create conditions under which individuals will not recognize themselves and will not be able to project into the future.

Change is important, adaptive, and we must teach the individual to adapt, but at the same time being sure that there are some elements that will be the pillars of our existence and will continue to offer us the awareness of our self and the consciousness of our past and our future.

> Here I am reminded of Ron, who suffered a serious injury to the frontal area of his brain, worked hard to regain cognitive functions, and then fought actively to achieve goals that he knew were possible (but some of the professionals who worked with him did not) because of his perception of his capacity to change. I will describe his case more fully in the next chapter because it gives us evidence for the support of our theory and practices.

The Mediation of a Search for Optimistic Alternatives

The next parameter I'm going to discuss is also a very important element in today's world, and has to be taken care of in the process of mediation. This is the search for optimistic alternatives to the outcome of our existence: of certain acts that we do, and decisions that we make. The need for this is strongly emphasized and increased by the fact that the world at this point in time often presents conditions that do not allow the individual to become too optimistic. As a consequence there are many people who literally are drawn to a state of passivity, concluding, "Why should I make efforts that anyway will not turn out to the good?"

The pessimism that we often observe in such individuals is, to a large extent, determined by life experience or by what they observe happening to others—exposure to conditions that are far from rendering the individual optimistic. This can be seen in decisions that parents make about their children or the decisions that society makes concerning the possibility of modifying the conditions of certain people living in society—all bringing about a kind of passive acceptance of a destiny that cannot be modified, cannot be prevented or corrected: "This is the situation, we have no ability to change it; this is the way this individual behaves and we have no way to modify it; this is the change that destiny imposes upon us and we cannot but adhere to a very pessimistic way of functioning." This also shows itself related to international political conflicts. The pessimism implied creates a state of immobilization, a state of passivity. It doesn't allow us to take action, to do what is necessary in order to prevent what is predicted.

The identification of and way of handling alternatives is very important. This must be a willful and conscious act. It's not done by itself. The tendency is to stay pessimistic. You have to want to say to yourself, "I can't accept this pessimism because I don't want to accept this destiny; I will do what I must in order to change this very pessimistic outlook by acting in a positive way."

Like most of my own orientation, my optimistic view of human potential has been in response to a need: the need to see human beings develop, to go beyond the limitations and dangers in which they find themselves. We therefore look for modalities of making development more adequate and more appropriate to *our* expectations and to *our* desires. I do not allow myself to accept the idea that there is nothing that can be done. I must look for ways to change what seems to be an unchangeable condition.

The choice of an optimistic alternative is a condition to have the individual become ready to engage in an active search for modalities of change. For many individuals, particularly those who have not experienced sufficient MLE, there are positive alternatives available but the individual does not see them or does not consider them within their grasp. This was a very important experience for me, where my need did not allow me to consider in a pessimistic way the future of certain children, those particularly who came out of the Holocaust. My greatest need was to see these children become able to act as competent adults despite the most terrifying experiences they had throughout their youngest period in existence. We said to ourselves, "We cannot lose one single child anymore; too many were killed, too many were maimed; we cannot afford to be pessimistic about their destiny, their future, the making of a happy and active human being" for each one of the children for whom we took responsibility. The *need* made me and my colleagues optimistic. Once we set ourselves an optimistic expectation and goal, we became very active in searching for the best and most promising modalities to materialize our view. It affected our thinking in a very creative way and our readiness to go beyond what existed at the time, searching for ways to help such children. Ultimately, this has been the source of the development of many of the methods that we have today in order to make these affected children become able to confront their future and become contributive members of society, even for those for whom there was little hope to see them achieve such goals.

One must choose from two types of alternatives (a pessimistic one and an optimistic one). It becomes a very important factor in the decisions you will make as to what to do, how much to do, and at what point to continue despite the fact that immediate success is not experienced. In certain cases, you may see your modalities of interacting with the child as very enriched by the search for ways to materialize your optimistic view. Having an optimistic view will make you very active, very creative, and will make you go out and search for a variety of ways to transform your interaction with the individual into very powerful mediation. In the next chapter we present the case of Ravital, whose mother would not accept her daughter's severe disabilities and fought for and found ways of overcoming them, in spite of *our* early pessimism.

I have experienced this in my work with many of the children who came out of the camps of death and who have experienced the most horrendous forms of human decline. On the other hand, *optimism is not enough*. If you make the determination that the individual, despite the present condition can go beyond the present condition, and direct mediation toward this goal you will mobilize the various forces—both in the child and in the surrounding society. This affects both the mediator (the parent, teacher, and other care providers—both professional and nonprofessional, including peers, siblings, extended family, neighbors, and so forth) and the mediatees themselves. This is not easy on either side, but it is feasible. We have experienced it numerous times, but we recognize that it requires a great deal of persistence.

My example in Chapter 1 about being with a group of children in a museum, looking at a painting that showed a precarious situation and the children's reaction to it is a good example of what I am talking about here. It shows well the choices that one makes once one adheres to an optimistic approach.

We often confront a child with a variety of deficiencies, and we ask ourselves, "Can this child be helped? Can this condition become transformed from an irreversible and unsurpassable barrier, enabling the child to reach out to levels of functioning—to speech, thinking, acting, despite the many deficits?"

> I recall a girl with Down syndrome who was brought to the hospital at the age of 7. She had some respiratory distress either because of a cold or whatever it was, or perhaps something that had to do with the structure of her respiratory system. The doctor told the parents, "What do you want? This is a child with Down syndrome and usually they contract such pulmonary conditions." And indeed, the child did not survive this condition.

This illustrates how many decisions are made regarding the correction of certain deficiencies in children because the pessimistic view is often accepted as the reflection of a biological condition of the individual. We have come up with an optimistic alternative by saying that the child with Down syndrome is an individual who can be helped, and through our positive and optimistic approach we confidently dared to say that the chromosomes that determine the condition of the individual are not necessarily the last word. We are ready to fight for the destiny or the conditions of the individual.

The Mediation of a Feeling of Belonging

Another parameter that we emphasize as a target of mediation, that parents, educational systems, and society in general should promote, is the feeling of belonging. The feeling of belonging to a larger system starts in the nuclear family, and extends itself concentrically into the groups in which one interacts (classrooms, clubs, study communities, sports teams, the nation to which one belongs) to becoming a member of the world. There are those who will tell you, "I have no need to have a family; I am a citizen of the world and the closer group does not matter to me." Do not believe them! Their description should not be taken seriously. They may indeed have an intensity of feeling with the whole world wherein they describe themselves as being adherents of universal values and so on. But real feeling comes from one's primary family group, which gives the first feelings of belonging, unconditional acceptance, and creates the foundation for meaningful emotional attachments. If individuals do not have a strong feeling of belonging to concentrically closer groups (such as the family), they are unlikely to experience the kind of intense and intimate support that more universal groups can offer, and are often perceived as distant or disengaged. This is why we are emphasizing the potential for primary family relationships for the developmentally delayed individual, as we described briefly above.

Nowadays, unhappily, the feeling of belonging is threatened. Relationships within the family are weakened, along with a diminished sense of belonging to the generations that preceded them. If you ask American children or other children questions such as, "Who are your grandparents? How many grandparents do you remember? When do you see your grandparents? How many times do you visit them? How much do you know about their existence?" the responses usually convey distance and lack of meaningful and frequent contact.

These responses reflect a kind of distorted "counterculture." The position is stated somewhat like this: "We are not the products of a culture. We produce culture." The assumption is a kind of freedom from cultural values, acting as individuals totally freed from any relationships. Adherents of this view say that they belong to the larger culture, but saying this means that they don't belong anywhere. I chose this particular mode of mediation to reflect that children who do not have a feeling of belonging are very unhappy people and will be very limited in their existential experiences. They live in their present; they live a horizontal life. They don't have the dimension of *verticality*, both in terms of what preceded them and the degree of belonging, attachment, and representation of what will follow them later.

> The capacity of the individual to project to the future is like the bow and arrow. The arrow is the projection into the distance. The individual projects into the future—plans (chooses a target), organizes (aims), cares for it (develops the technique of shooting), makes sure that the future will be better than the present for the self and for the benefit of those who will follow, generation by generation. But the distance by which this arrow will be propelled is strongly contingent on how far back you bring the bowstring. The farther back you pull the string, the farther and truer will be the projection of the arrow. The stronger you bring it back, the stronger will be your relationship to your past, and the farther your arrow will reach the future.

This is why the feeling of belonging to an environment that you really consider part of yourself—you experience it, you know about it, and you try to transmit it to the future—is what actually makes the individual not only live one's own biological life but actually makes oneself and humanity continue beyond the limits of the present.

HOW TO RESPOND/WHAT TO DO ABOUT IT?

We have learned a great deal about human modifiability through our application of the MLE parameters. We have often emphasized that ours is an optimistic approach. The consequence of our optimism, and the efforts to realize positive options, has changed our approach to the education and decisionmaking for individuals with severe genetic and other disabilities. Children with Down syndrome, for example, are now treated very differently, with more widely accepted expectations for learning and social adaptation. Initially, many were against such possibilities. One strategy we adopted was to have Down syndrome children undergo cosmetic surgery, to reduce the size of the tongue and minimize the epicanthal folds around the eyes. We did this to improve articulation and minimize some of the respiratory difficulties frequently experienced, and to reduce some of the facial stigmata. One such child who underwent this procedure later looked in the mirror and recognized the changes, and expressed pleasure at "looking more like everyone else, and her family." We had to fight against those who resisted surgery for children with Down syndrome, for reasons that I don't want to dignify by recounting here . . . and it is still resisted in some circles! The concept of doing this type of surgical intervention was considered radical at the time, and still is! But we firmly believe, and have observed, that by fighting for one you may change the whole belief system, working case by case.

We constantly directed and oriented ourselves to look for ways to accomplish this: If the child is slow, let us introduce certain types of exercises and conditions that will increase efficiency; if the child doesn't hear well, let us do something; let us intervene to affect the hearing and subsequent learning. An example of this is a case of a Down syndrome child whose respiration, language, and social interaction were impaired by a severe condition of drooling. We went and found a physician to explore the situation and found a way of doing a minor surgical intervention that stopped the condition. And this need renders us optimistic, reoriented, and enables us to choose an optimistic alternative. Interestingly, this acts in a very contagious way on parents and on society in general.

When we started to work with Down syndrome children, we brought the optimistic message that the child does not necessarily need to live in an institution, in a kind of isolation, and without the benefit of living in a family. It was done by making it clear that the child is best helped within a heterogeneous, warm, and active environment that is ready to mediate. We held that this environment may overcome the consequences of the chromosomal condition, and we made the whole environment cooperative in enriching the child's functioning. And the results we have today, 35 to 40 years after we started this program, are absolutely incredible. Youngsters with Down syndrome are functioning today on a much higher level than was predicted or even considered possible. Even with regard to longevity, children with Down syndrome are today reaching ages that previously were considered inaccessible for them.

By choosing an optimistic alternative, the possibilities of having Down syndrome youngsters become contributive members of society has been amply demonstrated. And by this choice we reversed the often-exhibited pessimistic outlook for the life of this child. There was a time when parents, being told by the "experts" and believing that their child with Down syndrome was irremediably mentally defective, would distance themselves, literally abandoning their child in the hospital, after being further advised not to return to see their child so as not to establish emotional bonding.

> I know of a situation (I did not have direct contact with this case) where a very prominent father, taking the advice described above, had not seen his Down syndrome son for 40 years. The child was placed from the very early days of his life in an institution. He had never been visited by his father. At the age of 30, the son became aware of who his father was, and attended a public lecture. Endowed with good language, which he developed despite the very difficult conditions of his upbringing, and good understanding, he made his way to sit in the audience and hear his father's speech. I don't know the outcome. The story in the newspapers did not mention whether the father ended up seeing or having a relationship with this boy, but I hope he did!

Unhappily, many such pessimistic options were, and in some instances still are, advocated by the medical profession. They are aware of the chromosomal conditions and they consider the severe outcomes of the chromosomes to be immutable or unchangeable. Today, however, we have Down syndrome youngsters who finish high school and complete their matriculation. They are able to become contributive members of society. A positive alternative that we have developed is to train youngsters with Down syndrome and other developmental disorders to act as caregivers for the aged and the handicapped. Their work has proven to be beneficial for those populations because they show great degrees of empathy, patience, sensitivity, and respect. We are now in the process of preparing and educating individuals with developmental and genetic disorders with the skills to enter into nuclear family relationships (marriage). To date, we have 16 couples married, and not one divorce! We want to give them their right to live their lives in the best and most enticing and stimulating conditions. This is the product of an optimistic view. We are now initiating a project to develop training courses for developmentally delayed young adults to prepare for the intimate independent living relationships of marriage.

The neurosciences of today, pointing out to neural plasticity and other new elements, tell us that even the genes are not the ultimate decisionmakers of the level and type of functioning of the individual (the increasingly recognized potential for epigenesis). This gives full support to our choice of a positive alternative. It is worth adhering to this alternative and to become active in searching for the best way to materialize it.

APPLICATION OF THE MLE PARAMETERS: A SUMMARY

The meaning of MLE is reflected in the way in which its parameters are applied. MLE is first and foremost a quality of the interaction between the child and the world that is strongly affected by the interposition of an initiated adult who, by this interposition, makes the child become attentive, focused, interested, and ready to learn. It focuses the mediatee's attention on the necessary qualities of the stimuli and on learning ways by which these stimuli can become part and parcel of a repertoire of cognitive functions that are necessary for better, more useful, and more efficient interacting with the world at large.

I have talked about how children who do not have MLE are frequently not able to benefit from direct exposure to stimuli. MLE is not necessarily a verbal interaction. It is not limited to certain contents. It's not limited to certain modalities of interaction.

We have asked the question, "Why is it that some people get MLE and some do not?" I have discussed the mechanisms by which MLE is elicited in the environment and the conditions that may obstruct it. To summarize what has been discussed earlier in this chapter: MLE may not be imparted by adults, or the learner may not be ready or able to benefit due to what we have described as *distal* conditions. There may be cultural conditions, accompanied but not necessarily determined by poverty or cultural difference/

deprivation. In many cases, these factors reflect themselves in the capacity and readiness of the child to learn new elements and to learn something that goes beyond simple perception. Yet, once children have had MLE, their capacity to learn is so great, their potential and propensity is elicited, they need less time, and they master well the things that have to be learned.

> An excellent example is that of the ultra-orthodox group (in Israel and elsewhere) who received a very intensive level of MLE (at home and in school) but may not have learned what they are supposed to learn in a modern, technologically oriented society. They are culturally different because they are oriented to their culture very intensively, and yet they differ from the surrounding culture due to a lack of exposure to the technical content of the modern, secular world. But they are culturally different and not culturally deprived. Moreover, the plasticity and rapidity by which they learn (the content of the modern world, when they need it) is to be attributed to the fact that they have been mediated in their culture. The same is true of the Ethiopians who immigrated to Israel, whom we have described earlier in this chapter.

CHAPTER 4

Mediated Learning Experience and the Nature of Change

In previous chapters, I have presented the reasons for lack of mediated learning experience by indicating that there are two types of reasons: *endogenous* conditions, representing physical or emotional barriers to being open to MLE; and *exogenous* factors, which include societal, familial, economical, and other similar conditions. I have also said that lack of MLE turns the individual into someone who is culturally deprived in the sense that one's own culture is not transmitted and is not used as a platform for further learning and accommodation.

THE OPTION FOR MODIFIABILITY

Here, the critical questions are: Are the effects of lack of MLE immutable, unchangeable? Are children who did not have MLE over a long period of time in their development, irrespective of whether this was due to internal barriers or the fact that it was not offered to them in an adequate way, modifiable? Yes, modifiability is possible even for individuals whose condition has not permitted them to have or use MLE, such as the autistic child and Down syndrome children in certain cases. Changes are possible when intervention comes in the form of a powerful mediated experience. If offered to the child at this level, at this level of resistance, MLE renders the individual more able and more capable of accepting the values, the learning, the experiences offered by existence in a certain environment.

To further understand this potential, it is necessary to describe the various modalities of mediation necessary for the individual, especially for those who have had different reasons for the lack of MLE that created conditions or interfered with becoming an efficient learner.

At this point in the discourse, I would like to address the issue of MLE in terms of its power to produce conscious awareness in the learner: Why does this kind of interaction, as we have defined it by the parameters of intentionality, transcendence, and the mediation of meaning (the major essential conditions), possess the power to enhance the modifiability of the individual? First, we consider the fact that the essential conditions of MLE *always* produce a consciousness, increasing or establishing a level of awareness within and between the mediator and the mediatee (reflected by reciprocity). The mediator is conscious and aware of the fact that a child needs something very special in order to benefit from encounters with certain stimuli. As I noted in an earlier chapter, the Bushman who doesn't talk to the children but knows how important it is for them to be able to observe what he does, to be able to understand the sequence, the order in which he is doing these kind of steps toward his goal of turning a tree into a canoe *will be animated by the consciousness of the fact that he wants his children or his group of people to learn how to do it.* He acts in a very different way from if he was doing it for himself. He will be much slower in his work. He will make every part of his activity more conspicuous, more observable, more clear so that the children he is mediating will be aware of each one of the acts he is doing.

When I am trying to make a child imitate, I do not act in the way I would do in my regular activity; I act in a way that whatever the child observes and sees will become obvious, clear, and will become a source of imitation—and I will intentionally repeat myself. If I want the child to learn some of my prayers or some of my songs, I will sing them in a very different way than I do when I sing them for myself. I will repeat often and with variations, to draw attention, build memory, and the like.

In this way the three partners involved in the process of MLE—the stimuli, the mediatee, and the mediator—are modified meaningfully by the intentionality of the mediator. As I've said, the mediator changes in order to become an accepted interpreter of the reality to be transmitted to the child. The child will have to be modified in terms of the level of sensitivity, alertness, and motivation in order to attend to what the mediator is attempting to do. And third, the object, the subject of mediation, will be chosen in such a way as to respond to the particular needs of the child or group.

THE DIFFERENTIAL APPLICATION OF MLE

MLE must (and can) be applied in differential ways in order to render it effective in responding to the particular needs of individuals, such as those with Down syndrome or other genetic conditions, severe developmental delays, hyperactivity, autistic spectrum disorders, and others, or to increase learning potentiality for all children. The essential point here is that the mediator must be attuned and oriented toward the necessary content and type of interaction that needs to be transmitted to the child with special needs. For the teacher of children within the normal-functioning spectrum, the important element is the content, the skill that has to be imparted to the student, and much less the particular modalities by which the learning of the child is improved. And teachers typically cannot spend too much time or cannot change the choice of certain objects and content of teaching so as to respond to the particularities and the special needs of these children.

However, the mediator—even if a certain content is included—devotes the major emphasis not so much on the content as on the modalities by which the learning experience will become a source of enhanced efficiency. Nowadays in most teacher-training programs, very little is emphasized as to how to render the individual a better learner. The teacher is encouraged to address the skills, the knowledge of the particular content that is prescribed by curriculum standards to be imparted to the students. This is the reason why so many children who are not able to benefit from the teaching of prescribed contents are literally falling behind, and are considered unable to follow the particular program of the classroom. Very little is offered to children in terms of modalities of learning, and that is why in attempting to improve the condition of many of these children we have developed a method we called *Instrumental Enrichment* (the Feuerstein Instrumental Enrichment Program, or FIE). This method emphasizes the need to *learn how to learn* that is so badly neglected in the regular classroom.

My Experience with the Survivors of the Holocaust

The theory of structural cognitive modifiability, developed along with our empirical data and observations, has become the theoretical impetus and support for a search for modalities of increasing the adaptability of the individual with special needs. The initial group of special-needs individuals that motivated me was the children and youth who were deeply traumatized during the Holocaust. We dealt with them on behalf of an organization called *Aliyat Ha Noar* (Youth Immigration), which was charged by the Jewish Agency with the ingathering of the thousands and thousands of orphans who lost their parents in the death camps in Europe and were themselves subjected to the most terrible conditions of life—where death was not the worst option—that were terrorized and went through the most difficult experiences a human being can imagine.

And the great question that I, as an educator of these children who survived the Holocaust and who were accepted into Youth Aliyah, faced was: "Can these children who have struggled for their life, experienced extreme degrees of hunger, cold, mutilation, in constant danger of being executed or being killed, as others were in front of their eyes—can they be saved? More than saved . . . can they be restored to normal and productive lives in society?" These children were not able to plan a moment in their lives because they did not know whether it would bring them to confrontation with the Nazi world and all its devastating consequences! And yet, in many of these children I found signs of an extraordinary capacity to identify themselves with the other and in many cases to endanger their own lives in order to make the lives of the other somewhat more acceptable—for example, the children who stole bread in order to give it to their neighbor. There was a young man who had in some way the honor of *tefillin* (enabling observant Jews to use phylacteries as prescribed in the Torah) bestowed upon him, and he went from one place to the other and gave a *tefilla* (the prayer ritual experience) to those people who were devoid of the possibility of making the prayer they used to make throughout their life. He endangered his life to do it.

The Importance of Restoring the Belief System (in the Mediatee and Ourselves)

On one hand, there were people who were totally disillusioned and deceived by human beings—questioning to what extent a human really could be good-hearted and empathic with the other. And yet there were many who were able to continue to believe and to have the need of empathizing with the other and keep them alive. But there were also many, on the other hand, as they were freed from the worst conditions, who were very seriously affected, traumatized with very little chance to survive. These children had to be confronted with a new world, and we asked ourselves: "Will we be able to modify them; will we be able to wipe out the terror from their eyes and give them a new belief in human beings and in the world? Will we be able to make them strive to a higher and more appropriate level of functioning in society?"

This question was strongly linked to the question of whether human beings were modifiable: Could they be changed; could they be developed in terms of their cognitive processes that have been underdeveloped due to the war (and more generally) and extreme conditions of life; could we turn these young people into those who would have a more optimistic view of life and thereby be more ready to engage in the kinds of activities from which they will be able not only to derive for themselves but derive from the world a better prospect than they had? Will we be able to teach them to plan; will we be able to set for them goals that were totally denied for them during their experiences in the Holocaust?

I remember that for myself that during the time of the Holocaust I was not able to plan ahead because I never knew what was going to happen in the next few minutes. The readiness to project myself into the future was very badly affected, and my question was whether people so affected could be modified. And further, when life presents a lack of this kind of predictability, is there the incapacity to be able to plan and to project into the future?

Structural Cognitive Modifiability and the Need System

So the theory of structural cognitive modifiability was produced by a need to offer the possibility of changing the cognitive emotional structure of the individual and provide new ways of looking into life, new tools to understand the world, new ways to rely on certain things that should be considered as being there. And there were these great questions! Emotionally, the search for a theory that would explain the modifiability that I believed in was the product of a need—the need to see individuals who had been so endangered and at developmental and behavioral risk become more ready to invest in life, not only for the self but for others. I needed to be able to withstand the terrible pressure produced by experiences that had the potential to create a pessimistic view of everything related to life, to human beings, to destiny, and to the future.

Our need to change this came from the feeling that we have to fight for each individual. We cannot afford to have one more individual succumbing to this emotional and cognitive condition. And so we looked for the theoretical support anchored in human modifiability as a basis for the activities that would make the individual be modified and reach higher levels of functioning.

Indeed, for the children of the Holocaust, to modify their pessimistic view of life, to counteract their lack of readiness and their capacity to think a step further, we had to address a number of behavioral manifestations and also cognitive and emotional modalities of functioning. For instance, the first day they arrived at school where they were supposed to start learning, we prepared for them beautiful tables and a rich menu. As the children came in and saw the bread on the table and some other fruits, they grabbed all they could and ran away to hide the food so that they would be able to eat it at the times they would need it, because they were not sure that they would have it again tomorrow. This was a strong demonstration of their lack of belief in the future, their lack of belief in the next moment. They had to grab for the immediate. This of course also had a very important bearing on their readiness to become involved in thinking and projecting something into the future and setting further goals than the immediate ones.

Structural Cognitive Modifiability and Emotional Engagement

In this sense, our theory of structural cognitive modifiability started by laying stress on our emotional engagement, as educators, on our need to make modifiability a meaningful and materializable phenomenon.

Surprisingly, I must say clearly that this concept of modifiability was at this time very badly received, and many people, both in the psychological as well as educational professions, questioned the possibility of modifying in a meaningful way the habits and behaviors of these children that were the product of a very long, prolonged exposure to the most inhuman conditions of life. And many of the children themselves had difficulty giving up their past adaptive behaviors—even if they were in many ways dysfunctional, at least they were familiar. We were "engaging them in a fight with their past!"

It was not an easy fight. Here I must go somewhat deeper to delve into the nature of recovering a lost past—the loss of parents, siblings, primary objects of self-identification. We wanted these children to understand that you can bring back your past and those of your parents by the life you live in the present. The poet Bialik quotes the Midrash in this way: "Through their death they ordered us to eternal life." For us, learning was the most important affirmation.

In the year 2007 I received the following letter from the husband of Tamar, a girl we had worked with during this period. She was writing to a friend:

> You asked me if I was lonely as a child in Israel. I was terribly lonely because all of the children surrounding me had adults to look after them but I had nobody. My yearning to have at least my mother hug me and kiss me and comfort me, I did not have. But I survived and I am still sane maybe because of my soul and some guardian angel. But I was lucky also. In the school I *had a teacher*; today he is a world renowned professor of psychology, *who dedicated all of his free time to me*. I was very sick after the Holocaust. I had a general infection in my body and I had to lie in bed a couple of months because my legs

were almost completely ruined. There was a bucket beside my bed that was collecting the pus which ran off of my legs. Thanks to antibiotics that were discovered at about that time I survived and my legs do not even bear a scar. And as you saw them in the picture, they do not look so bad and I can dance. Smile!! My teacher used to sit *every free minute he had from teaching in the school* beside my bed, teaching me Judaism, telling me stories, continuing my education, and singularly and marvelously acting out all of the plays of Shakespeare. He bought me books and played records for me. Afterward, thanks to him I could continue my regular education and play the piano. This was not given to the few other children who had gone through the Holocaust and survived. He did everything to make it easier for me to feel protected. At the end of a school term he became sick and went to Switzerland to recover. He used to send me small gifts and a special edition of the music of the Rachmaninoff Concerto No. II, which was one of my favorites. . . . I will be thankful to him until my last days. My first steps of knowledge in Judaism were due to him—he was the teacher of Judaism in the school. I will never forget him—that he *helped me back to life* as a child and added so much caring and knowledge to my life and opened my horizon to Judaism.

Here I must reflect that the Holocausts have not ended, and tragically many thousands of children and families face similar experiences—as we think of Somalia, Darfur, and sub-Saharan Africa as only a few tragic examples. But they can be overcome!

HOW DOES ONE IMPART *LEARNING TO LEARN*?

The answer is in the application of MLE. Intentionality increases the meaning of the learning experience. Transcendence makes sure that the learning experience will not be limited to a particular situation but will actually be something that can be generalized, transferred, and applied in a very large number of situations that can be predicted from the beginning and in certain instances even chosen. But important, the mediator orients the mediational interaction to the particular area known to be deficient in the mediatee.

For example, if I am dealing with a child with a speech delay due to either some sensorial problems, some problems in the articulatory system, or some problems of an emotional condition, as is—for example—frequently observed in the autistic child, and my interest is to make the child more able to use verbal interaction, I will address everything that I do in a way that will respond to the particularities of the needs of the child with the speech delay, irrespective of what is the reason for the delay.

Stimulating Attention and Language Awareness and Proficiency

Language deficiencies have an effect on the modality of mediation by which the mediator interacts with the child. As an example, for some of the children with a speech delay, the application of a method that we have developed over the years and that we have called *soliloquy* or mediated self-talk is a very effective way to impart to the child a vocabulary, a way of building sentences and the variety of dimensions of verbal interaction. In order to do it, I create around the child a linguistically rich verbal environment. I talk to myself in a way that immerses the child in a linguistic experience, in a verbal interaction, with gestures, even though the child is not expected to respond. But the child's lack of response does not prevent me from demonstrating in front of the child a verbal interpretation, a verbal description of certain acts that I am doing or I'm about to do. The enunciation of an act is accompanied by the appropriate gestures and demonstrates the particular objects that I am speaking about and shows the particular act that I am engaged in. Here is one such example, to be enacted with young children or those with significant language delays:

> "I'm taking the glass from the table, I'm lifting it to my mouth and I am drinking, I'm inclining it. . . ." I describe each one of the sequences of this act to the child while doing it. I do not condition my interaction and my verbal representation, my soliloquy, on the possibility that the child will answer me. I don't stop talking even if the child doesn't look at me. And yet I continue to present to the child the acts that I am describing, the acts I am doing, describing the feelings that I have, the plans that I make for tomorrow, the memories I have from the common experiences the day before. In this way, children with speech delays (for any number of reasons) are given a number of cues that enable them to become more verbal, more ready to express themselves, more ready to understand and involve themselves in a verbal and nonverbal interactive process.

The soliloquy method relies on *overhearing* and *imitation,* conditions in young children's speech development that have been well described and researched. We have recently (2013) published a book on this method: *A Think-Aloud and Talk-Aloud Approach to Building Language: Overcoming Disability, Delay, and Deficiency.* Today it receives very strong support from the findings of brain researchers, who are discovering many conditions of neural plasticity, including the existence of mirror neurons. Mirror neurons were first observed in research on monkeys, but they have been confirmed in numerous human subject studies. In the monkey studies it was observed that certain neurons in the monkey that respond to certain of the actions of the monkey also react in the same way when the monkey simply observes another monkey doing the particular act (which activated the monkey's brain during the actual performance of the action) (Umlita et al., 2001). This particular finding is of highest importance because it may explain much of the imitative behavior and the power of imitation in children as sources of learning. Thus, soliloquy not only responds to the particular needs of the child to be immersed in a verbal environment, but it appears that meaningful neurophysiological transformations occur through this exposure.

ACTIVATING AND MEDIATING THE BRAIN THROUGH THE MIRROR NEURONS

From this point of view, mirror neurons are a source of explanation of many of the phenomena that we observed but were not able to fully understand, especially as regards their neurological mechanisms. Most interesting is the behavior of the monkeys activating their mirror neurons as we described just above. This then leads to something very interesting, corresponding to our concept of transcendence. Umlita and his colleagues have observed that the monkey's brain not only responds to the direct observation (in the instances of observing the eating of nuts), but also in the same way just by hearing the noise of breaking the nut, or smelling the nut and shell as it is broken. This is very similar to what we discussed about transcendence: The individual learning about certain objects recognizes and understands not only the object but also certain of its functions or certain of the effects that this object may have on another sense. For instance, one may hear the noise of water coming from a bottle and immediately represent (mentally) the act of pouring water from a bottle—the mirror neurons generalize the activity from one sense to other senses. And thus, the brain may react in a very similar way to other known indicators of the experience—seeing, hearing, or smelling. Mental activation (what we term *structural learning*) thus becomes something that reminds or represents the object that has been learned previously.

The power of MLE is strongly understandable now by the new findings on the structure of the brain and the existence of neurons that are responsible for the imitative capacity of the individual. I will return to this in a later chapter. However, in this context, the mediator who approaches children with speech delay must be aware of the fact that the manner of presentation to the child—what is said or done—makes the child aware of the relationship between certain words and certain objects, acts that occur, facial expressions, emotions and feelings, and the like. The child who is offered this kind of mediation in an intentional way—related to the particular needs of the child—is exposed to a very powerful tool to affect limited or deficient linguistic functioning.

THE MODIFIABILITY OF INTELLIGENCE

Cognitively, the concept of modifiability that we formulated at an early point in our theoretical development was adamantly opposed by the then-prominent fixist theories of human development. For them, the belief that you can modify the IQ of the individual didn't exist. Actually, it was considered impossible that an individual whose measured IQ was low could be significantly modified, at the cost of any kind of intervention, to reach meaningfully and sustainably higher levels of IQ. The IQ was believed to be a constant and unchangeable mode of responding, reflected in levels of thinking, problem solving, acquiring information, and the like. The individual whose IQ was considered low was to be handled in a way that responded to the measured capacities, that were considered as unchangeable, and any attempt to see individuals who manifested (as reflected in the IQ results) low-functioning was considered a pipe dream.

Adapting Conventional Assessment Instruments

As if to confirm this position, some of the children whom we could not examine with the regular *conventional* tests and with whom we applied some developmental tests functioned at a much lower level than they would be expected to do, based on their chronological age. This was considered the measure of their capacities that were acquired through the period of their academic or developmental deprivation, or because they were genetically determined to be low-functioning individuals. They were considered not accessible to change.

In this context, our adapted interventions based on our theory of structural cognitive modifiability were very much against the *zeitgeist* of the times, philosophically and methodologically—both in terms of cognition as well as emotional elements. (I will address this issue in much more detail in later chapters of this book.)

But to summarize the issue at this point in the discourse, I can say that my need and the feeling of engagement generated the belief that modifiability was and is possible. Once this belief was generated, it created a feeling of responsibility and a high degree of creative thinking: "How will I do it best; what are the components of my interaction that will enable me to modify these above-described conditions?" To that end, I and my colleagues began to explore and develop alternative assessment tools and procedures (which eventually became the LPAD—the Learning Propensity Assessment Device).

Defining and Describing Modifiability

Let's start from the concept of modifiability. The concept of modifiability refers to the *propensity* of individuals to become changed in their activity, responses, and experience. To become modified through experiences means to remember those experiences and to act following the previous experience in a different way than one has done before. Modifiability represents a state of plasticity of the organism that, once it has experienced certain conditions, becomes able to improve, change, and develop other strategies, and avoid those experiences that have been proven to be a failure. Further, it enables the adapting of behaviors that will be more successful; the capacity of the individual to use present experience in order to go into the future; the readiness of the individual to set goals that do not exist in the immediate present and to use representational thinking as a way to prepare and plan how to reach particular goals. All these are included in the concept of modifiability—the changing of behavior, thinking, and the structure of thinking following experience. This is one of the most important characteristics of human beings and represents *the propensity and readiness of the individual to adapt to the new situations that are confronted.*

What Are the Characteristics of Modifiability?

Our intelligence is not a static phenomenon. I am modified by the fact that I learn another five words. I am modified by the fact that I am able now to put on my shoes myself and tie the laces. Modifiability is the propensity of the individual to improve one's behavior, to make it more adaptive following exposure to experience. Some people have great difficulties and they continue to do the same thing even if the outcomes of their experience are not positive or adequate, do not give them what is needed. This lack of flexibility is very often considered a characteristic of the low-functioning individual.

So we reiterate that modifiability is a change in the individual's level of functioning following experience and the expanded and differentiated use of the modalities of functioning. Mentally, the individual who becomes modified uses a number of cognitive operations in a more conscious way. The individual so modified is able to gather needed data in order to understand the experience undergone. One observes the outcome of the behavior and decides whether or not the desired outcome is achieved. Behavior is changed in order to receive what is needed, and so on. This is modifiability by a kind of control of one's behavior, comparing what one wants to achieve and what has indeed been achieved, and the behavior is modified in order to make it more efficient, adaptable to the particular needs, more satisfying—both in the situation required and for self-reference.

Today when we speak about modifiability, we are referring to a process that is more important than ever thought before, for modifying not only our behavior but also our operational thinking, and extending to the modifiability of the neural system itself. The deficiencies that the individual manifests in the course of life can be changed in terms of their operation and their activity:

> I don't do now what I did before because it turned out badly; I will avoid certain behaviors or I will choose certain behaviors because, according to the basic outcome, I've learned about them.

These kinds of changes are accompanied by a process of conscious awareness—the capacity to ponder and to reflect on what was done, what it resulted in, and the choice of more appropriate ways to bring more desirable results.

Modifiability and Neural Plasticity

Given what we now know about the neuroplasticity of the brain, we can confidently challenge the conception that our brains are the most stable and unchangeable part of our organism—quite the contrary! Concepts such as *neurogenesis*, *epigenesis*, *mental mapping*, and others have defined the potential for change. Our brains are our most flexible, most plastic organs (see Doidge, 2007; Schwartz & Begley, 2002), and the functions involved in certain of the brain structures are modifiable by activity imposed on the individual. This means we have the potential, through appropriate intervention programs guided by the provision of MLE, to modify not only the behavior of the individual but also the very neural substrata of the individual that permit the application of these changes to a variety of situations and in a variety of conditions.

The brain not only produces certain behaviors but also is actually shaped by the behaviors that the individual imposes on the brain. So, when we speak about the "structural" aspects of structural cognitive modifiability, we refer not only to the mental operations, to the way of thinking and planning, but also to the way of projecting to the future. We refer also to those meaningful changes produced in the brain structure itself, in its neural structure, and the way the various physiological changes are produced. This is a very strong support of our theory of modifiability that was denied for many years. Today, neurology points to certain types of activities that generate new neurons, a process that has been described as *neurogenesis* (see Doidge, 2007; Schwartz & Begley, 2002). Scientists are also beginning to consider and explore processes of epigenesis, or changing of the genes as a consequence of learning experiences, following the pioneering work of Eric Kandel (see Spector, 2012). It is also possible to lose neurons, in something that has been called "pruning." This occurs with disuse—a lack of mental activities. We have seen this in our work with brain-injured people, who have lost certain control of their functions due to some incident that has affected the brain. Our work rehabilitating these lost functions points to those that were inexistent in the brain (due to the injury) but became existent following the activity that we impose on it (what has come to be called *remapping*).

By way of summary, we have described the original need we felt to formulate a theory of cognitive modifiability; we developed and activated our theory to affect deeply traumatized youngsters, individuals who have not had the opportunity to develop cognitive processes according to their chronological age and were not able to benefit from their experience. And we have shown that this modifiability results in a wider and richer repertoire of activities on the part of the individual in response to certain stimuli, to certain experiences that are not only a change in the behavior—mental, operational, emotional behavior—but also affect the brain structure itself, generate new neurons, create new links in the brain, and, by this, produce new cognitive structures for the need of adaptation of the individual.

THE COGNITIVE COMPONENT

In our formulation of structural cognitive modifiability, the "cognitive" element is essential to the concept of modifiability. In order to modify an individual, the cognitive component is important, to build or strengthen the learning functions (what we have identified through assessment and observation of responses to mediation, and also relating to emotional/affective experiences that are to a very large extent strongly dependent on cognition).

What Is Cognition?

We start our discussion here with some of the very basic elements of cognition. We will come to higher-order levels later. By cognition, we refer to the great variety of activities starting from the sensorial—our five senses that gather data, observing certain elements in the outer reality, becoming aware of certain functions these objects are producing, comparing the various elements and creating relationships between them. When I compare two things that are totally different in their structure, in the material from which they've been produced, and yet I find something above and beyond the differences between them that they have in common, I am engaging in a "cognitive" activity. For example: Consider a glass of water and a tanker of 5 million tons of oil. They are different in size, volume, color, material, and yet they have their function in common—they are both containers of something, they are both vessels; they contain a liquid.

This comparison creates a relationship between two very different things and categorizes them under the same factor. The cognitive processes enable us to create relationships of causality—what has caused a certain reaction, a certain development, a certain event. The cognitive processes enable us to learn, to draw certain conclusions. They allow us inferential processes: If A, B, C, D, E are ordered on the level of size, and A is bigger than B, B is bigger than C, C is bigger than D, and D is bigger than E, then we will be able to infer from this that A is bigger than E even though we do not directly observe the size of objects.

Cognitive processes offer a great variety of operations of thinking. One starts from the input. It means the gathering of the data necessary to formulate some kind of proposition, and the elaboration of the data and to group and categorize them, create relationships between them; I turn them into elements from which I can infer the existence of other things that I have not directly been exposed to.

Cognition is actually the most adaptive function of our existence. Developing cognitive processes entails having the individual be able to be attentive and focused on certain phenomena that will be used in coming to decisions. The process involves creating certain rules by the help of which one infers from one set of data to another.

Cognition enables us to group, to categorize things that may be very different under the category tables. As an example, there might be a large variety of objects whose major common characteristic is that they serve as support for something, for food, writing activities, or a platform for working. We are inferring a table: It doesn't matter how high it is, or its size; it doesn't matter of what it is made, or what is its color. But of course we must differentiate it from other kinds of tables (according to differential criterial attributes). I may categorize the "table" according to its functions, the material it is made of, and so on. And the same is true for a variety of other operations that cognitive processes enable us to use and apply.

The Relationship of Cognition to Affect

Furthermore, cognition is at the basis of our emotional and affective reactions, and certain choices that we make according to these reactions are influenced by cognitive elements. We hold that the activity of modifiability is strongly contingent upon cognition. And I would say further that our choice of using cognition as the modality by which to modify the individual has to do with the fact that, in contradistinction to the basic emotions, the cognitive element is not only more adaptive and sensitive to modifiability, but it also enables us to modify our feelings. If I can use my cognitive processes in order to understand my behavior ("I am crying, what is causing me to cry"), and if I can, through my cognitive processes, identify the emotions in myself and others, I will be self-aware, empathic, understanding of both my and your reactions, because I will know what made me or you sad and so on, and this capacity to develop and apply feelings is strongly related to the use of cognition to understand the individual through the development of empathy. Cognition enables the representing of an emotional situation—how would I feel if I would be in this condition—and this makes me able to develop a process of identification with your condition.

Again, to understand why I am sad, I have to use my cognitive processes. Thus, there is a strong relationship between cognition and emotion. However, emotional elements are very difficult to change unless you use the appropriate cognitive functions. Piaget has described each *conduite*, as he called it in French, each behavior as adding two components, and as we said in an earlier chapter, this can be metaphorically described as the two sides of the same coin. The structural side responds to "What do I do? How do I do? Where do I do? How much do I do? How successfully am I doing?" and so forth. The other side of the coin is, "Why do I do it? What animates me to do this kind of thing?" One side is the structure of our behavior; the other is the energetic principle, the *reason* for our behavior. And as I pointed out earlier, I have added to Piaget's metaphor that the coin is transparent—that each side influences the other in a functionally conscious way. When you look to the structure "What am I going to do?" the question "Why do I do it?" will very much affect what I will do.

Phases in the Cognitive Process

In the cognitive process, there is first the *input phase*, describing the process of gathering of data; and second, the *elaboration phase*, where the data gathered are put together, discriminated, changed, placed in categories, subjected to inferential thinking, turned into a source of relationships, incorporated in operations, and so on. The third phase in the mental act is *output*, where whatever I've gathered on the input level and manipulated on the elaborational level is then the source of a product and response. You have to wrap up whatever you have done into a formulation of your conclusions, and into an execution of certain acts. This is the output level.

One of the problems we faced in the process of developing our theory of structural cognitive modifiability was how to make individuals more able to use their input, elaboration, and output phase functions in a more appropriate way. By observing children, who were in many cases low-functioning and considered unchangeable, we came to the conclusion that these children suffered from certain deficient functions that were responsible for their inadequate cognitive processes. These children could be observed to be deficient in the activation of their cognitive functions in terms of the three phases. In some instances, we could observe that the two peripheral activities—input and output—were significantly more deficient than the elaborational functions. And once we were able to improve the two peripheral functions, the better were the results and our modifiability was better achieved. In Chapter 7 we elaborate on this in much more detail.

DEFINING "STRUCTURE" IN SCM

The first term in the theory of structural cognitive modifiability is *structure*. By structure, we mean we identify the target of our change as reflected in the nature of the change. We refer to the fact that the individual is not just taught a certain behavior. The child who has learned one behavior in a very discrete way (in the behavioristic perspective) will not tend to generalize this particular behavior to a variety of situations, to a variety of operations. The newly acquired behavior is likely to be used only in the way it has been taught, without adaptive and/or conscious application.

When we speak about the structural aspect of cognitive modifiability, we set for ourselves the goal not of making the child acquire a particular behavior; rather, we want to modify the structure of thinking and by this ensure that whatever change has been produced will have a wide area of application and will be applied in a variety of situations. That's a very different approach to what is often considered cognitive education whereby thinking skills are often embedded in the curriculum, or lost in the approach that emphasizes the learning of facts as somewhat isolated aspects (through memorization) and then tested for what is remembered rather than what is understood and generalized (see Chapter 2 and the reference to the paper "Learning to Think; Thinking to Learn" [Feuerstein & Falik, 2010]).

The concept of structure that was beautifully described by Piaget, who was my teacher, is best formulated by three of the dimensions that he emphasized. The first characteristic of a structural change is that it actually affects the whole by changing the part that belongs to it. I offer a child a number of words, thus modifying the verbal repertoire. But does this enable the child to produce new words? Will the child apply grammatical rules in appropriate ways? This becomes possible only if I teach the child the structure of the language. Unless I teach the rules by which a sentence is structured, the fact that one knows 10 more words will be of limited meaning in the production of language. But if I teach a child how to decline a verb, how to modify the structure of the sentence in order to emphasize a particular thing, then I have changed the structure of the individual's language. And in this way, by changing the structure, the *part* that I am training will affect the whole to which this part belongs.

> One of our wise people described this distinction thusly: There is a heap of apples or nuts, and you take one nut from this well-ordered heap, from the whole. The minute you take it, the whole heap starts to move and starts to change and then it stabilizes itself again. You have

changed a part, and by changing the part you have affected the whole and enable in this way a meaningful change.

A second characteristic of the structure is that there are certain changes in the rapidity/efficiency of your functioning, implying *assimilation* and *accommodation*. This is reflected in the "fluency" or the pace of responding.

The third and probably the most important characteristic of structural cognitive modifiability is its generalizability and capacity for self-perpetuation. When you produce a structural change in the individual, you don't do it by teaching a specific element. If you taught a child how to put on shoes, that's a very limited element. But if you teach "structure" in the applying of structural cognitive modifiability, the acquired behavior will not be restricted to the level at which it was produced but will be taught in such a way as to perpetuate itself, continue, and go much beyond whatever you have trained. Expanding on the "shoe" example, one can expand the concept to other ways of securing shoes (straps, Velcro patches, slip-on types of shoes), and further to the relationship of the type of shoes worn and the activities being undertaken. Thus, learning does not occasion static pieces of information, but continues to develop and progress and generalize over a variety of situations, at a variety of ages. This particular type of change in the individual will enrich the functional repertoire in such a way that at each level of the structure it will be applied to that new learning or situation that requires it.

From this point of view, our concept of structural cognitive modifiability, going somewhat beyond that of Piaget, should be understood as an activity that makes the individual able to go beyond the immediacy and the limits of the acquired behavior toward much more varied, rich, complex types of responses.

APPLYING SCM THROUGH THE INSTRUMENTAL ENRICHMENT PROGRAM

Structural cognitive modifiability is implemented through a program, now called Feuerstein Instrumental Enrichment (FIE), that is based on the need to structurally modify the individual. Its almost 5 decades of use, with increasingly diverse ranges of populations and needs, have proven this last characteristic of Piaget, self-perpetuation, in a very beautiful way. We have offered children and adults our FIE program, with well-documented and consistent research results pointing to its efficacy. FIE does not have a specific academic content. The “content” that is included is used as a context in order to present learning activities.

> Here I describe one early research study (of the kind that has been replicated) (Rand, Tannenbaum, Feuerstein, & Mintzker, 1981). When we provided an experimental group of students with 200 hours of FIE, and a control group with 200 hours of additional academic exposure, we were able to assess their cognitive functioning 3 and a half years following the exposure. When we examined these subjects at the end of the “experiment,” the Instrumental Enrichment group had higher levels of functioning (both cognitively and academically) even though the FIE group had on the average received less academic skill teaching. Moreover, after the group had stopped doing the program, the differences in favor of the FIE group continued. They had continued to grow and in some cases even strengthened their levels of functioning, to the point that the differences between the control group and the experimental group had almost tripled. We have labeled this a “divergent effect” and consider it very significant. These results are shown in Figure 4.1.

Figure 4.1. Divergent Effect Diagram

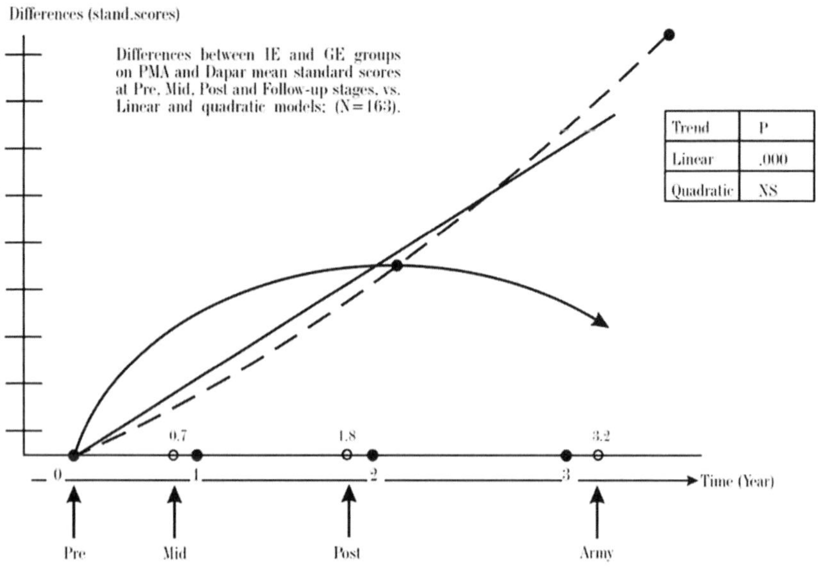
Differences (stand.scores)
.80
.70
.60
.50
.40
.30
.20
.10
.00
Differences between IE and GE groups on PMA and Dapar mean standard scores at Pre, Mid, Post and Follow-up stages, vs. Linear and quadratic models: (N=163).
Trend
P
Linear
.000
Quadratic
NS
0.7
1.8
3.2
0
1
2
3
Time (Year)
Pre
Mid
Post
Army

This is a very unusual result. Typically, when an experimental condition is terminated, there is what is called "a regression toward the mean," indicating that the differences between the experimental and control groups diminish. But this was not the case in this instance. We could rightly conclude that exposure to FIE, whose goal is to modify the cognitive structure of the individual, in fact did so, very strongly and sustainably. Because FIE provided the tools of thinking and learning, the more exposed they were to experience, the more they continued to benefit. This longitudinal study has been replicated in a number of other places and has shown similar effects. Its meaning is that modifying not only the behavior but its mental structure will have much greater and more meaningful results for the lives of those so taught, enabling and enhancing the possibilities to exceed to higher levels of functioning and to become more adapted to the great changes that occur in our time.

OVERCOMING THE BARRIERS TO CHANGE

I am now going to describe how modifiability is possible despite the generalized view that modifiability is not accessible to many types of conditions or the people who experience them. This challenges many long-held concepts and convictions, even in some cases by highly reputed experts.

Etiology

The first condition is the barrier that is set on individuals by the etiology of their condition. The etiology of condition is viewed by some scientists as a determinant for lack of modifiability. The causative condition may be genetic, physical, or even sociocultural. I have addressed this thoroughly in many other writings. Here, I want to discuss the genetic or hereditary condition that was invoked by Arthur Jensen as a determinant that cannot be modified. In his paper "How Much Can We Boost the IQ and Scholastic Achievement?" published in the *Harvard Educational Review* in 1969, he argues that we should stop attempting to modify those children who are functioning at a very low level because this is a waste of energy and resources, largely because these children are not modifiable due to the fact that their heredity determines very low levels of performance.

Although Jensen was writing in 1969, before neuroscience was opening new vistas into brain functioning, the concept that hereditability determines lack of modifiability has been stressed by many other authors, such as Herrnstein and Murray in their 1994 book *The Bell Curve*, which was widely read by the American public, and unfortunately by many scholars and policymakers. These voices advocated the concept of a lack of the option to become modified due to low functioning attributed to heredity. They believed that genetic conditions restrict the option for modifiability of the individual. These widely promulgated misconceptions die hard, even in the face of new evidence. Concepts of lack of modifiability still dominate the thinking and belief systems of not only many psychologists but—what is more dangerous and more damaging—also of educators and many of those entrusted with the design of programs for low-functioning individuals. But we consider the original causation (its "etiology") to be far less affecting the individual and not as an inevitable obstruction to the possibility of the individual's option to be changed, as we demonstrated with the condition of Down syndrome and other conditions. The present knowledge that we have points to the fact that the genetic determinant (among others) does not always "have the last word." I will return to this point later.

The Critical Period

A second barrier proposed to deny the option of becoming modifiable is that of the critical period. There is the well-held belief among biologists, psychologists, and educators that there are certain developmental periods in individuals when they are more accessible to change by learning. This is often presented as a reason for a lack of belief in modifiability. The individual who has gone through the proposed and accepted critical period of development and not acquired the skills and functions associated with that period is considered inaccessible to change. Depending on the function, as in language acquisition, for example, change is considered possible until the age of 4, 5, or 6 at latest, and any attempt to have a child beyond this age become meaningfully modified and more able to acquire the skills and use the related cognitive structures has been considered impossible. Those children who have not acquired speech until this age were unable to acquire proficient linguistic behavior. We have had many examples in which children of a much more advanced age have been meaningfully modified in terms of their linguistic behavior and their communication capacities. I present the case of Alex below because it challenges the critical period concept as well as other traditionally considered barriers, and was dealt with at an early phase in the revolution in the brain sciences, and so challenged what was then known but is now much more fully understood and accepted.

The Severity of the Condition

A third factor that has been considered a barrier to change is the severity of the condition and the multiplicity of the handicap the individual is suffering from. And the question is asked: Does the option of modifiability still exist even for individuals with a multiplicity of serious disorders? If one does not see, does not hear, cannot move, cannot speak, does not imitate—can these people also be considered as having the option of modifiability? Is it worth the time, effort, and resources to attempt to overcome these severe deficiencies? Or does one simply give up and relegate these individuals to a custodial life, under certain circumstances well taken care of with regard to their physical needs but ignoring their humanity?

TWO CASES THAT CHALLENGE THE CONCEPT OF BARRIERS

Here I present two cases that challenge the accepted belief that there are barriers to modifiability. In these cases, one sees the overlapping effects of the traditionally identified barriers to modifiability—with severe disability, one often misses the critical developmental periods. With some etiologies, especially before we have learned what we now know about neural plasticity, neurogenesis, and epigenesis, it seemed logical and appropriate to adopt a passive/acceptant posture. But these two cases will hopefully change this point of view!

> The case of Alex is a very eloquent challenge to the concept of etiological and critical period barriers. Alex suffered from Sturge-Weber syndrome, causing an electrical misfiring of the neurons of his brain, leading to a life-endangering epileptic condition of up to 10 to 15 epileptic seizures every day, starting at 4 years of age. He had to be very heavily medicated, and not always successfully, because the epilepsy was strongly affected by the condition of the flow of blood into the left hemisphere of his brain. The medical regimen left him almost vegetative. He did not develop language. He did not learn even to say the word *mama*. At a certain point (at the age of 8 or 9), his mother decided to seek surgery to remove the site of the dysfunction, and restore him to a nonmedicated state. He underwent a left hemispherectomy that removed the offending areas that included the parts of the brain (Broca and Wernicke areas) responsible for language

development and use. Much to the experts' surprise, after this procedure, Alex started to speak. His language was rather poor, but he was able to communicate his basic needs and enrich his repertoire over time. However, in spite of considerable efforts on the part of specialists over a period of 5 years, Alex never was able to learn to read, write, or do any kind of operational thinking, such as mathematics, counting, or to acquire number concepts.

Five years after he underwent the hemispherectomy, he was brought to us by his mother because of the very limited development that had taken place. His tested IQ had risen from 33 to 50, but he was still not able to learn reading, writing, and arithmetic. Those in the hospital who were working with him were convinced that there was nothing more to be done.

His mother did not accept his condition. She continued to search for ways to modify her child. Her need to see him develop was and continues to be a most important determinant of his development. She brought him to us and I examined him in front of an audience of more than 200 people. I was able to show that under conditions of mediated learning he was able to learn. Ultimately, after more than 3 years of intensive mediation in our institute, where he was integrated into a normal family living environment, he learned to read and write and do analogies and other advanced forms of operational thinking—to the point that he came up to a tested IQ level of 120. When he returned to his home country at the age of approximately 18, he entered and completed a college program in the area of accountancy and he has overcome many of his difficulties.

The great changes happened in him at ages much more advanced than the developmental literature considered possible—challenging the critical periods and severity of condition barriers to change. His speech came back at the age of 9, and then later he developed high degrees of cognitive and interactive sufficiency, including the ability to read, write, and perform mathematical operations, again against all the predictions of the experts.

As of this writing Alex returned to us for further assessment and mediation. He is now 32 years old. As part of this recent activity, an fMRI was administered. Those who administered the procedure and analyzed the resulting data, as well as specialists interacting with Alex—the neurologists, speech and language specialists, physical therapists and others—have become extremely interested in the function of his right hemisphere. Although all of the results and interpretations are not complete at the time of this writing, we can summarize the interest by quoting one of the specialists: "His brain is doing what it is not supposed to be able to do!" To which we add, we have much to learn further!

So the critical period is not necessarily an unsurpassable barrier for the individual. It certainly creates special needs, and specialized modalities and intensities of mediating and teaching that are necessary for the individual to be modified. But Alex and hundreds of other cases that we have had the opportunity to deal with in the later stages of their development have shown that modifiability is accessible even for individuals much beyond the critical period of development, with severe conditions, and even into adulthood.

Our colleague Dr. Hefziba Lifshitz from Bar-Ilan University (in Israel) has used MLE and dynamic assessment (LPAD) in order to assess the modifiability of an institutionalized population of elders and then, using the same methodology with populations of 20-year-olds and 40-year-olds, both of whom have had long histories of institutionalization, found these three populations accessible to modifiability (Lifshitz, 1995).

From this point of view, the option of modifiability exists. It depends, of course, on the conditions and on the special modalities that have to be offered to individuals *during*, *before*, and *after* the critical period.

The case of Ravital taught me the very important lesson that the multiple severity of condition as well as genetic and critical period issues do not present a barrier that cannot be bypassed. Ravital's case points to a number of things; first, to the importance of the need system that parents and caregivers have toward the individual and the way it affects their options to become modified; and second, it shows some very interesting modalities by which the changes can be produced in the multiply handicapped individual.

Ravital was referred to me in the hope that we could help this 12-year-old girl. She was brought to me by her mother, and the moment she came in, I saw difficulties that she brought to any attempt to intervene.

She looked like an ornithocephalic child, with a face like a bird: a very long nose covering most of her lips and mouth, a very small chin, bulging eyes (exophthalmia) that made her unable to see things except from very close distances. She had no speech whatsoever, and even the modulation of her voice was very, very limited. All she was able to vocalize was a screeching noise that was emitted primarily as a harsh kind of sound, at moments of frustration.

When she came in, she placed herself with her face toward the wall, and her mother had to take her by the hand and bring her and seat her on a chair in front of me. I started to present her with a number of tasks. She did not respond; she did not initiate any kind of behavior. There was a total state of aboulia, the lack of initiation of action. And at a given moment I took a certain amount of Plasticine and took her hand and started to make her manipulate it. I prompted her to roll it into a cylinder, and she did it as long as my hand was on her hand. The moment I removed my hand, she stopped. I worked for 2 hours to make this child respond to some of the stimulation that I gave her and/or asked the mother to give her, and there was a very limited awareness (on her part) or sense of success—she was almost totally unresponsive to my attempts to teach her something, to make her do something. So I told her mother that I did not see possibilities of modifying the child, at least not by me, and I doubted whether anything could be done.

The mother, who had come to me as a last hope, knowing my optimistic view about human beings, started to cry and said, "I came to you because I hoped you would be the one who would be ready and able to do something to develop my daughter. I cannot accept my daughter as an imbecile, as an idiot; I will not let it happen!" I then told her, "Well, what would you like to do?" She asked me to give her the possibility to come and learn from us how to work with her daughter and to be introduced to the various techniques that we had developed for stimulating the individual. I said that we would do it, and indeed Ravital's mother started to come each week and learned a number of our techniques, and she used some of the materials that we had developed specially for such low-functioning cases. But I must admit that I had very little hope of seeing Ravital develop.

Her mother reported from time to time the changes that she observed following her intervention according to our guidance and our suggestions, but we were not yet convinced about the possibility of really modifying the child.

After about 2 and a half years or 3 years, Ravital's mother came and told us that her daughter was reading and was also able to write! It was after a period where she hadn't come for about 3 or 4 months, and we were wondering why. Her revelation sounded like a pipe dream. But we asked the mother to bring Ravital to us and let us see how she does this. When Ravital came, her mother took out a little table, took out a number of letters, and told Revital to write her name. And indeed Ravital started to look on the table and search through the letters with her left hand. Her right hand was totally passive; she could not use it at all. So she looked with her bulging eyes and found the letters. It took some time but she wrote her name in proper order. Then her mother gave her a number of other tasks, and Ravital wrote each word that she was asked to construct without errors or hesitations. She knew exactly the order of the letters, the order of the syllables, the order of the sounds that she had been given by her mother. She was also able to do some mathematical exercises in addition, subtraction, and even multiplication. We were all amazed. She had all the precursors for reading and writing, and in fact, as she further developed, she learned to use the computer to execute these tasks.

I felt this as a slap to my face—telling me that my pessimism concerning the multiply handicapped individual had almost doomed this child to a state that was changed only by the strong need of her mother and her readiness to invest in her daughter in a way that nobody would try and do. And she succeeded.

As a result of this, we decided to take Ravital into treatment. She came daily. She started to learn to use the computer, and she learned to write on the computer. It was very difficult because her sight was very bad and she had to look and search for each letter, but with time she became more and more efficient and she was able to write long sentences and paragraphs on a variety of topics. Then she started to write sentences and paragraphs in a very meaningful way, conveying in her writing what she was feeling and thinking. She did not respond to dictation, but she initiated writing her thoughts in a very meaningful way.

In the midst of these extremely optimistic developments, we had the concern that Ravital could not do anything except with the mother keeping her hand on Ravital's right hand. We asked the mother not to keep her hand on Ravital's hand but instead to keep her hand on the shoulders. And this didn't change at all. We thought the mother may have used some kind of signs to make her do certain things, but it turned out to be absolutely the initiative of Ravital herself.

At a given point I wrote to Ravital on the computer, "Ravital, you are such an intelligent young lady. I admire the way you learn and you do such wonderful things. But, Ravital, why do you need your mother's hand always on your hand or on your shoulders?" She then sat down and in front of me wrote her answer, "Dear esteemed Professor Feuerstein"—and I felt another slap on my face—"Dear Professor Feuerstein, If you would be like me, always told that I am not able to learn anything, that I am not able to know anything and I am not able to do anything, and the only person who believes that I can, that I will be able to do it and I can learn is your mother, even you, Professor Feuerstein, would not leave your mother. You will want her to be with you."

Here I am paraphrasing what she wrote, but this was the essence of what she conveyed to me, that her capacities were developed and were engendered by the belief of her mother, by her need to see her child transformed. And indeed the only thing she could not learn to do was to speak or to emit understandable sounds.

Eventually she wrote her autobiography, about 20 pages, that I have and I hope someday to be able to publish. In this work I am not seen very favorably. She did not forget my reaction the first time where I declared myself unable to do something for her. But she was absolutely grateful for what had been done by teaching her the computer, by teaching her mother, and she is today a much more independent young lady who is able now to—at the age of 32 or 33—to care for herself, to cook certain things, to understand the world better, and to learn from experiences that were previously not accessible to her.

By describing Alex and Ravital, we want to show that the barriers against modifiability produced by the multiplicity of the handicap—sensorial, motor, cognitive, and so on—are not necessarily unsurpassable. They can be surpassed by the kind of need that we have to render the individual more able, more capable, more skilled, and more adaptable to life by our *determination* to do it, because of our need to see the individual become able to succeed, and by using a variety of techniques of mediation. We hope that today, after the research in the brain sciences, showing the potential for modifiability will no longer be questioned. This has great application not only for individuals who suffer from extreme challenges but also for broader education and the ability to increase the leaning potential of the many students who experience challenge in less dramatic but no less important and much more prevalent forms.

SUMMARIZING

We have discussed the three barriers that were considered as setting limits for the modifiability of the individual. We have presented just two of the many cases where we have demonstrated the possibility of bypassing these barriers. We have described our view about cognitive modifiability of the individual as a function of a belief system. In the beginning, there must be the need to see our fellow human beings as able to develop their attributes, their capacities, and their readiness to act in the sense of adaptation. The need makes us believe in the possibility of doing it. *We believed that it was possible because we needed to see it happen.*

But the fact that this belief is based on a need system risks making us sound biased and *unscientific*, and science does not accept such biases. So the question must be, "What are the theoretical scientific underpinnings of this belief in the human modifiability and the possibilities of practicing what is necessary in order to render modifiability, not only as an option but as something that materializes itself in the life of the individual?"

CHAPTER 5

Sources of Support for the Theory of Structural Cognitive Modifiability

In this chapter I will elaborate on what we consider to be important sources of support for the theory of structural cognitive modifiability, and the practices and programs derived from it. Perhaps the most satisfying and powerful source of support, for both the theory and production of modifiability, has been the results pouring in from what I call the "new neurosciences." A plethora of research is being done, and frontiers are being pushed back, showing the brain's capacity to be modified in response to external stimulation. Elsewhere in this book I have mentioned the writings of Norman Doidge and Jeffrey Schwartz, as well as the work of Rizzolatti and his team at the University of Parma identifying the mirror neurons and other aspects of neural plasticity. These have been the pioneers in understanding and disseminating these findings, and they strongly support the tenants of my theory and consequences of my applications. I will have more to say about this source of support later in this chapter.

THE DOUBLE ONTOGENY OF HUMAN DEVELOPMENT

We use the concept of ontological development, or the naturally occurring life cycles, to describe the critical aspects of human development, drawing upon the work of Tomasello and others (Tomasello, 1993; Tomasello, Kruger, & Ratner, 1999).

Let's now come back to the first determinant of support, the double ontogeny, or development over time, of the human being. The development of the human being is determined by two factors: The first factor is the *biological* that is the obvious cause of our existence. Our lives are dominated and become possible by the biological processes that animate us, enable our actions, our thinking and learning. So the first component of our developmental ontogeny is biological. Of course, this has a very strong impact on our lives, the level of development of the individual, the capacity to master certain biologically and determined factors, and so on.

The second determinant of our functioning and our structure is the *environmental*, sociocultural, economic conditions in which we live. The two systems, the two sources of development—the biological and the environmental—do not always interact in harmony. Our educational development, our capacity to master and integrate what we are exposed to in our environments, is beginning to be identified as a source of influence on our biological condition. There is now emerging evidence (not without controversy as to the relative or proportional contributions, as I have addressed elsewhere in this book) that our educational, psychological, and experiential knowledge contribute to our ontogeny. We do not have to accept what biology imposes on us. We can fight against certain formerly limiting biological factors. For instance, if we are in some way affected by sickness, we fight against it. We find ways by which to curb the impact of our biology; we don't accept it as it is. We are able to modify biological conditions by science, by knowledge, by that which we absorb through our exposure to our environments.

But as I say, the two systems do not always live in harmony with each other. The biological determinant is not left alone to perform the way that science and the material conditions of the body determine. We are able to modify these conditions and thus affect in a very meaningful way the destiny of the individual.

Consider the problem of low birth weight. The work of Professor Pnina Klein, who has examined children who were born with a weight at birth of below 1,500 grams, showed that such children were expected to experience certain cognitive and intellectual developmental deficiencies. A child with 1,000 grams of weight at birth was considered to be much lower-functioning, at least predictably, than the child who was born at a weight of 1,500 grams or 2,000 grams. There was a high correlation between the weight at birth and the level of intelligence. Professor Klein studied this phenomenon in relation to the type of environment that the parents gave the underweight child, and she found out that the way these parents interacted with the child, talked to the child, supported and enriched the life experiences and stimulated development made a difference. When she examined these children at age 3, whose parents were very active mediators, stimulating their children, she found that the results were absolutely amazing compared with those of children who did not have this kind of mediation (Klein, 1996). The correlation between weight and intelligence was totally washed out by the impact of the environment. The quality of the environment, the type of stimuli offered to the child, was such that it affected children who, despite low birth weight, were able to function much beyond what had been expected and predicted by level of weight.

> An interesting case that supports Klein's findings is that of quintuplets who were referred to us at the age of 5 and a half. They were born with extremely low birth weights and had very low developmental weights for their current ages. They were considered mentally defective. Their family was very poor, but their parents (particularly their mother) were active in stimulating them, and wanted them to develop well. Our dynamic assessment showed them to be functioning in many respects within normal ranges and to have good functional potential. We then worked with them for a period of almost 3 years. Three of the girls were able to be placed in normal kindergartens at the outset of treatment and 3 years later were observed to have regular skills and age-appropriate development. The two boys had more difficulties. One needed considerable additional instruction, and within 1 year was placed in a normal school program.

These are wonderful illustrations of how the environment modifies the biological condition of the individual and may actually counteract the effects. This is one of the very important sources of support, showing that a properly applied environment enables the surpassing of difficulties produced by the biological condition. The double ontogeny says, "Yes, biology determines much of the life of the individual," but the environment, the sociocultural and educational determinants, the financial conditions, and so forth are able to modify the biological conditions in a very meaningful way. For many learners, this experience has not come to them in a systematic, meaningful, or persistent way (due to conditions of family, environment, or their own developmental limitations) and thus they need to be the object of mediation. The goal of MLE is to help such children respond to diverse but significant stimuli meaningfully and differentially.

ISSUES RELATED TO THE DOUBLE ONTOGENY

This brings us to a consideration of related issues in the area of environmental stimulation, enrichment, and mediation that ultimately affect the two factors comprising the double ontogeny. They respond to the question, "What are the mechanisms of structural change?" An elaborated response (and conceptual model) is enabled by the revolution in the brain sciences.

Imitation

Imitative behavior plays a very crucial role in the development of cognitive processes, emotional interactions, and the capacity to experience empathy toward the other. Imitative behavior is developed in a normal automatic way as children are constantly exposed to models. At a given point, to focus or enhance the learner's awareness and responsiveness to stimuli, MLE can use the imitative process as a way of learning how to learn, how to select certain stimuli, and how to become aware of the need to treat particular stimuli with greater attention and more time focused on them. Imitation in MLE is strongly contingent on the way by which the adult or other children set themselves as models, with the *intention* to act as models and with the *awareness* of the meaning of this way of modeling the behavior of the child. This can be done by intentioned parents and teachers who serve as models of imitation for the child. Teaching the child how to (and to want to) imitate is one of the most important mediational tools to turn the child into a good learner. The goal of mediation in this instance is to teach children to imitate, to go beyond chance encounters with models, to choose models and respond to them differentially instead of reacting in a haphazard and or chance-occurring way.

We know that we can make children imitate at very early stages in their development. But the kinds of speech, for example, or the way by which children will use mimicry in order to communicate feelings and understandings of what they experience becomes a focus and goal of our mediation, as a function of our awareness of how to mediate to children the imitative behavior necessary for them.

Imitative behavior will continue throughout life to affect the behavior of the individual. The great diversity of models to which children are exposed will allow them to make a free choice regarding which models, at given points in time and space, will (and should) be incorporated and assimilated.

Furthermore, the combinations of these models will allow the formation of a behavioral pattern that will be a mosaic of the various models that have been previously experienced and imitated, in addition to internalized choices of behavior that have been developed. Ultimately, responses to the environment (the impinging stimuli) will be specific to the individual, not restricted to the models that were previously experienced. However, the mediator is often called upon to change certain behaviors acquired by the individual through imitation and that are no longer appropriate for the particular age or for the particular environment to which the child must respond and adapt.

Overcoming Attention Deficit Behavior

We see the potential to overcome ADD behavior being strongly related to the imitation processes we have just described. We are very suspicious that the great epidemic of attention deficit disorders that are considered today as being due to deficiencies related to genetic conditions or certain hereditary characteristics are really (to some extent, although not necessarily exclusively) the outcome of lack of MLE, particularly in the area of imitation. Or conversely, children imitate some of the deleterious stimuli that they see in their parents and other behavioral models. This is not to deny the seriousness or complexity of attention deficit disorder but rather to suggest that, contrary to some thinking and the beliefs of some advocacy organizations, it can be affected by cognitive modifiability interventions and is not some type of inborn "trait" of the individual, as we differentiate below.

INTELLIGENCE AND COGNITIVE DEVELOPMENT AS *STATES* RATHER THAN *TRAITS*

The second source of support for the theory of structural cognitive modifiability resides in a consideration of the level and quality of *behavior* of the individual as a *state* rather than a *trait*. When you speak about a trait, you refer to something that is *not modifiable*. A trait is, by definition, a presumed stable condition of the organism that is basically supported by inherited genetic determinants, by chromosomal determinants, and the like. Much of the thinking in psychology and education accepts the genetic inevitability of some conditions (see our discussion of the question of intelligence from the perspective of Jensen and Herrnstein and Murray elsewhere in this book), thus considering intelligence and cognitive potential human traits that cannot be substantially modified. If you think about a characteristic or function as a trait, there is very little place for modifiability. If, on the other hand, you consider it a state, the functioning of the individual may be the product of biological conditions or of a variety of other environmental factors, but it is not stable. A state is conditioned, created, or produced by factors that are by themselves not fixed, but are constantly evolving in the individual. A state is something that is produced by certain conditions, even those that are biological, or even genetic.

Implications for Modifiability

If traits are considered permanent and even pervasive and part of the mental/emotional personality structure of the individual they will not be considered as readily modifiable. Traits have been attributed more to genetic hereditary phenomena, the sources of which are considered unmodifiable.

However, when we speak of a state we consider that a certain condition of the individual is occurring and produces transient effects that do not leave too many lasting effects even if they occur over long passages of time. The state can be overcome! Certain conditions may appear at a given point in the life of the individual; other conditions may be imposed that may modify the condition that has produced the state. A state, by definition, is a more modifiable condition of the individual. Behavior, feelings, and ways of thinking can be very different according to the condition in which individuals find themselves and the conditions that have produced the state.

This has very important implications for the way we refer to the learning-disabled individual, the dyslexic, the dysgraphic, the aphasic, and so on. These and many other phenomena have been customarily considered traits and therefore not considered accessible to meaningful change.

In recent years, even some traits are starting to be considered accessible to change. More and more studies have pointed to the possibility of affecting the expression of our genes: having certain genes modified by certain modalities of functioning and imposing on the genes certain types of activities that were previously considered inaccessible to them (epigenesis). For example, researchers are beginning to observe changes in cellular differentiation as a consequence of external stimulation (Reik, 2007).

Thus, our identification of intelligence and cognition as states rather than traits supports the potential, and positive responses, to explain and manifest human modifiability.

Further Defining the Difference

What does this mean? It means that if you change the conditions, you will change the state of the individual. Yes, children with Down syndrome have great difficulties because of their slow reaction to a variety of stimuli. They may appear inattentive because of slow reactions. They may be unable to focus on certain stimuli long enough to be able to learn them. Or they may have the need to focus beyond their ability to sustain attention. There are a number of conditions in their biological makeup that are responsible for this. But knowing these conditions will make us search for modalities by which these conditions will be in some way overcome or moderated, and by this the state of the individual will be meaningfully altered.

To further the differentiation between state and trait, consider that children with Down syndrome tend to be hypotonic, or exhibiting initial flaccid muscle movement, particularly in the peribuccal area affecting the formation of the mouth, lips, the articulatory systems, often limiting the capacity to learn to talk in an articulated way. Many of these children mumble without moving their lips and without projecting their voice in a way that will make their speech understandable. So you have children who do not learn to speak appropriately, even into advanced ages. And if one speaks in a way that is not understood by one's companions, the person will probably end up with very limited communication and verbal interaction skills. Here we consider our *soliloquy* method that I described briefly in Chapter 4 as a means to produce more adequate speech.

We have tried to counteract this condition by teaching a child with Down syndrome to protrude the lips in concert with hearing the *boo, baa, baah* sounds (each requiring a different configuration of the peribuccal muscles of the mouth, as I described in Chapter 1). We have done this at the age of 3 months and continued for a long period, and children learned quite rapidly and early to imitate the protrusion of the lips and eventually learned to speak in a very clear and understandable way. This reinforces the individuals interacting with them to continue to talk to them and to enrich their language (another aspect of the application of *soliloquy*). And this whole series of developments is due to the simple intervention of making the child able to speak in a way that is understood by others.

My description of working with the Down syndrome child is illustrative of how learners acquire many behaviors through imitation, acquiring, correcting, or replacing them with other modalities of behavior that are more appropriate in terms of age, place, and in terms of the roles the child has to play. MLE brings a much higher degree of awareness of the condition of the individual, and intentionality to have these changes produced.

The child comes back from kindergarten where there is the potential to imitate other children: perhaps children who have tics or bad verbal habits. This imitation will be inappropriate and dysfunctional and we may have to expose the child to different modalities of interaction. These are *states* that require the introduction of different conditions of imitation in order to produce the desired changes in the child's behavior, in some cases overcoming cultural or limited exposure to stimulation. Sometimes persistent effects of "states" become attributable to "traits. Here is one such example:

> We have seen more than one young boy who did not learn to read for reasons having to do with the fact that the act of reading was to identify with his sisters, and the child wanted to be more like his father, who showed a very limited interest in reading. So the fact that they lived in an environment in which certain objects of imitation were not chosen because of their gender identity, and since their sisters were proficient readers compared to the father who was a declared nonreader, so the children identified themselves with the father and became a very bad reader. In more than one instance they were diagnosed as dyslexic and because of their great difficulty acquiring reading, the dysfunction was attributed to some kind of genetic disorder (to a trait). We, on the other hand, considered the reason for the lack of reading as resulting from a lack of identification or an attempt not to identify with the sisters, in order to identify instead with the father. Once I asked fathers to act as a model of reading and to read with their sons, there were no more problems. And one young man whom I am thinking about in this example, who had learned to read approximately at the age of 10, became a very important engineer and his reading was a major way of advancing himself.
>
> This was true also with another boy who was a very bad reader, to the point that his school wanted him—at the age of 17—to start a manual profession because he was not able to read the materials he needed for a "more theoretically oriented profession." This young man was also described to us as having a genetic disorder that manifested itself in a state of dyslexia. We involved this young man in a series of courses and discussed with him certain of the issues related to his lack of reading. He turned out to be a person who advanced himself in a very demanding profession where he had to read incessantly new demanding and technical materials. He had to learn by heart certain things. He became not only a proficient reader but also an excellent student and a very high-level professional.

These examples show how MLE plays a very important role and serves to create the conditions for the individual to change the state of functioning. The counterpoint to this phenomenon is seen in the phenomenon of an epidemic rise in the number of individuals diagnosed with deficiencies in reading and writing, which has jumped in the last 20 years from 0.2% (of true dyslexic people due to certain characteristics of the brain structure) to about 20% of population. This is a good news/bad news phenomenon, as improvements in diagnostic procedures and awareness affect numbers of reported incidence, but many also cite deterioration of life conditions (environmental toxins, nutritional deficits, and so on) as possible causes for the increase. There have been a number of studies over the last several decades, well summarized by Pressinger (1997). In the academic world, individuals with learning disorders (dyslexia and its variations) are given legal rights to access special accommodations at the time of matriculation and entrance examinations. I would characterize this as an instance of a trait that is considered to be the reason for a deficiency and which in many cases turns out to be actually a state produced by some very diverse and different conditions.

We have described this epidemic of learning disabilities as a condition of *disabling learning* rather than a learning disability. Rather than a trait of the individual it may well be a condition of the teaching (as mentioned in an earlier chapter of this book) and a condition of the environment that affects the readiness and the capacity of the individual to learn to read.

THE ISSUE OF MEDICATION: TO MEDICATE OR NOT TO MEDICATE?

Yet another example of this situation is in the heightened occurrence of individuals with learning difficulties being medicated, frequently with Ritalin. Without regard to its potential negative side effects, medication does little to correct learning disabilities. It is thought that by taking Ritalin the child will become better able to learn because it will affect the trait. It is not understood that even if the medication affects tendencies toward impulsivity or inattention, it in itself will not affect the process of concentration. We will have to create the conditions by which the individual, who has been affected for some reasons in the capacity to concentrate, will be given opportunities for learning appropriate to the condition.

It is time to question to what extent one should immediately use medication instead of searching for conditions to enable the individual to develop thinking and social interactive skills appropriate to the environment thereby enlisting the readiness to change behavior in the direction of good learning and adaptive functioning.

HOW TO EFFECT CHANGES IN
THE *STATE* OF FUNCTIONING

From our point of view, the concept of state requires a better understanding of the conditions responsible for the individual's level and nature of functioning—emotional, cognitive, behavioral, and social. We must assess the conditions conducive to the development of the state and make a difference on the outcome.

MLE works to change the ineffective repertoire of interactive modalities with the environment or the self and create the belief and understanding that one can indeed be modified. In this way, those disabilities that are said to be genetic, or to have some chromosomal substrata, or are considered a deficiency by which the neurological system is malfunctioning, are instead seen (and experienced) as *conditions* that have produced certain states. Change the conditions and you will change the states. And what is more important, in spite of the habits that the individual has acquired in response to the existing (pre-mediation) conditions they can be changed by producing another habit. This means that in order to have a habit extinguished, you must produce another habit. Many of the conditions of an existing state are *remediable* by creating new and appropriate states of functioning. This is actually one of the great developments that we have offered to many of those who are low-functioning—even those labeled and presenting with severe disabling conditions—with very appropriate results, as the examples I have presented hopefully illustrate.

> We have many adults come to us and tell us that they are dyslexic. When we assessed one man's activities, we saw him as somebody who has produced some very important literary and cognitively rich productions, but he disclaimed them: "But I am dyslexic!" We had to totally reverse his way of thinking about himself, proving to him by showing him his "nondyslexic" actions. For him and others, difficulties in reading may be the result of bad habits formed in the course of their studies, and not of the more formal reading deficiencies that are considered evidence of "dyslexia." One mediational strategy is to expose such learners to four or five pages of written material, help the learner "overlearn" the content, and then have them recite what they have learned. These pages, once learned, are recited in front of us. The understanding of these paragraphs was checked again by a method where we turned each sentence into a source of answers to questions that we posed. The experience of fluency and competence,

often for the first time, has great and meaningful effects on the way the learner perceives the "disability."

In the example above, I describe how we change a habit by a acquiring a more appropriate habit. I could go on and describe many more of these phenomena. The phenomenon of impulsiveness plays a prominent role in many of the disabilities experienced. Some people declare their impulsivity to be a genetic, hereditary, and, in certain cases, an immutable condition. This becomes one of the implications of the way advocacy groups have promoted special interventions for individuals diagnosed as ADHD (for example, two such groups are the CHADD [Children and Adults with Attention Deficit/Hyperactive Disorders] and the ADDA [Attention Deficit Disorder Association], whose motto is "helping adults with ADHD lead better lives."

We have seen individuals, once they knew the importance of their paying attention, the importance of not being impulsive, modify their behavior that was considered previously as belonging to a genetic disorder or cultural identity—that is, to a disorder of the individual's traits.

> For instance, we had a young man who was said not to be able to attend to a particular topic or a particular subject or stimulus for more than a few minutes. He had to change his environment and the activity with which he was involved in order to be able to sustain his attention. And this of course was considered the reason for a very limited learning capacity. We placed this young man in front of certain situations, and we explained to him the importance of paying attention, working slowly, not responding before he was sure that indeed he had the right answer, to peruse and look for a systematic way to gather all the sources of information in the particular situation. And by showing him the way by which systematic search enabled him to succeed, for the first time his behavior changed. And again, what was considered his trait, not modifiable except by medication or by other modalities, was shown to be modifiable by enlisting the volitional act. We gave him a whole set of systematic ways of checking his thinking before responding and this changed his behavior in a very meaningful way over a long period of time.

The answer was to mediate a systematic approach to build new habits, by repeating effective new behaviors and offering opportunities to understand how this type of behavior affects efficiency of the results obtained. Habitual behavior cannot be modified except by creating new habits. A new habit is created, first of all by rendering the individual aware of the importance of the meaning of the new habit to be acquired. Second, we have to offer the possibility of repeating and crystallizing the behavior and turning it into something that will become more and more familiar; it means almost being automatized and not necessarily contingent upon certain situations.

On the other hand, we have to understand that certain conditions of life require a certain degree of impulsiveness in order to survive. Some people who are confronted by a danger have to be able to respond quickly, being cognizant of all the consequences of being too slow. This would be the only way to survive in imminent danger. But in general, some impulsive behavior is due to a lack of mediation of regulation of behavior. It means that when confronted with a given problem that requires a response, a way of solving the problem, one must say to oneself:

> "Well, in order to solve the problem, I will have to go over a number
> of things that are in my repertoire and find out from them what
> would be the best solution to this problem, after I have learned all
> its dimensions. I may find a very appropriate solution in terms of the
> type of problem. But in the particular environment in which I find
> myself, I will have to conclude that in this case, this solution, which is
> wonderful otherwise, is not acceptable."

So the control of impulsiveness is possible by instituting a modality of asking questions: "Is this the place where I could do it? It would be very good if I could, but it's not the place and here I will not succeed." In this sense, impulsiveness is a state of the individual that can be changed, modified by a thoughtful and appropriate way of making the individual acquire a different habit, a different way of thinking, and a different rhythm of control.

I have tried here to point out the great importance of the way we define certain behavior. Do we define function as the consequence of a trait that will be very difficult to be changed, or do we define it as a state that we can change if we introduce new habits and behaviors by creating new conditions and changing the conditions under which the state came into existence?

MEDIATED LEARNING EXPERIENCE AS A *THIRD* ONTOGENETIC COMPONENT: SUPPORTED BY THE NEUROSCIENCES

We now add a third source of support to the theory of structural cognitive modifiability, from our perspective: that of the effect of MLE on not only the behavioral functioning of the individual but on the very neurophysiological structures of our brains. Our clinical observations and the bourgeoning results of the new neurosciences have encouraged us to add another component to the double ontogeny of biology and the sociocultural—that of MLE contributing to what we now describe as a *triple ontogeny* of human development. First, this reflects the interactive nature of MLE as a determinant of development. But this belief also has come to us from a very unexpected source. It is the neurosciences that bring us an enormous amount of evidence that by modifying the cognitive structure, the emotional behavior, and even the various spiritual manifestations of our thinking (see, for example, the innovative research of Gallesse [2003, 2009], Goleman [2006], and others), of our life, we actually modify the neural structure and matter of the brain. We will address this more fully in the next chapter.

This third source of support came from a very unexpected direction. When we were formulating our theory of structural cognitive modifiability, the major stumbling block, the major source of disbelief, came from the fact that neurosciences considered the brain totally inaccessible to change. The blood-brain barrier and many other factors—the genetic, the stability of the brain, or the presumed lack of capacity of the brain to recuperate from certain adverse conditions, vascular or otherwise, and the fact that the brain was "known" to lose neurons daily, with "diminished" learning capacity occurring with advanced age—all these argued against the concept of modifiability. To certain people, the critical period barrier was also a reason for this belief in the lack of human modifiability.

So as we postulated the propensity of the individual to become modified, the reasons for the disbelief were basically reasons taken from the existent level of knowledge in the neurosciences. See our earlier discussion in Chapter 4 of the barriers of critical period, etiology, and severity of condition that supported this perspective.

However, the relatively newly available noninvasive methods of assessing the brain's activity in real time permit us today to look at the phenomena that produce the changes. And this leads us to describe and understand the brain's neuroplasticity—our brain may well be the most plastic part of our body. Very significantly, this concept and the evidence for it are approximately 20 years old, and are accumulating at a very rapid pace.

HOW THE NEUROSCIENCES
HAVE CONFIRMED AND SUPPORTED
SCM AND MLE

Here I would like to make a personal declaration. For many years, having observed the modifiability that we produced by application of MLE in spite of the presumed immutability of the brain, I asked myself, "Can it be that behaviors acquired by the individual (e.g., learning) result in any effects on the brain itself, on the matter that determines it? Is it not possible that so many mental activities in existence in the individual's repertoire in some way change the brain itself?" And these questions came as we observed major and significant changes in cognitive functions!

> For example, we saw children who were unable to learn to create analogies, where they had to reduce relationships between two domains, or between two objects, finding what is common and what is different. This required adducing the relationships of commonality and difference and applying this self-produced relationship to a different area of functioning. These are complex mental operations, but through MLE and systematic teaching we produced changes and enabled the efficient use of these cognitive adaptations, even in individuals said to be very low-functioning.

This confirmed the great flexibility of the cognitive structures that could be mediated in the individual and the capacity to modify individuals to learn to do syllogistic thinking, to employ permutational relationships, to learn to use inferential processes and other mental operations. Systematic and persistent mediation showed that these capacities were within the individuals' repertoire, and with repetition they become fluent. Further, this fluency could then be applied in a variety of situations, becoming more and more distant from those that they had been taught and learned. So I asked my question, but I didn't dare ask it in a loud voice (although I was not the only one . . . there was a substantial group of people thinking as I was): "Is this change that we observe in the mental behavior of the individual possible without the concomitant change in the brain in its various manifestations?"

Changes in Understanding How the Brain Functions

At the time I raised this question with a well-known neurologist and he came up with the idea that the brain functions as a hologram rather than in a localized manner that responds specifically to one type of operation or problem. His speculation was that you did not have to have only the intact Broca and the Wernicke areas in order to explain speech in the left hemisphere of the brain, but any part of the brain will actually contain the totality of knowledge, of fact functions. This was an anticipation of much of what we have more recently learned regarding the functioning and structure of the brain, and was prescient. I also recall asking the prominent neuro-scientist Karl Pribram how we can ever understand what the brain is doing when an individual changes from a very low concrete level of functioning to somebody who can use abstract thinking and can become able to apply whatever is learned in one activity to other different activities. He answered, "Feuerstein, be patient. It is coming." And here I am, grateful to see that my basic hypothesis that *behavior changes the brain no less than the brain determines the behavior* has become evidenced by the existence of noninvasive methods of studying the brain in a real-time fashion.

Noninvasive Technologies to Study the Brain

The noninvasive technologies that are now used to study the brain enable us to consider the great changes produced by a behavior on the brain. The changes are both physical and functional. It is now clear that the brain is more modifiable than any other part of our body. This goes counter to all the knowledge and understanding that we have had previously about the brain. These techniques, such as the MRI, fMRI, SPECT, CT scans, TMS, and Evoked Potential EEG, are able to detect changes in the brain produced by our behavior.

Once we used to think about the brain as a one-way development. The brain develops and then this development stops and there begins a gradual but constant loss of neurons, eventually creating an impoverishment of neural structure leading in turn to a diminishing of the mental and emotional capacities of the individual. All this is today totally a matter of the past. There was a time when a patient with a brain injury was considered modifiable only for a very brief time. If the function lost was not rehabilitated within 6, 7 weeks, or a few months at most, there was no more reason to invest; it was considered a lost function. The belief that brain functions can be regenerated was considered almost heresy. This position determined the modalities of treatment, the length of treatment, and the intensity of treatment for millions of people who have been unhappily affected in their brain functioning by one or another condition.

But now the noninvasive modalities have shown us that a variety of functions can be modified, and—most important—that modifiability is effected in the individual's brain by the behavior imposed on the brain. New behaviors create new structures, pathways, and neural elements themselves. They will change the blood flow that will affect and be affected by the locus in which certain mental operations take place. They will affect the neurotransmitters, and affect even the generation of new neural matter with new synaptic connections that were destroyed, so to speak, by necrotic processes in the brain.

The examples are multiple. I described earlier the case of Alex, the young man who had his left hemisphere removed. We have many others with similar kinds of results. In these cases we observed changes that happened after many years of treatment. The results and success occurred when we offered a treatment based on MLE, and affecting changes whose possibility was considered not possible given his loss of his left brain. In Alex's case we were told, "Well, he has learned to read 5 years after an ablation of his hemisphere, but once he will leave the door where he has learned to read, then the reading will be totally forgotten." Here the denial (of the "experts") was that of the possibility of structural change. Well, Alex did not forget. However, our further observation and assessment of him, after he left our institute, showed that he not only maintained what he learned, but he extended his learning far beyond where he was when he left us.

Our work with Ron presents further evidence of the potential to change the brain:

Ron was an individual who lost a good part of his frontal lobe (recognized as a syndrome called *moira*). And his behavior was typical of a frontal lobe loss, with the lack of capacity to take into consideration the environment in which he found himself, affecting social judgment in the way he behaved. His "executive functions" were very badly affected. The changes that we observed were so dramatic that he became, following extensive treatment, one of the most gentle and considerate people that I know. I remember, early in his exposure to MLE, the way he came into my room just by using his leg, kicking the door to come in, screaming out like a small child, "Well, look what she (the teacher) is giving me to do! I will never be able to do it! Take it away from me!" and "Why do you have that cow (my secretary) in your office telling me not to come in to see you?" But 3 years later (it took us 3 years), he came to me and said, "I want to go and make a BA in psychology, anthropology, and sociology," and he said it in such a way that it showed that he knew exactly what he would love to do, in spite of its difficulty. Not only this, in his whole manner, he became one of the most considerate and gentle persons, in contrast to the insensitive and aggressive behaviors that were due to his initial condition of injury. There was no coming to see me without bringing a little gift. He finished his BA with flying colors, completing multiple major areas of study.

Cases such as these reinforce our belief that the kinds of changes that are produced by the behavior conveyed through the process of MLE become a very active agent in producing the types of structural changes in the neural system that have been proven possible through extensive, focused, systematic, and ongoing research.

At our international institute we have an Institute for the Cognitive Rehabilitation of Brain Injury where we are applying our theory and techniques. It is one of our great hopes that we will be able to study the effects of our work on the structure of the brain in order to come up with clearer evidence about the changes produced by certain modalities of interacting with the brain. A small research grant by the Crowne Family Foundation is starting us on this very important and exciting endeavor. The great discoveries in the last 10–15 years by those such as Rizzolatti and his team at Parma (c.f., Rizzolatti and Craighero, 2004) and Merzenech and his various research team members (c.f., Merzenech, 2004), and other researchers, first on the identification of the mirror neurons and broadening to other functions, structures, and potentials have given us confirmation of our theory of modifiability, enabling us to offer a scientific basis for what we have observed and considered as a true phenomenon of human modifiability. We will discuss this further in the next chapter.

CHAPTER 6

Materialism, Spiritualism, the Mirror Neurons, and Cognitive Modifiability

The relationship of mind and body has for me become an important area of concern, as an observantly religious person, and as a follower of research development in the brain sciences. The research developments in this area that I am aware of generate optimism that the relationships will become better understood and amenable to much of the technology that is developing and will be further refined. Thus, in this chapter I want to share my thinking, some of which is speculative and some of which is beginning to be supported by the research.

Much of what I have been describing in earlier chapters, particularly in Chapters 4 and 5, has totally changed my views and the views of many others concerning the dependence and focus on materialistic determinism in the neurosciences, and the structure and function of the brain, particularly with regard to the spiritual and idealistic aspects of our brains. The matter of our brains, its material, often referred to as the *hardware*, has traditionally been believed to determine the nature of what we refer to as "mental spiritual phenomena." The concept of epiphenomena—that our spiritual life isn't anything else but a kind of manifestation of the matter (the hardware)—is being thrown into question by rapidly accumulating neurophysiological technology (e.g., fMRI) that the noninvasive modalities of assessing and observing the brain in response to real-time stimulation have enabled us to see. To put it simply: There is gathering observable evidence that spiritual activities (mediation, religious practice, and so on) change the nature and functioning of the brain. Some suggestive research to support this comes, for example, from the work of Richard Davidson (2004), who studied the brain processes of meditating monks, and found changes in structure and functioning related to their meditative practices. This has been further elaborated by Daniel Siegel's (2010) writing about "mindfulness." This gives us the opportunity to question the relationship between the material and spiritual as it has been described by the traditional scientific conceptualization of determinism. Our development of the theory of structural cognitive modifiability and the practices of MLE has intensified our focus, and has challenged many of the issues that we have long considered relevant.

CONSIDERING HUMAN BEHAVIOR THROUGH THE SPECTRUM OF MLE AND QUANTUM THEORY

The development in physics of quantum theory has given us a perspective in parallel that can be applied to help us think about the importance of the volitional actions of humans, and the way things are observed and reacted to, as described by the work of Jeffrey Schwartz (see below). From this perspective, the "observed" means that we modify our experience just by the act of observing it. MLE focuses experience in certain intentional directions and creates structural changes in behavior. Much recent research is validating the potential for external stimulation to change the structure of the brain. All of this creates a real revolution in the way we may consider the brain/behavior interaction.

Jeffrey Schwartz, in his 2002 book *The Mind and the Brain*, devotes a chapter to the theoretical role that quantum physics may play in reframing the science of what we know about the brain and its potential to be modified. In his view, it offers a totally new paradigm, both for the "hard scientists" in the physics domain and for those of us working with human behavior. A specialist in treating obsessive-compulsive disorder, or OCD, he developed the term *self-directed neuroplasticity* for the changes he observed in patients through the replacement of OCD behaviors with positive self-direction. Speaking of quantum physics, he says:

> Physical theory thus underwent a tectonic shift, from a theory about physical reality to a theory about our knowledge. Science is about what we know, and what we know is only what our observations tell us. It is unscientific to ask what is "really" out there, what lies behind the observations. Physical laws as embodied in the equations of quantum physics, then, ceased describing the physical world itself. They described, instead, our knowledge of that world. Physics shifted from an ontological goal—learning what is—to an epistemological one: determining what is known, or knowable. (pp. 273–274)
>
> . . . for quantum physics describes a world in which consciousness is intimately tied to the causal structure of nature, a world purged of determinism. (pp. 276–277)

We add to the second of Schwartz's statements that this "purged" world is filled up with consciousness to compensate for the vacuum created. Later, Schwartz extends the relationship to a consideration of what is essential reality, and further to a definition of *matter* as a representation of primary reality. We think that this has important implications for the importance of consciousness in the application of MLE to promote both cognitive modifiability and neural plasticity, as we have indicated in a number of places in this book. Here we bring the issue into the context of material changes in the brain, and join even the "hard scientists" of neurophysiology to begin to question where and how spiritual aspects of human experience effect changes in neural structure in the brain, and in particular its physical matter (here we refer back to Gallesse, 2005, 2009; Rizzolatti & Craighero, 2004). Later in this chapter I will pose a number of questions that now must be asked, given what we know and see on the scientific horizon.

As I have said earlier in this volume, this new avenue of exploration brings a very meaningful support to the theory of human modifiability not only in terms of certain behaviors, but in terms of the structure that manifests itself in behavior, not only at given ages—thus disproving the critical period hypotheses—but also because the neurons can be lost in situations of "disuse" that have been described as *apoptosis*.

Today we know that even aged people may benefit from certain cognitive and spiritual behaviors that modify their neural system that is affected by their age. This is support for the theory of modifiability not only in terms of the way it acts upon children in the early period during the development of the brain but also throughout the course of life and under certain conditions restoring even some very adverse effects on the brain. Thus, the revolution brought about today in the neurosciences by new research methods and perspectives (a willingness to formulate, search, and hypothesize conditions) has led to a condition where new research results and speculations are coming to us in almost overwhelming proportions. My point here is simple: We can start to consider dimensions of spiritualism through noninvasive modalities of observation of brain functioning in order to investigate in a very meaningful way the relationship between matter and spirit.

From my perspective, I am increasingly seeing evidence that matter produces spiritual behavior, generating essential spiritual elements in the individual, and I have come to believe that spiritual thinking and behavior produces changes in the gray matter of the brain. And this imposes on us a different view of the relationship, as we are now at the beginning of an era that is able to consider differently many of the dynamics by which the human being has evolved and develops constantly by existing, by the presence of certain stimulations, by the presence of certain activities.

The demarcation between material and spiritual as affecting brain functioning and modifiability is vague. I would like to point out the fact that we are dealing with brain-injured people who have suffered loss of brain matter in various parts of the brain, and that this loss was, by necessity, accompanied by the loss of certain very important functions both with regard to "skills" and self-perception. And these people, following a very intensive treatment process, have not only regained their functions, but have experienced changes or recovery of aspects of their personalities and belief systems. Although there is an opposing view among neuroscientists that these aspects of identity reside in the brain and are recovered through its ability to repurpose networks to regain function and identity, we have yet to disprove that there also exists a "spiritual" recovery of powerful dimensions of their existence. Here is a meaningful example:

> A well-known architect in Jerusalem suffered a stroke, totally losing his speech. He was completely aphasic in terms of nominal aphasia—unable to name things, unable to repeat things, unable to imitate. I tried to make him say the word *table*, and all he could do was make mumbling sounds as he worked hard to articulate the word, contorting his mouth in a dyspraxic effort. He didn't know where to put the tongue in order to say *table*. I repeated it numerous times and he was not able to evoke it by himself, or to imitate sounds, words, or syllables. This man, after 3 and a half years of hard work at a rate of 2 to 3 hours a day, learned to speak. Today he's a fully remediated individual who has a very large studio with many people working with him, and he's able to communicate with no difficulties, and in particular in this area of activity he became a proficient, fully remediated human being. And to the point of this example, he is changed in other, more "spiritual" ways as he experienced a new enthusiasm, commitment to human beings, and a renewed sense of self—reflected in his internal perspective and strong need to share his experience with others.

I want to return here to the case of Ron in the last chapter, and add details that relate to the material/spiritual dimension. When I consider "spiritual" dimensions of experience, I think about a belief system that encompasses aspects of self-reflection and adherence to philosophical/religious principles and beliefs, usually with a belief in God, but not necessarily. When I described Ron and his recovery from his frontal lobe injury, I left out some details that are relevant here.

> When he came to me after 3 and a half years of treatment, he said, "I would like to go study anthropology, psychology, and sociology at the university. So how do you feel about that?" I answered, "Listen, at this time, at this point, at this level of functioning, you show you will certainly be a wonderful student." He went and had to discuss it with his rehabilitation psychologist, where he received a discouraging evaluation and prognosis. He was told, "Listen, I've been working for the last 20 years with frontal lobe syndrome people. I have not been able to make any one of them able to perform on a level that will enable them to become rehabilitated intellectually, cognitively, and behaviorally." When Ron told me this I asked him, "How did you react when he told you this?" I was fearful that Ron would react violently to this encounter. Instead, Ron reported, "I said (to the "expert" voicing the negative opinion), 'Yes, you are right,' but when I left his office I started to cry, and I cried bitterly and said to myself, 'I will not get the help that should have been given by his accepting my program (because the approval of Ron's plan by his psychologist would have qualified him for financial support), but I will pay it from my own pocket, from the compensation I am getting for my condition.'" And he did it, and for 3 years he studied and he finished his BA with multiple majors, showing a high degree of proficiency, despite the negative predictions of his psychologist. *It is not an exaggeration to describe him as spiritually transformed in terms of his belief in himself and power to affect his own destiny.*

What does this mean? Is it possible that this condition of rehabilitation has happened without any kind of changes in the hardware of the individual? Later, at a presentation at Tel Aviv University, Ron offered to speak to the audience, saying,

> "I want to warn you to keep away from Reuven Feuerstein. He is a dangerous man; he will not let you be what you were before. He will change you. He is really able to formulate the kind of changes that can be produced in the individual under certain types of intervention."

WAYS IN WHICH SPIRITUAL MEDIATION
AFFECTS THE MATTER OF THE BRAIN

There is an increasing need for exploration of the possible relationship between cognitive processes, mental operations, and spiritual existence—the latter not just as epiphenomena of the matter, but as actually the constituent elements that modify the matter itself and not only the behavior. So when we speak now about structural cognitive modifiability, we refer not only to changes in the behavior but also to the changes that happen in the brain itself. And the neurosciences are beginning to provide evidence, and gather data, supporting this potential. I fully expect future research will allow us to go beyond to understand how changes in brain structure change matter, change the spirit, and how the spirit changes the matter.

The Mirror Neuron's Relationship to the Spiritual/Materialistic Dichotomy

One of the most revolutionary elements that now enable us to understand many other things, even though we don't totally understand the phenomenon itself, is the existence of mirror neurons. Mirror neurons observed by microscopic electrodes inserted into the brains of monkeys, the firing of these neurons was registered by the then newly discovered technology of real-time tracking (such as MRI, PET, and so forth). It was observed that the firing of the electrodes from the mirror neurons was the same when the individual *observed* another having an experience as it was when the event was directly experienced. This meant that observing a certain act (not necessarily the object) imposed on the object—as for example in one study the breaking a peanut (in a monkey subject's presence) or eating a banana—produced the same firing as though the individual did it by itself. The observer's neurons were mirroring, with the same pattern of firing, when the individual observed someone else performing the act. This is the work of Umlita and his colleagues that I referred to earlier.

These findings have been confirmed in human studies, using noninvasive observations of the brain as it is being stimulated. To summarize, the mirror neurons in individuals observing a meaningful act will fire in the same way as they do when the act is directly engaged in. And the mirror neurons will "migrate" to other areas of the brain to stimulate activities that take over for lost or inefficient functioning—causing what is now described as the *remapping* of the brain. Thus, many of our observations of substantial changes in learned behavior that we were never able to explain previously now become understandable—particularly in their structural dimensions. That is, when we describe cognitive distance—learning that occurs when one is separated from direct exposure or contact with an act or object—we can posit that the mirror neurons are being activated in the *doing, observing, or hearing*. For instance, going back to what we discussed earlier, we could not understand how the small child described in Chapter 1, only 3 days old, when exposed to the protrusion of the tongue in a certain rhythm, hundreds of times, started to make the movements of preparing the lips to protrude the tongue. We now view this as a function of the mirror neurons, as the child protrudes the tongue following the observation of the act. It means that the individual's neural system is acting in potentially the same way by observing the phenomenon as by acting directly.

The Mirror Neurons and Imitative Behavior

I have earlier discussed the importance of imitative behavior in language acquisition and other aspects of cognitive development. The mechanism of imitation is also better understood from the perspective of mirror neurons. Imitation is a constant phenomenon throughout our existence. At certain times we imitate in a kind of automatic way, as is done in early childhood; then we imitate in a kind of deferred way. I imitate when I observe meaningful actions. I imitate without being conscious that I do so. And it's a well-known phenomenon that people who live together for many years imitate each other to the point that they even structure their facial expression in a way that is amazingly close to and similar to each other.

One can extend this relationship to a broad range of behaviors. It relates to a great number of phenomena that describe and form the social life of the individual, feelings of empathy and of readiness to understand others' reasons for doing or feeling a thing. It is probably the most important phenomenon that permits us to better understand what is happening.

Many neuroscientists who have studied the mirroring phenomenon predict that mirror neurons will do for psychology what DNA has done for biology. The mirror neurons will become a most important source of evidence and support for human modifiability. We have discussed earlier how MLE can affect our mirror neurons and we will return to this issue later in this chapter. MLE is consistent with neurological findings in that it does not just present individuals with an object to be acted upon, but makes the acts relevant to the individual's interests, to the individual's need to learn about the object and to learn the relationship that the act has imposed on the object.

We can explain language in much the same way. The mirror neurons may be the only way to explain language acquisition and development—particularly with regard to the processes of imitation. I have discussed earlier the issue of making a child imitate the way to protrude the tongue, and will not repeat it here. But to go further, from the perspective of the mirroring functions of the neurons, the most interesting observation is that the protrusion of the tongue goes in the opposite direction of the observed model; it means the child is not doing the same thing as the model. The model puts out the tongue and, if it were simply the imitation of the same movement, the child would have to retrieve the tongue back into the mouth in order to go in the same direction as the model. We saw this in Ravital, who was described in Chapter 4. When we tried to teach her to pull out her tongue she was unable to do it. On the contrary, she pulled it back. She made the imitational act in the direction in which the model went. And this meant pulling back the tongue rather than protruding it. So all these things were not explainable without the mirror neurons.

We know that certain autistic children are unable to imitate, and they have great difficulties in learning and in co-vibrating with their environment because of their incapacity to use models of imitation in order to become socialized and experience the social world as a source of learning. Again, mirror neurons may be a great source for understanding this behavior, and eventually one may consider modalities of intervention that will take into account these findings.

Mirror Neurons and the Modifiability of the Brain

Mirror neurons, representing a very recent development in brain plasticity, have brought some very meaningful contributions to the issue of human modifiability. One of the pioneers in this research is V. S. Ramachandran, who wrote in 1995 and predicted that mirror neurons would provide "a unifying framework" and thus explain a number of mental abilities not heretofore well understood, but clearly observed. He thus linked the mirror neuron phenomenon to a potential "great leap forward" with enormous implications for cultural transmission. He was correct, as reflected in the research of Rizzolatti and Craighero that we mentioned earlier in this chapter.

These researchers, and others working in the "new neurosciences," summarize the situation well. For my theoretical formulations, I have increasing confidence that MLE may be very meaningfully interpreted and elaborated in terms of the mirror neurons. The total body of research on neural plasticity helps explain why MLE is effective in modifying the individual's level and nature of functions. To take an example that brings us back to the focus of this chapter—the relationship of material and spiritual functions—there are now data available that relate the violence to which children are exposed to the activation of their mirror neurons. There are many mechanisms that are not yet fully understood. One is that if children are presented with models of violence, they will activate (unconsciously, emotionally, behaviorally) mental processes, even as a *potential source of pleasurable feelings*, and by this develop some kind of addiction to violence. And because of the nature of the development produced by the mirror neurons, the access to some of the more conscious/awareness factors will be very meaningfully effected.

Mirror Neurons and Genetic Heritability and Stability

The mirror neurons also offer us some insights into the way by which certain generalizations with the issue of transcendence are affected. They offer a very clear model of development of the individual in relation to environmental stimulation. Certain behaviors become modeled by exposure to certain types of activities, leading to changes in the structure of the brain itself. This represents, from our point of view, very strong support for the theory of structural cognitive modifiability, and extends to questioning the belief in the fixity produced by certain genes that are inherited.

The genes that are the building blocks of the genome were recently considered the way by which one could explain certain characteristics (stable, fixed, immutable) of the individual. However, new developments have thrown doubt on whether they are reliable sources of information. Today it has been shown, starting with the innovative research of Nobel laureate Eric Kandel (2006), whose innovating thinking and research opened our awareness to the concept of epigenesist, which says that even our genes are not necessarily part of our *fixed* traits.

DEFINING MATERIALISM VERSUS SPIRITUALISM AND THE CONCEPTUALIZATION OF HUMAN BEHAVIOR AND POTENTIAL

Traditionally, materialism has been associated with a perspective on observing the world and accepted models for orienting scientific inquiry. As we have indicated earlier in this chapter, and elsewhere in this book, the revolution in the brain sciences has given us encouragement to question the assumptions relating to the nature of human behavior and ways of differentially understanding the spectrum of behaviors and neurocortical responses generated. We are not alone in this consideration, as it is of great interest to philosophers and a growing number of scientists who see the potential for new paradigms of study and focusing research.

To simplify the process of differentiating and place it in a somewhat narrower context for the science of studying the brain and linking it to understanding human behavior, we have searched the literature and will identify those contrasts that we see as relevant. Our selective criteria are organized around implications for scientific inquiry that will clarify the confrontation that we see as happening and necessary in understanding the relationship between brain and behavior.

For materialists, matter is one substance, and it can be objectively studied and manipulated. Spiritualists accept a dualism—matter and mind. For materialists, human functioning can be fully described by an analysis of the matter (of the brain, nervous system, biology), but for spiritualism human functioning is more than just the "objective" matter. Now it is possible that evidence may be found that spiritual experience may change the nature of matter. In materialism, there is no need for an organizing spiritual concept. In contrast, spiritualists believe that there may be influences on the matter of "supernatural" forces, and this clearly pushes the scientific paradigm in new directions!

Materialism is closely associated with determinism, autonomy, self-consciousness, and the notion that an inherent meaning of life is illusory. The spiritual conception is one of freedom and the potential for free will. From the determinist perspective, human beings are a part of nature, like all other animate and inanimate objects. The "pure" scientific view is that what is not known awaits discovery, which often closes off perspective and inquiry, and creates a "blinder" effect. The spiritualists believe that what is not known presents an opportunity for transcendence that then transforms that which is "objective."

Simply put, materialists want to research the *how* of existence. Spiritualists, on the other hand, search for the *why*. Semantically, the polarities are reflected in the difference between "knowledge" and "faith," and between "perception" and "speculation." For us, this has the potential to inform our theory for both understanding and facilitating cognitive modifiability—helping individuals overcome and structure their learning and their very beings. If this process extends to the very neurophysiological structures of the brain, it implies that matter changes spirit and spirit changes matter—in what we have referred to elsewhere in this book as a "reciprocal" relationship.

THE CONFRONTATION OF MATERIALISM AND SPIRITUALISM

We believe that future research will bring the philosophical and scientific domains closer together, as some of the "hard" neuroscientists have begun to explore. We are very much encouraged by the work of Vittorio Gallese and his colleagues, whom we referred to in earlier chapters and who have published a number of papers exploring this nexus, including "The Roots of Empathy" (2003); " 'Being Like Me': Self-Other Identity, Mirror Neurons, and Empathy" (2005), and especially "Mirror Neurons, Embodied Simulation, and the Neural Basis of Social Identification" (2009). We are heartened by the growing attention being paid to the confrontation between materialisms and spiritualism among both scientists and philosophers and among brain researchers, like Gallese, looking into the brain mechanisms for sites and effects on brain functioning of spiritual thinking, ethics, values, and religious beliefs. We are also interested by the work of researchers such as Richard Davidson (2004) on observing brain functioning in response to meditative (Buddhist monks) practices. Another indication of the interest in this confrontation is the number of conferences devoted to consciousness and awareness and their implications for a wide range of behavioral conditions. Although many of these are focusing on hard scientific findings, this does not preclude future discoveries widening the findings to spiritual factors.

Raising the Critical Questions

At this stage in the confrontation, we feel the best effort should be directed toward raising the critical questions. The answers to these questions will serve to frame the debate that is already under way, but from my point of view has a long way to go.

Here we identify questions that seem to us to be important in framing the debate between an entirely materialistic view and one that includes the spiritual in an intelligent and open way:

1. How should we handle the issue? What should we be looking at related to both the scientific and the spiritual perspectives?
2. As we confront the potential that materialistic conceptions are being challenged, are we open to considering a broader understanding of the relationships? I have a colleague who both devoutly observes Jewish rituals and practice (often labeled for the purposes of this discussion as a *believer*) and is also a practicing

behavioral neurologist. He participates in a group of similarly inclined individuals who are systematically exploring the biblical references and commentaries looking for confirmations of the cognitive and behavioral aspects of scripture. We ask, and are increasingly convinced, whether this is the way that the brain sciences are bringing new knowledge regarding the potential for structural and functional modifiability, and the mechanisms to produce it. Although I do not have an intimate knowledge of this, I strongly suspect that others from diverse religious and philosophical perspectives are pursuing similar lines of inquiry.

3. If evidence is found for a spiritual component of consciousness and identity, can we continue to do science and conceptualize human behavior and potential in the same way? Can the tenets of the materialistic view of the world (strictly interpreted) remain viable?

4. The brain sciences now clearly point to the possibility that the neurons, as part of our gray matter, are modified by types of mental activities that cannot be considered in themselves matter. It is increasingly possible that spiritual activities can change matter. What does this do for both scientific inquiry and for understanding exposure to activities in the spiritual/ethical and moral realm?

5. This casts a new light on the cognitive processes of hypothesis formation and the nature of thought. This is why we are so interested in the way Gallese and his colleagues have approached this issue! What is the effect of our interpretation of the world around us, irrespective of the objective meaning of the "data"?

6. If all this is true, then there are several levels of confrontation— between definitions of science, between neuronal structures and mechanisms in the human brain, and thus can we deny that the neural structures represent a matter that can be changed? Do we broaden our horizons as to what can be changed and what changes them?

These are the challenges posed by the future of research in the brain sciences. But we must beware. Confrontation can lead either to efforts at accommodation or tendencies toward polarization and denial. It is still early in the process. We hope and anticipate that concepts of brain matter and its modifiability in form and function, through elements that must be defined as spiritual, will benefit from the confrontation with new knowledge that we cannot avoid by calling them spiritual, and thus consider them beyond the pale of serious science!

A NEW AND BROADER PERSPECTIVE
ON THE MODIFIABILITY OF THE BRAIN

A very important conclusion to be drawn from this is that it is the duty of society to provide the individual with those elements that have proven to be so important in the making of the human being, in creating and determining the level of functioning, of cognitive, emotional, behavioral, social development, to ensure that the individual is reaching the highest level of functioning needed in order to adapt to the demands and changes in society.

The same is true for a variety of other elements that have to do with the plasticity of the brain. Unhappily, the reductionist methodology character-izing much of scientific research has not (in the past) allowed the consider-ation of various diverse types of behavior in the ways they affect the brain. Nevertheless, there is an increasing number of elements that have been and can be studied using new technologies that permit us to establish that cer-tain changes in the brain can be produced by systematic and intensive be-havioral experiences.

All this enables us to better understand the effects of cognitive invest-ment, the nature of the environment, the richness of the stimulation, and the intentionality of the stimulation typical for MLE, and deemed to be promotive of neural plasticity (Kleim and Jones, 2008). The new develop-ments in neural plasticity, energized by the activity of the mirror neurons, play a very important part in this development and may become a great source of further explanation for these phenomena. Even more so, they actually will turn a pointing finger from the responsibility of the individual (it is his or her fault) to the responsibility of society (to provide restorative or developmental resources) toward the individual. Now that we know how important the world of stimulation is in shaping the structure of the brain and its behavior, and the level of functioning of the individual, it will become an extremely important support for the role of society in the making of the human being.

I quote here the former Venezuelan Minister of Human Intelligence, Alberto Luis Machado who, in his attempts to implement government poli-cy to modify the level of intelligent functioning of the citizens in Venezuela, said, "If indeed modifiability is proven to be possible, then it will be the responsibility of the government to provide the individual with these inter-ventions which will modify him. The possibility becomes the responsibility of society." And indeed he called upon us to help him!

CHAPTER 7

How Mediated Learning Experience Produces Structural Cognitive Modifiability

What are the ways by which structural cognitive modifiability is brought into action to create, sustain, and elaborate the cognitive changes that we define as modifiability? This occurs through a careful observation and analysis of both the needs and development of the learner, and the nature of the tasks to be responded to. These are embodied in the operational concepts of the deficient cognitive functions and the Cognitive Map. In this chapter I want to offer some observations and elaborations of how these conceptual frameworks "operate" to make MLE effective.

MEDIATED LEARNING EXPERIENCE TO MODIFY THE CAPACITY FOR HIGHER-LEVEL THINKING

I start this aspect of my discussion by reflecting my essential optimism regarding the potential for all individuals to achieve higher-order mental processes, utilizing complex mental operations. One of the important things that evolved through our observation of the effect applying MLE to the cognitive functions is the way by which the task that the individual is called on to act upon is characterized by the state of the learner's cognitive functions, and the demands of the task (the Cognitive Map). This led us to consider both the nature and propensity for higher-level thinking in low-performing individuals. This brings us to a debate that has had a long and contentious history in the psychology of learning and intelligence. It requires some explanation and review—both iterative and historical. I began to discuss it in earlier chapters, and now return to it here in the context of acquisition of higher-level thinking/learning.

Level I and Level II Thinking

Two levels of thinking capacity have been differentiated by Arthur Jensen: *Level I* and *Level II* type thinking. What is Level I type thinking? Level I type thinking is limited to the simple reproduction of what has been learned. Children manifesting this type of thinking can reproduce; they have memory and they can reproduce certain things that others have done. They can reproduce what is told to them, but they will not be able to combine various sources of information to produce new information because they are (presumably) limited in invoking an independent use of thinking in order to solve certain problems. Our "metaphorical" way of describing this characterization is that there is a straight line from the input to the output; it "comes out like it went in" with no transformation or elaboration.

In terms of what is referred to as Level I thinking, Arthur Jensen (1969) would hold that when children (confined to Level I thinking) are placed in front of a task like the kind we present in our LPAD Set Variations instrument (see Figure 7.1) requiring making a figural analogy, they will see that there is a circle with two lines, the circle is black and white, and yet will propose as an answer:

> Here I have a square with two lines; here also I need to have a square with two lines. (Focusing on the circle,) I will choose number 4 saying,

Figure 7.1. Set Variations B-8 to B-12, Level A, Problem 1

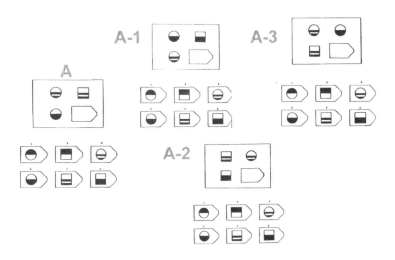

here I have a circle with black and white, and here I will place also the circle with black and white.

This shows the reproductive nature of Level I type thinking that Jensen attributed to individuals—both culturally different and culturally deprived and socially disadvantaged children, or those who by virtue of their heredity would never be able to go beyond it. Jensen says that being limited to Level I thinking makes any attempt to produce Level II thinking unproductive, so one should not bother trying to teach them (Jensen, "How Much Can We Boost IQ and Scholastic Achievement?," 1969). Despite the fact that Jensen's work is close to 50 years old, it seems to confirm the assumptions (and expectations) of many educators for low-achieving students. It may not be a flattering recollection, but we must ask ourselves how much thinking and planning that pervades special educational curricular development continues to be reflected—covertly or overtly.

Our view is very different. Jensen describes Level II thinking as the form of thinking that makes the individual able to exceed to higher levels of abstraction and go beyond the concrete and the reproductive. Level II represents a productive, creative way of thinking. The individual constructs reality rather than only reproducing it.

The differentiation between Level I and Level II thinking and its presumed limitations in the population is accompanied by some very interesting historical facts. Jensen's approach is based on the proposition that the level of functioning of the individuals is very largely determined by their heritability, genetic makeup, and chromosomal conditions. Jensen relied very heavily on the findings of British psychologist Sir Cyril Burt in the 1940s on identical twins, showing strong correlations between identical twins who were separated and placed in extremely different environments (1940). Burt presented data to point out that the environment did not affect the individual, and that the correlations between their IQs were very similar, supporting Spearman's long-term emphasis on the *g* factor in intelligence. Decades later Leon Kamin (1974) became suspicious of these data. When he looked for the documents that related to Burt's conclusions, he showed that either they did not exist or they had been falsified. But even after he exposed this in his 1974 book *The Science and Politics of IQ*, Jensen (and others, including Herrnstein and Murray in their 1994 book *The Bell Curve*) continued to rely on the Burt conclusions. A number of other scientists continued to hold that this theory of immutable, unchangeable intelligence accounts for up to 80% of the variance due to the genetic makeup of the individual. Earlier I noted that these kinds of research conclusions are still being promulgated.

The "Light" That MLE Sheds on This Question

Our experience over many years with the application of MLE challenges the Level I/Level II distinctions. In many instances the productive capacity of low-functioning individuals can be enhanced, going beyond the rote-learning types of activities to which they are exposed. For these individuals and for those whose thinking uses the superordinate types of concepts and modalities of functioning in a plastic, flexible way, MLE elaborates thinking that is adaptable and generalizable and both extends the nature of the thinking and overcomes the resistances presented by new situations.

APPLICATION OF MLE TO SPECIAL POPULATIONS

Our work with brain-injured people who have been treated for long periods of time in order to teach them to regain speech or to regain thinking shows the effect of the application of MLE. We have had individuals who came to us with very resistant forms of aphasia, dysarthria, and apraxia. Through a very focused modality of mediation we have seen the remission and recovery of lost or deficient functions. We are even able to help people who were for a long time without speech and yet are able to regain their verbal expressive skills.

MLE offers the individual tools to go beyond what has just been learned and transfer it to a variety of situations. To be effective, we must learn through observation and initial interactions (the intentionality and transference parameters as described in Chapter 2) not only what is the level of modifiability—the capacity of the individual to widen skills, understanding, and awareness—but also about the nature of investment that individuals require in order to become modified.

When attempting to modify functioning, the Level I aspects (primarily at the input and output levels) are more resistant to change, until we mediate the elaboration functions (moving toward Level II thinking) that are, somewhat counterintuitively, easier to modify. Thus, we have discovered, somewhat to our surprise, that MLE can be productively directed toward the elaboration levels of the cognitive functions, and then will positively affect both the input and output levels. I suspect that much of special education curricular thinking is somewhat stuck in the view that one must mediate input levels *before* moving to higher levels of cognitive processing. A legacy from Piaget?

Parameters of MLE and Their Mediational Distance

To this end we have conceptualized MLE as a series of stages that are different in terms of their distance from the objective that we have. I want to teach a child something. Given the nature of the child's special needs, I can teach in a variety of ways. I interpose myself between the object and the child and I present an experience. I show it, I ask the learner to describe it, and I arrange that it should be appropriately observed and registered— in other words, I bring the cognitive functions into play, overcoming or strengthening those that are deficient or impaired. This involves data gathering, giving meaning to what is registered, becoming precise, thinking about meanings, and so on. The mediation moves toward levels of increased abstraction and complexity (two aspects of the task that need to be addressed for the learner to bring cognitive mastery or flexibility to responding— elements of the Cognitive Map), less proximal to the objects within direct exposure, responding to verbal instructions, using more concepts and a variety of symbols and linguistic modalities for understanding and extending what is experienced. And we know that as MLE "takes hold," the learner is modified, creating the self-perpetuating quality that we have described earlier. The mediator does not have to tell the learner to do this or that; what is mediated helps the learner by encouraging synergistic thinking. This returns us to a consideration of the process of mediational distance that we described earlier in this chapter. We can offer a concise summary: by becoming less and less dependent on the mediation process, which can be characterized as an *interiorization*, turning the mediating agent into a part of one's own self. Following the mediational interaction/experience, the learner becomes less and less dependent on the mediation of activities. As described earlier, when individuals learn to change themselves, we refer to this as *vicarious* mediation. It can be described as the ability to mediate to oneself what previously was done by the external mediator.

The transformation from lower to higher mediational distance occurs as the mediator—an external source of interpretation, knowledge, and modalities of functioning—becomes instead an internal source of thinking and of modalities of interacting with tasks. We have heard children (both within the normal spectrum and with special learning needs) tell themselves, "Don't rush; you have to look systematically through all the possibilities." By doing this, they were orienting themselves to the kinds of mediation that they experienced across the task, showing that they have internalized the mediation.

Responding to Individual Differences

In the application of mediation there are great differences between individuals. Some become affected in a very immediate way, and they will change their style of thinking, perception, and the rhythm and the nature of their responses. They will pass from an impulsive modality of interacting with tasks to one that is more deliberate and thought-through. It means we can learn about the needs of the individual, and by this not just say, "Yes, this individual is modifiable," but also be able to establish the type of program and intervention that will enable going beyond present levels of functioning.

As a relevant case example that illustrates much of what we have been discussing, we are now dealing with a young man, 28 years old, who was considered from birth to be suffering from a severe state of mental deficiency. He was believed to have a condition called microcephalia (a very small cortical cavity) and other deficiencies in terms of his very poor language achievement. This individual was kept for many years in a nondemanding program that provided little stimulation and mental challenge. He was brought to us in order not only to assess and evaluate the possibilities to modify him but also to find appropriate ways to mediate him—type, extent, amount of intervention, and the degree of resistance to be overcome. Upon observation and assessment we discovered that this individual required a very intensive restructuring of his perceptual behavior, verbal interaction, and understanding of the tasks to which he was exposed, but that he had the potential to become interested and able to deal with them. In the beginning we could show this young man—using our FIE instruments—a combination of things that were absurd, impossible, but he didn't see the absurdity. For instance, from FIE-Basic (our program for building cognitive functions for young children) we showed him a picture of a strong man who worked very hard to lift a weight, and then a small child carrying the same weight on one finger of his hand. He did not consider this absurd, and he did not experience any disequilibrium, partly because he didn't compare the two images. He didn't consider that the two weights were the same, or that the two people who raised it were different—the one being a strong athletic man and the other a small child. Comparing these two types of behaviors would have made him conclude, "Oh, no, that's impossible; it's absurd; it cannot be that the child is able to do with two fingers what the other cannot do with two hands." He was not sensitive to the situation because he did not compare. He didn't have in his repertoire of responding the mental operation of comparison and therefore did not experience the absurdity of this presentation in the inappropriate reality.

The mediational strategies in this situation are clear: We have to make the learner see, understand, and articulate the similarities and differences. The learner will then, following this comparison of the various components of the task, come up with a solution to the absurdity. It is an aspect of critical thinking, where we try to create in the individual a variety of cognitive modalities to analyze situations. This is of very great importance in terms of adaptability—cognitive, social, conceptual, and so forth. And this can be achieved by learners with special needs, contrary to much conventional thinking. If one attempts to understand situations, one will be in a much better position to plan the types of behaviors needed to overcome certain difficulties confronted during learning and life situations.

THE APPLICATION OF MLE TO THE DEFICIENT COGNITIVE FUNCTIONS

As we have said, MLE is directed toward changing deficient cognitive functions in the individual. When we speak of deficient functions, we do not refer to the operations themselves but to the prerequisites of behavior needed in order to produce an operation to create the conditions for appropriate employment of operations. The deficient functions are not restricted to low-functioning individuals. Every individual may have a deficient function in one of the areas that we will describe. Most people, however, are able to overcome the particular deficiency by modalities of exposure and intervention, acquiring a variety of strategies and types of functioning to reduce or avoid the effects of the specific deficiency. For example, there are people who have deficiencies in spatial orientation. They may be very intelligent people who are extremely successful in a variety of areas, for instance in mathematics, but they might have specific difficulty in orienting themselves in space. This was said to be true of Einstein! The deficiency may become more or less conscious to the individual, and the person may find strategies to compensate by using a variety of verbal modalities of describing the orientation, by using other, better developed functions to overcome the effects of the particular deficiency.

When in lectures I describe deficient functions, many of the people from the audience step up and say, "Do you know that I have this difficulty?" My response is: "Yes, you have it, but in some way you were able to make it despite the deficiency."

We know that certain deficiencies may appear under certain conditions of stress or distraction. We know that some very serious accidents happen to people because of this. Examples were given to me by pilots who responded to instructions given to them by their navigator. The navigator told them to turn to the left because there is a rock on your right side, but the pilot turned to the right despite the instruction, due to a momentary confusion or because of something related to a more constant impairment of orientation in space.

Cognitive Functions as Prerequisites to Mental Operations

We consider deficient functions as affecting three stages of the mental act—(1) input—that is, the phase at which the individual gathers the necessary information in order to operate appropriately; (2) elaboration, the phase at which the individual uses the information gathered in order to elaborate, combine, and infer from information gathered to other information needed or produced; and (3) output, the phase at which we formulate operations and emit responses that affect the outcome of our elaborative process. The elaboration phase can be considered the center of one's mental life, of the intellectual power of the individual. It is where we process the information elaborated upon and combine it with other sources in order to come up with some important responses to our questions, to our needs for adaptation and our ways of responding to certain situations. In the output phase, we come up with a conclusion that has to be formulated and conveyed in a way that for both oneself and the other will become a source of understanding and of appropriate functioning. The three levels are present in each one of our acts. We look at things, we understand what has happened, and we respond appropriately to the elaborated information that we have gathered.

Relationships Among the Phases of the Mental Act

Within cognitive functions, the relationship between the various stages is very strong. The nature of our information gathering is very meaningfully affected by our elaborative thinking. To give an example, imagine observing an automobile accident. In order to gather the information necessary to decide which car is responsible for the accident, I have to gather the kinds of information that will permit me to come up with a valid conclusion. For instance, I have to know from what direction the two cars came, which car had to stop, how fast the cars were moving (by looking at the tread marks left by the car as it attempted to stop, and so on). Here the elaborational process orients the perceptual process—the information gathered, the level of precision, and so forth. I will then formulate conclusions: I have to be able to say the car coming from this direction had to stop but didn't. This process is made meaningful by the goals that the learner sets regarding the level of elaboration. If no goals are set, independently or through mediation, the information gathered will be very different and there are very limited possibilities of analyzing and responding to "the problem." This example shows that there must be integration among the three stages of the mental act. However, the elaboration functions are the best way to evaluate the modifiability capabilities of the individual.

WHY DO WE FOCUS ON
DEFICIENT COGNITIVE FUNCTIONS?

A key question is why we define and focus on the cognitive deficiencies rather than on the existent cognitive functions.

Our observations in using the Learning Propensity Assessment Device (LPAD) have enabled us to use the clinical method of Piaget to explore and intervene (mediate) with the individual as to the ways in which problems are responded to, revealing a number of reasons for deficiencies in the individual's functioning. We don't speak about a deficient individual. We speak about certain functions that are deficient, do not appear in the individual's repertoire, are impaired, or do not appear at the necessary moment in the functioning of the individual. Consider my example of the pilot just above.

We point to those functions that are deficient because of our goal to correct them. You don't correct a function that exists or is appropriately employed. In order to remediate, you have to define the nature of the difficulty as a target for change. It's why we, even with our optimistic orientation, find it necessary to formulate the reasons for failure, for inadequate or impaired functioning, in a very clear way in order to set the goal of modifying with appropriate clarity. We are out there to change certain things in individuals' functioning by improving their cognitive deficiencies. We must make a special effort and become able to distinguish at what level the individual failed, what caused the failure, and at which phase of the mental act (input, elaboration, or output) we should direct our mediation.

Deficiencies at the Input Level

An often-observed phenomenon on the input level occurs when an individual is presented with a certain task visually and must operate on it by focusing, analyzing, and perceiving all its dimensions. We have observed children whose perception is blurred and sweeping. They do not attempt to act on the particular stimulus by giving the necessary time and perceptual scope to fully gather the relevant information. The individual just "sweeps" across the perceived element and certain very important dimensions are neglected, ignored, or perceived in a very imprecise way. Actually, this describes many children who are diagnosed with attention deficit disorders.

The great value of isolating input factors and not turning them into a global designation of *learning disability* or *ADD* makes it possible to focus on the nature of the cognitive deficiencies, such as identifying a failure in the individual's gathering of accurate and consistent information. This will affect other aspects of cognitive functioning. It gives us a target for mediation. It also means that the individual is acting/operating deficiently in one particular situation and does not necessarily mean that the same deficiency will be apparent and as sharply perceived in a variety of other situations.

Continuing with the same example, the deficiency of blurred and sweeping perception will prevent the learner from recognizing the differences in the letters b, p, and d in writing or print. The individual may not see what is on the left and what is on the right, what is up and what is down. Yet in other situations (or modalities—the auditory, for example), the learner may be very focused, interested, and invested, and able to gather clear and consistent input. Another intervention is to use the tactile modality, where the learner must pay attention to the features of a shape successively by exploring using the haptic sense (touching) and then must confirm the perception through graphic (drawing) and visual (discriminating what was explored visually from other similar forms) modalities, as illustrated in Figure 7.2. To reiterate, the great value of this analytical process is that it does not lead to a kind of globalization in defining the individual's functioning that we consider limiting and inappropriate.

Another interesting phenomenon that we have observed in children who manifest a sweeping perception is that they tend to look for the solution *before* they have defined the problem. This has important implications for the elaboration processes that must follow. They respond immediately by pointing to something that is salient in their rapid perceptual sweep. They retain a vague perception of what they have seen, and they immediately go on to something that seems to them to be appropriate in order to respond

Figure 7.2. A Drawing of the Tri-Channel Attentional Learning Test;
** Showing Mediational Options**

to the problem; they do not look at all the parts of the presented stimulus. They do not differentially treat the element(s) needed to solve the problem. The nature of the perception and the effort of the individual to perceive the stimulus appropriately to formulate the problem is strongly related to the gathering of information. In general, our way to correct such deficiencies is to create habits in the learner to use cognitive functions automatically, consistently, and so on. There is a reciprocity between input and elaboration: If the problem has been adequately formulated, then perception will be oriented by this formulation, but if the input is inconsistent or inadequate, then the problem will be misperceived. If the individual has not formulated the problem adequately, then this will affect the result because of what we term *episodicity*, or experiencing objects and events as disconnected, unrelated, and random instead of as an integrated and connected whole.

The Way That Deficient Functions Reflect
the Three Phases of the Mental Act

We have pointed out the impact that the input level has on perceptual deficiency and the way you can correct the deficiency on the input level by mediating at the elaborational level: initially by defining the problems. Another very meaningful dysfunction relating input to elaboration is the tendency of the individual to approach the task and to search for the answer in a very unsystematic way. At the input level, it occurs when the learner is very impulsive, pointing to the first thing the eye falls upon without being aware that what has been identified is indeed the salient aspect. This may reflect a deficiency of elaboration: The mental processes are not regulated because the elaboration was not used to correct and orient perception.

Impulsiveness is probably one of the most commonly observed phenomena in children who are referred to as learning disabled or even as mentally retarded. Somewhat counterintuitively, in many cases children considered to be mentally deficient are much more easily modified and changed on the elaborational level than on the input or output levels. This is due to the fact that the input and the output were very often exercised in a way that created habits of functioning, and these habits can be substituted only by other habits. The target for correction in these children is to make them more able to regulate their behavior, to formulate hypotheses, and regulate them through processes of mental operation: "This cannot be it. I thought it may but it cannot be," and "No, I don't know yet enough in order to be able to respond." In this regard, when we observe behavior because of a lack of systematic searching, we look to the elaboration level to find reasons and strategies to overcome impulsive, inappropriate responses.

In many cases you have a very interesting phenomenon where the individual gives you an inappropriate answer, and upon your demand is able to tell you, "No, this is not the right one. Now I can tell you what it is." The mediation is directed toward rethinking. So, impulsiveness is a very important element that affects the functioning of individuals on a very large variety of modalities of thinking: for example, in perceptual and visual graphical modes where the child has to draw or compare certain things according to certain models. Impulsiveness will be visible and will deleteriously affect the functioning of the individual in all three phases of mental operations.

We produce conditions in the LPAD that compel the child to regulate behavior. In certain cases, we ask the individual not to respond before going over all the dimensions of the task and establishing the reasons for a correct response before eliminating the incorrect ones—"This is no good because"—and then coming up in the end with the appropriate answer. We build in the individual an awareness of the nature of the right answer: "They (the incorrect choices) are no good because they don't have the right color"; "They are not good because they don't have the right form." This makes the learner less impulsive by establishing elaboration and output phase functions. Other strategies include the capacity to use logical evidence to formulate the reasons for accurate conclusions. Here, the individual brings evidence for what has been asserted as appropriate, why is it appropriate, why is it not appropriate, with justification for the answers, affecting the readiness to invest in the task to be sure that the appropriate solution to the problem has been produced.

Other Aspects of Impulsiveness Affecting Cognitive Functioning

When the individual acts an impulsive way, the time necessary to define goals and to plan to achieve them does not occur. Tasks are responded to in a way that doesn't leave time and space for perception, experience, and response. This leads to a kind of short-circuited form of activity that does not allow for a clear understanding of the goals, of responses, and of ways of planning to reaching the best results.

Impulsiveness is a form of action that responds to one particular characteristic of the task. It does not really regard the totality of the situation, and therefore it is a kind of behavior that doesn't consider a number of elements that have to be considered before deciding what and how to respond to a particular stimulus. The response comes without any kind of time distance between the perception of the stimulus, the experience the individual has, and the response. This kind of behavior does not allow for a consideration of how the response may affect—in a variety of ways—one's life, the other's life, and there are no opportunities to adjust the nature of the response. This has significant social and interactional implications.

Planning behavior is totally impaired by impulsivity because behavior requires a distance from the stimulus, from the experience encountered, in order to plan behavior in a way that will correspond to a well-established and well-prepared kind of goal ("this is what needs to be done and this is how we will do it"). What is my goal in responding to an individual who has offended me? What do I want to obtain with my response? If I can't plan ahead and I respond in an impulsive way, it may lead me to very inadequate behaviors that I may regret. Impulsive behavior does not allow me to consider what will be the end result of my behavior. Thus, one of the goals of MLE is to create in the individual the propensity to put a distance between what is heard and what is done, to ensure that one has all the necessary information in order to respond, to choose certain types of responses from one's repertoire to find that which is most adequate in terms of my goals. It means planning ahead to be able to control impulsive behavior by setting a distance between an experienced stimulus, a perceived stimulus, and appropriate choices of responses.

From this point of view, many of the deficiencies and failures of the human being in a variety of situations are related to impulsive, unplanned, unsystematic behavior. Without planned behavior, human beings may make very significant and in certain cases vital errors. It's why this particular element is of great importance in the provision of MLE, as we attempt to create the habits of functioning that engender planning behavior and create an awareness of its importance.

Temperament Versus Situational Factors in Impulsive Behavior

Deficient functioning may be related to certain basic temperamental inclinations of individuals. Some individuals tend to use a very limited, inadequate, inappropriate, and incorrect source of information in their response; others will assess and scan the stimuli or the task demands before acting. This has to be related to the particular individual but also to particular situations. There are people who live in certain situations that do not require them or do not allow them to plan ahead—for example, these people might live in a state of insecurity where they are not really called upon and permitted to plan their behavior.

I remember my condition during the Holocaust. I was in a labor camp where planned behavior was not possible because of the fact of the great insecurity in which we found ourselves. We couldn't plan more than the next 5 minutes ahead because of the changes imposed on us from outside and by people who did not respect our needs and who wanted us to be in a state of existential stress. We could not predict what they were going to tell us, when they are going to free us. And so, planned behavior was something that was not possible or even necessary because any plans you made could have been totally neutralized by the authority imposed on us. So we, like all others who live under such conditions of life where the future is not predictable, could not learn or develop the habit to plan ahead.

When I came to Israel from the conditions of the Holocaust, I came to one of the *kibbutzim* in Kfar Etziyon. I remember being told that there was to be a meeting of all the members of the kibbutz. When I asked what the subject of this meeting was, they told me we were going to discuss a 5-year plan of construction of our place. When I heard this, I was literally shocked.

"Five years? You try to plan ahead 5 years? Will you be able to maintain the conditions that will turn your plans into something possible?" And they told me yes, of course, we have to plan because we will establish ourselves forever in this place. Unfortunately, the 5-year plan was not really materialized because the War of Independence broke out approximately 4 years after this planning and the plan turned into an unrealized dream because of the tragic end of the kibbutz as it was occupied by the Arab legion during the War of Independence.

For some people, it is 5 years that they can predict ahead; for others it is only the next 5 minutes. I will never forget that during the Holocaust, when I went out the door of my room I could not tell when I would be back. Security and predictability are necessary to create habits of planning, predicting, acting. It is not necessarily due to genetics, heredity, or other factors. It may well be the environment that encourages certain modalities of long-term planning.

When we mediate through the LPAD or the Instrumental Enrichment program we say: "Take your time; you don't have to rush. On the contrary, don't answer me; wait until you feel very sure that your answer is appropriate." And from this point of view, we mediate the important feeling of security in the individual, the feeling that time is not the factor that determines the nature of the response: "I can wait; I can think!" This is in contrast to many experiences in classrooms and teaching situations. We produce in the individual planned behaviors by inhibiting impulsiveness, encouraging a systematic, careful, and reasoned search. It means the individual will not be pushed to be too rapid in the scanning or responding. Rather, to take the time to plan ahead, to bring up a number of hypotheses, to check on these hypotheses, and to come up with the right answer is not something that is done rapidly. Rapidity is only one aspect of efficiency. What interests us is the product of a thought-through, planned, and systematic search that permits the individual to formulate and understand the process of arriving at the right answer.

MEDIATIONAL INTERACTIONS AT THE INPUT PHASE

The mediator has many options to work with the parameters and interactions with the mediatee. We have discussed the issue of impulsiveness as the outcome of deficient cognitive functions that have many effects on a wide range of behavioral responding. Here, we broaden our perspective. Although we continue to focus on how MLE is directed toward modifying deficient cognitive functions, we broaden our discussion to describe how the mental operations are also affected by the application of MLE. In this way, we begin to bring aspects of the Cognitive Map into the discussion.

From the perspective of mediational interactions, the mediator creates situations where the individual has the opportunity to repeat the same principle or operation learned and also to repeat activities challenged by variations in one or another aspect of the repeated function. We have produced a series of tasks incorporating this experience in FIE and the LPAD requiring the need to respond to the nature of tasks. In addition to affecting the deficient cognitive functions the mediated repetition achieves the goal of producing both crystallized and fluid thinking.

The Lack of Verbal/Conceptual Tools

A dimension to consider is what happens, and what is needed (through mediation) when the cognitive deficiency is characterized by a lack of verbal, conceptual tools. In the figural modality, concepts such as horizontal, vertical, obtuse, and diagonal may not exist in the learner's verbal repertoire. More broadly, concepts such as relationships between two things also may not be present.

> I recall examining children regarding the concept of relationship by asking what the relationship is between you and your brother; how are you related? And we hoped that they would say: "Our relationship is that we belong—we are born to the same parents and the relationship between us is the fact that we belong to the same family; we were born to the same parent or parents." However, many of the children heard the word *relationship* and said: "My brother is very kind to me. He relates to me very well." They interpreted the concept of relationship as the nature of the interaction between themselves and their brother, not the nature of the conceptual relationships. It is not an incorrect interpretation, but it is a rather limited or constricted one.

This reflects the lack of the concept of a relationship. Further, it shows a deficiency whereby the child perceives the relationship purely in social/interactional terms, and also lacks the labels that permit the individual to identify and use relevant mental operations. This deficiency can be corrected by enriching the individual with appropriate verbal tools, enabling the identification of the nature of the task that one is confronted with.

This occurs in many modalities: for example, asking a child for the relationship between a circle and a square, seeking the identification of commonality that they are both geometric figures. But one can mediate for differences as well. We can mediate at differing levels of sophistication: Here, our example above focuses on seeking a relationship—the containing of elements of commonality between the two compared objects and their differences. In the FIE-Standard instrument of Family Relations, the teaching objectives and focus of mediation helps students understand these concepts through learning how the members of a family represent complex and interacting relationships—mothers and fathers are parents, husband and wife, sisters and brothers to members of the "extended" family, and so on.

These can be considered "content-oriented" interactions. Children may need to be taught certain basic concepts that they may not have in their repertoire either because they are culturally different, they come from a world in which these concepts were not used, or because they have never been able to learn despite the fact that they live in an environment in which these concepts (and the relationships upon which they are based) are used. If the concepts were either not used or not experienced specially oriented interventions are required to equip individuals with the tools—verbal and perceptual—and the comparative behavior that will permit them to become more able to deal with the problem at hand. In formal learning environments, such as classroom situations, teachers who ignore this may overlook this deficiency and not realize that they need to address or attempt to correct it.

These investments will modify the cognitive style and structure of the individual. Without changing the verbal efficiency, expressive or receptive, the individual may continue to fail and will then be considered as reflecting a lack of a capacity to learn and to think that leads to the imposition of a *label* rather than developing a qualitative description of what can and must be learned through the provision of MLE. This is the guiding framework for MLE interactions.

Lack of Orientation to Time and Space

Many learners lack stable systems of reference, creating a lack of orientation to space. The spatial element may play a very important role. The philosopher Kant considered time and space *a priori* conditions of the mind—one cannot have an experience that is not framed in time or space. For us, this brings together input and elaboration functions. One must have a perceptual orientation and a vocabulary to describe what is perceived. To put it concretely, each experience occurs at *some* time and in *some* place. If you tell an individual to look above, behind, forward, right, and left, and the individual is not able to orient by these terms, there will be no stable system of reference in space that enables a response to certain instructions. From this point of view, the deficient functions on this level do not really reflect a lack of propensity to learn, but just the fact that the individual does not have these systems of reference available.

The same is true for time. Individuals from certain cultures may not have a time perspective, or may have a different concept of time; they do not see time in the way it has to be seen in order to refer to "before" and "after," elements that are very important in order to orient to temporal aspects of experience and to determine causality principles. For example, if you ask a Bedouin how long it takes to ride from his village to the sea, he may respond, "Two and a half cigarettes." Jared Diamond (2012), in his book *The World Until Yesterday: What We Can Learn From Traditional Societies*, describes this phenomenon well with regard to indigenous/aboriginal cultures such as those in New Guinea or the Brazilian jungles. A lack of temporal relationships will distort the way individuals see things and the way they understand the relationship between a cause and an outcome. Time and space are actually the crossroads by which an event is defined. The definition of the event will be meaningfully determined by the capacity to say what has happened *where* and what has happened *when*. Time and space orientation are very important components of proper mental operations. And my discussion of this emphasizes the importance of verbal labels for the cognitive frame of reference.

Object Constancy

Another factor that is very important in the acquisition or development of appropriate functions of the individual that may be missing is the constancy of the object across changes in certain of its features: Is it the same object when it is seen in a changed orientation, or when it is made of a different material, or when it fulfills a different function? The possibility of considering certain objects as constant beyond transformations that happen in their orientation, their function, or what they are made of is very important in order to be able to relate to the object irrespective of the way it is presented, the way it is produced, and the way it has been used. I have to be able to see the constant part, the common element in the object, regardless of where it appears, how it appears, for what it is made, what its size is, and so on.

Cognitively, we may find some constant functions shared by two objects that differ greatly, and this function may stay constant despite the fact that the objects are so different. A glass of water and a big tanker have something in common between them. What is the common element? They both are vessels. Despite the great difference between them, the function they fulfill gives a certain (conceptual) constancy to these different objects.

The same is true for a variety of other situations in which changes in the object do not alter their basic characteristics. If you take a square that is placed on its apex instead of its base, it will still be a square even though its position is changed in space. Some children perceive a square as a triangle if they only see the apex as a part and not its totality. Surprisingly, many otherwise high-functioning individuals will impulsively label the rotated square as a diamond, before self-correcting on the basis of cognitive information.

Thus, constancy may be determined by function, structure, or other elements to be discerned—perceptually (input) and conceptually (elaboration). Individuals often do not search for the common elements and/or may consider them different and not included in the repertoire of constant functions that characterize the similar objects. Constancy may be marked by the commonality of the orientation, the structure, or the function.

The Need for Precision

Another deficient function on the input level is the lack of need for precision. In gathering the data on a particular stimulus or event, individuals may not invest what is necessary to do it with the precision that will allow the application of the data, once gathered, to be operated on—categorize, label, place in a certain order, and so forth. They do not use all the data or do not apply a level of precision necessary to operate upon the problem at hand.

Impulsiveness may not play a role here. If the child invests all the time necessary but there are elements that are not considered as important because they are not precisely gathered or processed, this lack of precision will render very difficult the particular operation required by the task.

For instance, if the student is not precise about describing certain stimuli—for example, describing objects as "smaller" or "bigger" rather than using specific measurements to compare sizes—then when asked to use the data they will not be able to draw conclusions or make comparisons because of the vagueness of their descriptions. Precision in data gathering must become a need and a habit on the part of the individual, and the learner has to know that without being able to take into account the various characteristics of the object it will not be possible to correctly solve the problem.

Here, the mediational interaction will be to create an awareness of the need to be precise as a condition for appropriate responding. As is true with all cognitive functions, there is a relationship among the three phases of the mental act. If at the output level you are required to give some answers related to the object with the degree of precision that is necessary and imposed by the output, you will relate and refer to your object in a very different way. For example, when perceiving a complex shape, how many *loops* did you see? How many *lines* did you count? The relevance of precision is related to the demands of the task, but without a need and readiness for precision I will not focus my attention and actions on the relevant details and necessary operations.

Responding to Multiple Sources of Information

The individual must often refer to two sources of information at the same time—not being distracted by one source so as not to see the other, but combining and bringing the two sources of information together.

Many tasks require children to refer to more than one source at one time, requiring them to pay attention and integrate multiple sources. This is true for a large variety of tasks: verbal, visual, figural, and also in terms of the way by which a child applies information in academic subject areas such as mathematics.

In a mathematical operation—for example, in a problem requiring determining the cost of objects purchased—you will have to know how many pieces you have bought and what is the cost of each piece. And then these two sources of information will enable answering the question: "How many pieces have you bought, how much did you pay for each piece, and how much did you pay for all the pieces?" These are multiple sources of information that have to be brought together to produce the necessary operations, and thus understand the manipulations of data and ultimate solutions of the problem.

So the use of multiple sources of information in solving a given problem is important, and many of the children who struggle will tend to relate only to one source of information at a time. We have found this to be an issue with many individuals who have learning difficulties or who have been subjected to culturally different or depriving experiences. Many, but certainly not all!

MEDIATIONAL INTERACTIONS AT THE ELABORATION PHASE

The discussion above relates primarily to input phase deficient functions. I will now address some of the elaboration phase deficient functions from the perspective of how MLE interactions may improve them.

Defining a Problem to Be Solved

One of the first deficiencies that we observe in many children when they are confronted with certain tasks is that they are not able to define the problem; they are not aware that there is a problem that requires a solution. And by not being aware, they do not carefully consider (compare) the nature of the stimulus they are working on.

The foremost issue is *knowing* whether there is a problem—experiencing a disequilibrium that is recognized in a certain situation by being confronted with conflicting information. Disequilibrium occurs when one becomes aware of the conflict and must search for ways to resolve it, defined as information that the learner needs and does not have in order to understand the problem. I must define the problem and the best ways by which I can solve it. I see something that seems to me to be totally inappropriate as compared to what I know about this thing. It means that in order to feel that there is a problem, I first have to compare what I see with what I know. It's by this act of comparing that I will create the kind of disequilibrium that will make me go and look for an answer. The disequilibrium is produced by the incongruity, inconsistency, or inappropriateness of the perceived, compared to the known. When recognizing a problem, I will look for a way to resolve it and restore my state of equilibrium.

Picture someone walking along a riverbank in an industrial city (Pittsburgh, Philadelphia, or Providence, Rhode Island) and seeing the water on fire. How can that be? What do I have to know about the situations in industrial cities? What is the geography, chemistry, history, and so on that will inform my understanding? And what will I learn along the way? Finally, what conclusions will I draw that I will apply to future observations and in the formulation of rules and principles for understanding and elaborating future encounters? This of the implications of this way of processing observations—for the classroom and one's being in the environment. The search for an explanation creates a disequilibrium (a feeling of loss, confusion, or conflict) and a readiness to change our position to go from one state to another to resolve the conflict and achieve and do things that will be the expression of our disequilibrium. It takes us away from a static condition, causes us to take action, to "go off of our track." Put another way, it represents a "positive" disruption of our present state in order to solve the problem. The level of focusing, investment, and concentration in individuals is strongly contingent upon the elaborational process that requires a very different approach from inattentive, unfocused behavior.

I want to summarize the operations that take place. One does not just see something (perception), but one compares it with what seems possible and with what one knows. Comparison is an elaborational act: by comparing what is presented with what was known before, and relating it to one's knowledge of natural phenomenon. And once the comparison is made between what is *understood to be seen* and what is known, and they are found to be not congruent, one needs to go out and look for reasons why.

To give another example, Piaget based many of his findings on the observation of children's behavior at different levels and stages of development, on the assumption that perceiving is *ipso facto* comparing. He did not go and look at the extent to which the individual compared in order to ask the questions, in order to fill the incongruity. He considered comparison something that is absolutely identifiable with the perceiving process itself. By thinking this way, Piaget believed the inappropriateness of certain answers given by children was due to the fact that for the individual a particular problem didn't exist because the child did not see the problem, so the child has nothing to compare.

The Role of Questioning in Mediation

How to make the child able to formulate the problem? In working with children, we make this possible by a series of mediational questions: "What am I going to ask you to do? What does this task require from you? What do you have to do? What are two reasons that make a chosen answer a good one?" This issue is addressed in Chapter 9. The process of questioning means the elucidation and the formulation of the problem that will then be conducive to the kind of research, focus, and precision and use of various dimensions and sources of stimuli necessary in order to solve the problem. In many cases, children are much better at elaborating the problem if they are properly mediated. And once this is done, you see a total change in their approach to the perception of the stimulus, to the focusing behavior that is required in order to respond to the questions set by the elaborational process.

Selection of Relevant Information (Cues)

A second element in the elaborational process that determines the nature of the input and output is the limited propensity of the individual to select from a large number of stimuli those that are most relevant to the problem defined, and to pay attention to only those details that are really important and related to the problem.

Many children bring in a variety of irrelevant elements. The lack of a need to distinguish between relevant and irrelevant details or elements is due to the fact that the individual does not focus differentially on the various details. If you cannot distinguish between what is more important and what is less important, you will pay the same kind of attention to details that have nothing to do with the formulation of the problem. The orientation that the mediator has to offer is how to select from a variety of data those elements that are relevant to the particular problem.

An irrelevant element is often chosen by the individual because the formulation of the problem has not been complete or is not detailed enough to enable the conclusion: "No, this has nothing to do with it; the fact that it is this color doesn't have anything to do with it." Good formulation of the problem developed by comparative behavior enables the individual to select those elements that are relevant to the problem as formulated, and to ignore others because they are considered irrelevant in creating the right response.

Developing and Applying Relationships

The enunciation of a relationship permits us to go over to other parts, to other domains, and apply them. If I have to consider two objects that have something in common and something different, what is required is to create a relationship between them, and to determine in what ways they are similar and dissimilar. And once you have this formulation, you can apply the operation of analogy. I impose a relationship analogous to the relationships I've established somewhere else.

This kind of comparative behavior is of greatest importance; it is the basis for each cognitive operation. The lack of comparative behavior is probably the cause for a limited investment on the input level—if one does not have to compare, one will not search:

"Why must I see exactly what are the dimensions of the thing? Why do I have to go and look for things that do very different things and are common? Why do I have to make hypotheses about what is common for the two things?"

The whole process of thinking will be determined by the type of questions that my comparative behavior will elicit (see again Chapter 9 on mediational questioning at the end of this book). This shows us the real measure of the effects of elaboration on the input level. When we make the learner conscious about what must be looked for in order to elaborate, what the elaboration requires, the learner will become more systematic, searching for and applying relationships to a variety of conditions, situations, and problems.

An interesting example is the Jewish ritual of the Passover Seder, the night commemorating the Exodus from Egypt. The children participating in this are enticed to ask questions that differentiate the special characteristics of the Seder night and the highly ritualized meal that everyone participates in. The questions, which are systematized around a number of different rites that are performed at the meal, are meant to create the consciousness of the reasons for having this special evening set in the way it is done. The child asks four questions that frame the rest of the ritual, the answers to which are designed to tell the story and deeply understand its meaning. The questions begin with the iconic, "Why is this night different from all the others?" As the questions are answered, the story is told and the ritual unfolds.

Comparative behavior in this ritual is the way to make the individual search for an answer. And the answers are given in both narrative and questioning forms. In this way, important historical events are mediated by creating the conditions (rituals that are specially constructed) so that the individual will ask the questions and both receive and perceive the kind of historical perspective through a process of cultural transmission. Even the adults are encouraged to ask questions (even though they already know the answers and have repeated the experience many times throughout their lives) to be reminded and reconnected to the generations through the story of the Exodus. Another beautiful and important element in this process (of mediation) is that the Seder takes place within a family framework—the family gathers together, people who are familiar with one another respond to the questions, children are offered rewards for responding, each question they ask will be considered a very important performance, and the children who answer will be rewarded. The Seder ritual epitomizes the great role of comparative behavior, accomplished through the enunciation of relationships between certain events. Hypotheses generated by questions are then checked against others, and in this way the individual learns both to develop hypotheses and to check these hypotheses using comparative behavior.

Many other religions and cultures also transmit culture through questions around rituals and through important culturally historical events that are repeated from generation to generation, and become metaphors for living lives in communities.

The "Narrowness" of the Mental Field

This is defined as the amount of data, the number of details, the number of issues that the individual is aware of and able to deal with at a given moment. If the learner is not able to keep in mind multiple dimensions, then it will be difficult to widen the source of information onto a variety of fields and the learner will experience (and deal with) in a piecemeal way the tasks that are presented. In certain cases, the narrowness of field is also linked to limited memory, affected by the inability to use a number of data in order to respond. Some children handle this in a very interesting way, and we have created a metaphor to describe this process that we call the "short sheet phenomenon."

> If you are in the bed and the sheet is too short, when you try to cover up your head, your legs will be uncovered. If you try to cover your legs, your head will be uncovered.

It means if the learner tries to focus on two details, then five others are forgotten. When the focus is on the five, the two others are forgotten. This comes to the fore not only in memory tasks but also in a variety of other situations, leading to piecemeal responses. And of course this will not enable the individual to deal with problems in a way that integrates multiple elements.

The narrowness of the mental field is a recognized phenomenon, and we are able under certain circumstances and with certain modalities of functioning to have the child become able to widen the field of data perception and gathering, and integrate them into a common principle, with common elements in it. We know that we are all limited in the amount of elements that we can keep in mind at once, but the individual can widen this field by using a variety of operational modalities of thinking and by using categories rather than details. And one of the ways to change the individual is by appealing to the categories to which the required elements belong, thus creating the cognitive elements that permit recognizing and distinguishing the data to which one is exposed. Mental operations here are strongly contingent upon the possibility of the individual to manipulate the amount of data and the differences in data in order to create new types of information that are the result of connecting, of relating types of information in a very efficient way

Rapidity of response is also an issue here. Learning to read is a good example: In order to read, you have to bring together a number of data so that you will be able to turn the various components (sounds and letters) into a word, and words into phrases, and so on. To turn reading into a source of understanding, one needs efficiency—being rapid enough to hold on to details, but also being precise in getting the meaning of the words and phrases read. For this, you have to keep in mind a number of things. This requires being able to keep in mind a sufficient amount of data as the learner increases the ability to integrate a complex process—reading and comprehending.

This is evidenced in those who suffer from Korsakoff syndrome, a condition where the individual speaks a kind of salad of words. To a certain extent, behaviorally this is due to the fact that the affected individual cannot keep in mind what has already been said, which results in the person emitting words that do not relate to one another and do not become structured as a phrase with a specific goal in mind.

In the LPAD 16 Word Memory Test, the learner may have great difficulties in remembering more than three, four, or five words. If offered the idea that they can subdivide the 16 words into four categories, that the words may have shared attributes, then the words that belong to the learned groups are much better remembered because they expand the width of the mental field. An interesting perversion of this learning is the child who adds to the words *horse*, *dog*, *cat*, and *mouse* in the heard list the words *elephant*, *moose*, and so on—animals that were not included in the list spoken to the child, indicating that the category is understood but the boundaries of input are fragile.

Other higher-order mental operations, such as logical multiplication or permutations, are not possible unless you are able to keep in mind a given number of data. And it's why we mediate remembering many things by dividing them into categories. This becomes a way to deal with people with memory deficits.

An Episodic Grasp of Reality

This describes a condition where each observed phenomenon is considered by itself, with no perception or attempt to relate the stimuli to one another: The learner does not sum up whatever has been observed, take the components of one experience, and relate them to a totality that represents the bigger, integrated picture. Instead, each part, each component, is perceived as an episode by itself without any attempt to create a relationship between one particular part and the (potential) totality in order to understand the meaning and nature of the occurrence. As long as the individual relates to the world as a series of isolated episodes, without links to what has preceded or to what will follow, one will be unable to organize the various components into a meaningful whole that has a significance and meaning.

Again, the role of comparative behavior is related. A primary reason for restricted forms of thinking is the inability to look for other aspects of the situation: "What else must I see? What other things are occurring here that are related?" In order to create a comparison, I must take two episodes, bring them together, and then create a relationship that is the product of my thinking. If I relate to each object as an episode by itself, there is no way to compare two events and link them to each other in terms of common elements and different elements or in terms of perceiving a progression.

In this sense, an episodic grasp of reality represents a state of inertia of the mind. The active operational mind links objects and events that have been experienced, doesn't leave them in isolation, in their uniqueness. If you ask a child to copy a complex design (as we do in the LPAD with the Complex Figure of Rey), and if each detail is registered as an episode by itself, the parts become "dismembered" from the whole object. In Figure 7.3 we show the complete Complex Figure, along with an example from an examinee (in the LPAD) who showed an episodic grasp of the complexity of the task. The figure shows the stimulus that is observed and copied, and the ways in which the examinee perceived and reproduced it, with the parts not integrated into a coherent whole as presented in the original stimulus. This can also be seen in many children's drawings of the human figure. If one arm is on one side, appropriately placed, but the other is somewhere else, we

Figure 7.3. The Rey Complex Figure: The Complete Figure and an Example of a Fragmented Reproduction

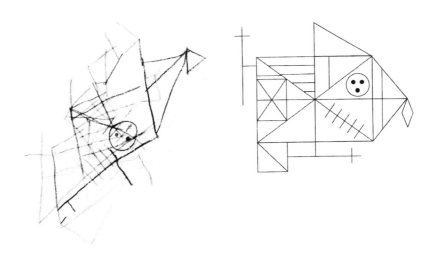

can conclude that the child's concept of the human body is "episodic." This illustrates the need to bring together complex parts by creating a synthesis, creating the necessary relationships among the elements.

Unhappily, our exposure to the media often reinforces this kind of episodicity. Things are shown without ensuring that a certain order or certain relationships exist between the events presented, usually in a very rapid time frame. This results in our being exposed to "sets of episodes"—rapidly presented, highly salient, but not well-connected stimuli—that do not allow the individual the time or the need to find the link between events portrayed. Malcolm Gladwell (2000), in his book *The Tipping Point*, describes criticisms of the very popular children's television program *Sesame Street* with regard to this observation. He points to the rapid segments, the lack of integration of topics, and the loud noises and other stimuli, and attributes this mode of presentation to the adult's conception of what is interesting (and marketable). He presents the contrast to another children's program such as *Blue's Clues*, which is explicitly constructed to bring young children information in a systematic, repeated, and connected way (but not coincidentally is often very boring for adults!).

Thus, one of the critical goals of MLE in modifying the individual is to create relationships between the various elements of the field and to look for the meaning of these relationships by comparing things, by creating relationships, by considering the changes that happen in the course of the development of the event and so on—often in a very slow, deliberate, and repeated manner (differentiating *Blue's Clues* from *Sesame Street*). In this way, MLE is directed to the need in the individual to relate to the elements in the field in a way that creates a significant meaning to the information and the making of mental/cognitive relationships.

The Need for Logical Evidence

This is often one of the most central deficiencies on the elaboration level of the mental act. The need for, capacity, and tendency (three closely related elements) to use logical evidence to determine and justify our judgment—our acts and ways of interacting with others—imply that whatever I say or do has a meaningful logic that is understood by me and accepted by those with whom I am interacting. The process of justification also presents opportunities for the mediation of sharing behavior—both conveying to others what I know and have concluded, and receiving confirmation from others that what I have communicated is accepted, understood, and valued. The "logic" is accepted and understood by those whom I address and with whom I interact.

In contradistinction to certain modalities of responding that are purely subjective and emotional, a "logical" response is shared by my interlocutor. The simple example of a lack of logical justification comes from observing small children: "Why do you do it?" "Because." "Why because?" "Because of because."

Acting on and using logical evidence is only possible if a person thinks logically, using a range of elaboration phase functions of the mental act—the mental operations that we have been referring to throughout this discourse. If it is logical, it will be compelling, not only to me but also to everybody with whom I will interact. And those with whom I interact will feel that whatever I say is acceptable or must be accepted, provided that I can bring the evidence explaining the particular act. This is the experience of the mediation of sharing behavior, as I have described it above.

One of the phenomena in some individuals who are deficient in this particular area is the tendency to try to convince their partner about something that is purely relative to their own needs, to their own way of feeling about a thing. But the feeling and way of thinking does not in any way compel the other because it represents only the individual's subjective reaction to the particular issue they are discussing. "I like it this way" does not make the other compelled to like it, too. And the way by which individuals attempt to explain their behavior and thinking will be contingent on the way that logical evidence is present in the responsive interaction.

From this point of view, the lack of logical evidence in the process of coming to a solution and conveying it to others is a deficient function that creates many problems for the individual in interaction with others—it is a form of egocentricity, of considering whatever I feel as of necessity being also what my partner should feel. Many of the difficulties in interrelationships between people, not only among individuals but also in groups, are very meaningfully and deleteriously affected by this lack of need for logical evidence, leading to a lack of searching for ways by which the dialogue that I have with the other will be shared by the other *because* it is logical and acceptable.

Here, I must emphasize that there is a functional relationship between this deficient function and a narrow mental field and episodic grasp of reality. The gathering of sufficient and integrated data and operating on the "logical evidence" of the experience allows summing up, categorizing, ordering, and responding in a systematic and efficient manner. As we relate events to one another, we learn and interpret phenomena in an appropriate way.

> As an extreme example, if an individual has an encounter with some type of behavior that has hurt him or her, and even if the actual episode of being hurt is of minimal importance (that is, there is no serious injury) but the individual feels that one has been in some way mishandled, then the individual may overreact in a way that may lead to a response that is a source of disastrous results—such as physically striking out. In this way, the individual does not consider all the implications of an impulsive response. The person does not look to the thing that may be the result of the behavior, with negative implications for self, the other, and future consequences. Such is a response devoid of logical evidence, and thus logical responding.

How do we mediate in such circumstances? One way is to expand awareness of consequences and needs for self and others. Does the event justify a behavior that will end up eventually by potentially seriously hurting or even killing somebody? Do you want to have the son, or mother, or wife of the harmed other deeply affected, made sad or destroyed by your response to this episode? Further, one can look to one's own relationships, to one's own children and family. How will their lives be changed by an emotionally impulsive action? Here we are describing empathic respond-ing, which has a strong cognitive element. In fact, as we described Piaget's formulations earlier in this discourse, we explained that we view the cog-nitive and the emotional elements as intimately interrelated. When a lack of logical responding occurs, we must look to the emotive factors, and find the connective relationships. In the FIE program, we have developed several instruments that link these factors—Identifying Emotions, From Empathy to Action, and Thinking and Learning to Prevent Violence (from FIE-Basic).

If one is able—instead of responding immediately and (for example) attacking the individual who was the source of the discomfort—to repre-sent and imagine what the effects of the attacking behavior will be, one can put a distance between the stimulus experienced and the response. And by representing these effects to oneself, one may become much better able to control and understand the process of responding, generating behavior in more peaceful and adequate ways of settling the conflict.

We believe that much of the violent behavior observed in many cultures can become modified and translated to a more adaptive behavior by making the individual able to overcome tendencies resulting from an episodic grasp of reality, in favor of more considerate and thought-through behavior. The need for logical evidence as a way to interact with the other, and also with oneself, is dealt with by using MLE to prepare the individual to give up ego-centric views and become able to respond in a way that will be shared by others. There are feelings that I may be able to make my colleague feel with me, but this has to do with the kind of empathic conditions that we create in our feelings with and for the other. This is a very cognitive process that we have addressed in an explicit way in the development of our Instrumental Enrichment program—embedded throughout various instruments and in several specially constructed learning activities. But to summarize this very important issue, the way to convey to an individual the sense of our under-standing of the shared situation is to use logical evidence and relate it to emotional responding.

MEDIATIONAL INTERACTIONS AT THE OUTPUT PHASE

The Interdependence of the Three Phases of the Mental Act

In considering the issues of the output phase, I start with the observation that one cannot speak of the three phases—input, elaboration, and output—as being independent of one another. They are totally *interdependent*—each one of them creates the conditions for the other phases to function appropriately. Output often depends upon a consciousness that the learner has about the output of the thinking; the fact that I have to present the outcomes of my thinking to an "audience" makes me look in a very different and adapted way to the sources of information that I must convey. I will gather and formulate the data in a way that reflects the conceptual and functional aspects of the problem at the input level, and elaborate it in a meaningful way that allows me to present (respond) at the later output stage. So, in applying MLE as a process of intervention that improves the cognitive functions, we must understand how the output is connected to the two earlier phases, and direct our mediation to its relationship to them.

> Here is an example: The policeman who enters the scene of a traffic accident knows he will be asked about who was responsible, what the conditions of the road and weather were, what were the indications of who was at fault, and so on, and he will have to convey this to a judge, to the involved parties, and possibly to lawyers, and he will have to consider what information to gather, how to interpret it, and ultimately how, when, and to whom to convey the data (the output level). Precision and accuracy is vital in a process such as this, and the policeman is trained and experienced to perform this process. The outcomes depend upon it!

If the educator limits the intervention to simply answering the question, neglecting the data that have to be gathered by the learner and must be elaborated in the two earlier phases, and goes only to the output, then important aspects of the mental act will be neglected, and thus will severely limit the kind and depth of knowledge that must be acquired. In this way, examinations are usually based on a predetermined list of answers that the examinee must conjure up from memory. We don't care how the students come to the conclusion; we don't ask the examinee to differentially and critically consider the data; we simply require the answer! In the assessment process, the student is not obliged to go through the process of the data gathering and analysis of the data's meaning. Thus, knowing what is required at the output level will determine what I must do at the two earlier phases of the mental act.

This issue has recently received attention at the educational policy level in several countries: In the United States, there is the development of what is being called a *Common Core Curriculum* or *Common Core State Standards* that emphasize critical thinking skills and move away from the emphasis on testing for facts, requiring students to develop a list of things that must be learned by heart; in Israel, the Minister of Education has recently imposed a moratorium on various aspects of testing in order to force a consideration of the process of evaluation of what students have learned. Both of these developments are too early in their implementation to know their impact, but they signify positive intentionality related to the issues I have addressed above.

The Motivational, Energetic, Affective Aspects

These play a very important role in selecting the kinds of elements to be considered at the output phase. We know that emotional factors have great influence on choosing what should be taught (mediated), responding to the prejudices of the teacher (and curriculum objectives) and the particularities of the learner. Piaget recognized that both cognitive and emotional aspects influenced intelligence and behavior. He called them "two sides of the same coin." I have added to the metaphor by saying that the coin is "transparent" and that MLE works on the edge of the coin that connects the two sides. For me, the relationship between cognition and emotion is critically important. The affective domain directs learning to the meaningfulness of the activity, and sustains focus and energy. To differentiate, the cognitive aspect refers to the structure of the response ("what" is it, "where" is it, and so on) and the emotional aspect refers to the energetic principle regarding the question "Why do I do it?" There is much more to say about this issue, but I refer the reader to what has been written elsewhere (see the Annotated Bibliography at the end of this book).

Factors Affecting the Nature of the Output

A number of factors affect the nature of the output. We have identified them in our formulation of the deficient cognitive functions. Here, I will offer some observations regarding them, to place them in the context of our discussion of the provision of MLE. There are extensive discussions of them in numerous other writings (see the Annotated Bibliography).

Egocentric Communication. What do I mean by egocentricity in communication? Most simply, this refers to a person who cannot consider the differences between the self and the other. All of us begin life as egocentric, but we begin to differentiate as we interact and internalize the significant others in our lives. If the learner's communication is egocentric, it represents a significant cognitive deficiency, especially if it is not mediated through modifications of input and elaboration phase functions. In failures to communicate at the output level, it might be described in this way: If you ask me a question and you believe that I already know the answer, why should you bother to ask me? I consider the question irrelevant because I already know the answer. My question (or other forms of interaction) is not a matter of my desire to know, or my need to have you understand my knowing, because I presume that we both know the answer so it is not necessary to go into an elaboration. Thus, no differentiation or elaboration is necessary. Another way to describe egocentric communication is that it is a "one-way interaction."

> I observe a person eating voraciously. If I know he is hungry and attribute his eating to the presumption of his deprivation, I will not explore (elaborate) issues of preferences, styles of eating, or cultural factors (for example, eating with fingers rather than utensils—as is true in many parts of the world). I will then miss important potential aspects of understanding and communication.

Difficulty Projecting Virtual Relationships. At this level, I must restructure the kinds of relationships that are required for responding. I don't have the data in front of me, and I have to take what I know (and have elaborated) and reconstruct the relationships between the various components that I know. I must recollect my experience and bring it into action—hence, the *projection* of it. What are the various elements involved in the question or problem I am responding to? The learner may neglect the evidence of the various components, and will come out with an incomplete or distorted response.

> In cognitive psychology, the phenomenon of perceptual *sharpening* and *flattening* has been described. The issue is that some aspects of direct experience may be so threatening or so salient that in recall they are emphasized or suppressed to the detriment of the reality of what has been experienced. In witnessing a traumatic event—for example, seeing people jumping from the collapsing World Trade Center towers on 9/11—at a later point in time one is likely to recall only the most salient (and frightening) parts and not other important but less traumatic details.

This is the projection of a virtual experience into time and space, influenced by emotional factors.

Blocking. This is an element caused by the emotional reaction of anticipating that I will not be able to respond. It is something that I know, but for some reasons I will not, or have not in the past, been able to respond positively. This is closely related to issues of projection of virtual relationships, as very powerful experiences have persistent aftereffects. Consider those individuals with word retrieval difficulties (a kind of expressive aphasia) or the many students with perceived "math phobias." They know what they want to say, and they have the potential to acquire the facts, strategies, and operations, but they experience the frustration of not being able to do so. The mediator must know this situation in the learner, and work to overcome the blocking because of the emotional reaction to the anticipation of failure.

Trial-and-Error Responses. This is observable in children in a variety of tasks that they are asked to perform. For them, trial and error is a way of responding with an inadequate process of critical thinking: They do not retain (internalize structurally) the strategies and solutions learned and relate them to the various possibilities that are presented in the current task. That is, they do not compare the current task with those previously encountered, consider the strategies or rules previously employed, and apply them to the current situation. Rather, the first thing that comes to mind is acted upon, without considering the various possibilities for a solution. It is a manifestation of an impulsivity . . . answering before processing the information and lacking the integration of a mental processing that results from an internal elaboration prior to responding. At the output level, this shows itself as doing the same inadequate thing over and over again, with random and unplanned actions, and if by chance one succeeds, not registering what was done to cause the solution to be reached. In such a situation, the inadequate response is repeated relatively endlessly.

> Consider our behavior in programming our computer or "smart" telephones, and learning a new and complex procedure, both in the learning and the remembering of what we did in the first successful iteration. Trial and error responses, if they do not lead to the emergance of an organizing principle or meaningful strategy, are continued endlessly, inefficiently, and frustratingly. What do we do when we must reboot our television remote control device?

Lack of Verbal Tools for Communicating. This is one of the most common determinants of a lack of communication in interpersonal interactions. There may be a lack of need to expend the energy and work to convey in words what is internally understood—we don't feel the need to do it, or perceive that those whom we are communicating with are not getting enough information from us. The individuals know the answer, have solved the problem, but they have neither the patience, the experience, nor the motivation to work to convey their knowledge to others—especially in words (language is a "second-order" level of experience, after the primary or first level). Those who have studied communication processes from the perspective of transformational grammar and communication such as Noam Chomsky, or Bandler and Grinder have described deficient communication that leaves out the source of the action, the nature of the action, the outcomes, and so on. We see it here clearly in deficiencies of output functions related to the language of communicating.

> Here, the learner frequently has elaborated an accurate response but does not have the right words, cannot sequence sentences, and the response reflects a lack of the right linguistic elements to communicate the understood relationships and solution. The use of language as a mode of presentation that is accepted and mutually understood is missing: "I know it but I do not know how to say it." "I do not specify what the *it* is, or who did *what*." It may be a matter of imprecision on a format of communication (writing a word and misplacing a phonetic element, a function of affective/motivational factors, a grammatical or syntactical inadequacy—a matter of learning), or a more serious matter of expressive aphasia as we considered above. I have seen the critical comments on students' papers from teachers who did not acknowledge that the students understood context and syntax, but misplaced small elements in words (mixing or misplacing vowels) that changed the meaning of a sentence. Had they understood this distinction, they could have helped students greatly improve the structure and precision of their communication.

Lack of Need for Precision at Output. This element is closely related to trial and error responding and the lack of verbal tools. The individual who is not accurate in responding often does not know it because the critical analysis (awareness) of the response is not available (this becomes a potential target for mediation). We have often seen this in children diagnosed as

ADD and ADHD. They do not need to be fully accurate. They have no need for precise communication because they have worked out the solution long before, and for them it is "old business."

> Further, parents often do not require precise communication—they do not correct imprecision, ask for clarification or elaboration, and in other ways do not engage with their children in focused and meaningful conversation. Many children respond with gestures that are a somewhat primitive substitute for language . . . a grimace of annoyance instead of a discussion of what is being felt, experienced, understood. Thus, there is no need, and little reinforced experience, to answer in a fully precise way. The children may not have been mediated to be precise. The mediator must say, "Tell me exactly what you mean, where it is, why not somewhere else?" "What is the *it*? Who is the *they*?"

In some ways, this refers back to egocentric communication and the lack of precision in verbal output. This is also a typical phenomenon of lack of MLE observed in perceptual/motor behavior, as the learner must look at things and examine them carefully, affecting even more the visual transport with complex situations where one must go from more simple arrays of information to those which are filled with details that require discrimination, differentiation, memory, and the like. That which is perceived in the simpler modality is not transported as a model into the more complex situation. The transport reveals a lack of stability and retention of the critical elements.

MEDIATIONAL QUESTIONS AS THE "BACKBONE" OF MLE

I summarize this chapter by considering the issue of questioning in the provision of MLE. In the next chapter I will further my summarization by discussing some of the outcomes of effective mediation. But I consider this such an important, and perhaps not fully understood, aspect of MLE that I want to offer some observations, and then follow this up with an additional chapter by Shmuel Feuerstein on the role of questioning in the three levels of the mental act. The nature of the questions posed to the learner and responded to determine what information must be gathered, and how it will be understood and analyzed. This, then, is reflected in the responses generated perceptually, behaviorally, and verbally.

I am proposing the strategy of mediational questioning as a "logistical" element, relating to how to provide MLE. This contrasts with the structural elements that are embodied in the operational concepts of the deficient cognitive functions, the cognitive map, and the parameters of MLE that I have discussed throughout this book. It relates to how I started the discussion at the beginning of this chapter, providing a functional look at the way in which the three levels or phases of the mental act are interdependent, determining mutual effects upon one another.

My last observation here is that this interdependence stimulates, expands, and differentiates the need system of the learner—something that I consider critical for the provision of MLE and the promotion of cognitive modifiability.

CHAPTER 8

Making Mediated Learning Experience Effective

Summarizing and Integrating

Here I will begin to summarize much of my thinking expressed in earlier chapters of this book. I say "begin" because my thinking about the implications of theory and practice are constantly evolving. But I can start by saying that when we think about how MLE produces cognitive modifiability, we consider the process of change. We consider the structure of thinking and learning, as well as changes in the neurological structures and functioning in the brain. We approach the concept of change from different perspectives. (See my discussion in Chapter 1 regarding the proximal and distal determinants of MLE.) But I can bring things together by looking primarily at aspects of a program that are necessary to produce change, such as their intensity, their duration, and how they are adapted to the changes in learners' functioning. Ultimately, these changes will reflect themselves in the structure of the acquired learning—its persistence, resistance, flexibility, and generalizability. I will address these qualities as well in this chapter.

As an example, when we work with brain-injured people, we literally have to produce new structures to replace those that have been destroyed by the adverse conditions of their injury. And the question is: What is the nature of the program and level of intensity that must be offered in order to create anew those lost structures that were related to the injury and the affected functions—the localization of the injury, where it was, and what was the most severely affected area? We need to determine how intensive an intervention should be. How many hours per day? How do we plan and adjust the MLE to the needs and possibilities for the available functioning of the learner and the dimensions of the intervention? More specifically, what are the levels and types of presentation necessary, and how do we adapt the MLE to the needs (and changes) in the individual? These are the questions that we respond to in this chapter.

MEDIATION FOR GENERALIZATION

An important quality in modifying the cognitive structure of the individual is creating learning propensities that enable the learner to go beyond the particular learned experience and applying it to a variety of other situations. This is what we refer to as the generalization of the learned technique, operation, or experience. It can also be viewed as a transformation of knowledge, projecting the learned principle into a new learning situation. For example, if one is only able to apply an operation in the specific case where it has been learned, there is very little transformation of the individual.

So the nature of the change produced in the individual following mediation with a variety of experiences has to be evaluated against the level of generalizability of the learned effect. When children who are offered mediation on very difficult tasks are given modalities by which the learned element can be generalized to a variety of situations, we see the nature of the change. This is not just a process of adding meaning to what has been learned, but adding to the individual's modalities of functioning by constantly adapting the MLE to help the learner respond to new situations based on experience—that is, being restructured to challenge and stimulate further learning potential. Here, and with regard to mediation to formulate cognitive relationships (see below), we emphasize the role of repetition and variation in exposure. We have developed a schema that we refer to as the "cylindrical model" to characterize this process. In Figure 8.1, we show how the mediation begins at the center of the top of the cylinder, and moves both outward to higher levels of complexity and abstraction and also around the circumference to engage in different (but supporting) modalities of experience. In this way, we show the nature of the necessary repetition. This model has been the subject of considerable description and elaboration in our literature, and the reader is encouraged to learn more about it by referring to references in the bibliography.

Let us take the issue of memory as an example. Having a good memory does not always mean that what I recall is generalized to other contexts. If I repeat exactly what I have learned, even if I retrieve many complex details, I may not have been modified. If, however, I identify rules, relationships, implications of meaning beyond the manifest details, I have adapted what I have learned and will be able to transform my experience and generalize far beyond the immediate exposure. This is what learning theorists have referred to as "far transfer." So we can offer a dictum: *If generalization does not take place, we cannot speak of modifiability.* Many children who

**Figure 8.1. The Cylindrical Model for Dynamic Assessment
and Cognitive Modifiability**

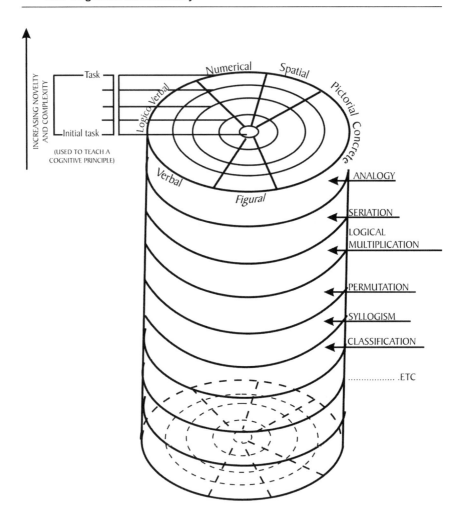

memorize whatever is written in a book have very little opportunity to exercise this modality of functioning to generalize, and as a result, they will not necessarily have an increased readiness to solve problems that have similar elements but that have very different appearances, situations, and dimensions. Many of my observations elsewhere in this book refer to these important phenomena and concepts. Thus, one of the changes that we are looking for is a change in the capacity to transfer what has been mediated.

MEDIATION FOR RETENTION
AND PERMANENCE

In many cases, permanence of a learned element and the retention of it has to do with and is greatly enhanced by the process of conceptualization. For example, keeping in memory a number of elements is strongly contingent upon the conceptualization of grouping into categories.

> For instance, in one of the memory tests in the LPAD (the 16-Word Memory Test), the individual is presented with 16 seemingly random words to remember. If the learner discovers, or is mediated to find among the 16 words a number of categories, the learner will be in a much better position to retain the large number of initially randomly presented words by decreasing the number of discrete objects by grouping them into four categories according to their shared characteristics and thus more easily retaining the individual words. This process has sometimes been called "chunking." Retention in this instance is the nature of change produced in the individual's learning process by mediating modalities of organization of the data gathered, by this to become more efficient in remembering, retaining, and associating these things within particular categories.

We had an interesting and surprising example of this resistance.

> We were mediating a young girl to respond to the 16-Word Memory test. She had great difficulty recalling the words, and inconsistency in learning and retaining the concept of grouping. Considerable mediation was directed toward her putting the words into groups according to their shared attributes. Many trials were offered, and various strategies were attempted to teach her the concepts but she continued to have difficulty understanding and integrating. She was very frustrated, and time ran out before the mediation could be brought to a successful conclusion. Immediately following, those who had observed the process expressed their discomfort with the mediation, stating (in summary) that it seemed like the child was being unnecessarily stressed, and that perhaps the mediator should have been less persistent and demanding. Then the following was reported: The psychologist who brought the child to the session said that 4 days later, when she visited the girl's school, the girl came up to her and said, "I know all the words now . . . can I say them to you?" And she

recalled all 16 words, in their categorical grouping! And then she said: "When can I go with you again to learn? I want to do more learning!"

Such is the nature of MLE. It is not always comfortable for the mediatee.

The mediator must challenge and reinforce, by finding ways to bring a positive learning experience to the student. But in this example, as with so many others, active and positive persistence often penetrates resistance, and the learner experiences change and joins the mediator in the learning process. The example above is striking but not unusual in our experience.

MEDIATION FOR THE FORMATION OF RELATIONSHIPS

There are other elements affecting the capacity of the individual to learn a particular operation or task, and to become able to infer from the learned elements other instances in which the same relationship may exist. This is true not only in analogical thinking but also in a variety of other situations in which the individual has to infer from the learned relationship to a variety of other relationships that are encountered. This is our definition of mediated transfer. It also requires that we return to a discussion of the role of repetition and variation in the process of learning.

Rote learning seldom offers the opportunity to identify and use conceptual relationships. An individual who learns a certain number of words may retain them. The individual who learns how these words are changed in terms of their meaning or their temporal elements is in a much better position not only to learn a particular part of the language, but also to go beyond and to advance thinking through semantic structural understandings. The mechanism for this learning process is in the exposure of the learner to frequent repetition, but presenting the learner with variations of the same task so that it is never responded to in the same way. The MLE objective is to present the learner with a variation that teaches a principle or provides exposure to an aspect of a task that reinforces a rule or formula that becomes the basis for an internalized generalization—a kind of *aha*!: "So that is what this means; this is how I can apply this to something sort of similar." In this way, the learner either discovers or rediscovers a relationship in the variation, identifying the elements in the particular problem that relate to the relationships discovered.

THE AMOUNT AND NATURE OF NECESSARY MEDIATION

In Chapter 1, I described exposing the newborn child to a model of protruding the tongue. This is an excellent example of assessing and then providing the amount and quality of mediation necessary to overcome a potential developmental and functional difficulty. Our concern there, and for all decisions regarding the provision of MLE, is the extent to which the learner needs more or less exposure to the particular identified function (in the case of the infant, tongue protrusion). To what extent will one require less repetition as responses are observed, related to the need to adjust the amount and nature of the mediation? This is often observed as we regard how the first exposure affects subsequent exposures.

What does this mean? With observation and calibration, mediation as a consequence of the learning experience may (and should) become less necessary, or the nature of the mediation offered may be less direct in order to produce and achieve a given way of functioning. At the beginning, I need to be extremely insistent in mediating the individual and very close to the task that the individual has to do—I almost have to show him what to do, modeling the behavior by doing it myself. By the end of the process, I will not need to model, but rather will orient the learner verbally, without any other kind of modalities. We have described this as *mediational distance*, and consider it a very important aspect of the provision of MLE.

The Degree of Mediational Distance

In the provision of MLE, we have derived a scale that permits us to evaluate the changes produced in the individual following mediation in terms of the lessened need for mediation in the course of the exposure to a learning experience. These described "degrees of mediational distance," which we labeled as "required mediational intervention," or RMI, help the mediator to both observe the learner's need and adjust the mediational intervention according to some guidelines for the nature and amount of distance that the learner requires.

The teacher who responds to a student's need for assistance must decide how active and direct to be in providing help. Should I answer the question directly and fully, modeling or doing the problem, or should I ask orienting questions to help the student search for correct solutions? If the former is needed, and not provided, this may lead to frustration. But when do we withdraw the direct assistance, and under what conditions? Our discussions of RMI issues in the application of MLE—how and what to observe, when to move to higher levels of distance, under what conditions of task demand or modality of responses needed—address this critical issue in the provision of MLE (see Annotated Bibliography for references).

This is important because we want to know to what extent the individual becomes more and more independent, less and less needing the mediator's imposition in order to be able to respond appropriately to the demands of the task. This is related to the widely applied concept of "gradual release of responsibility," originally described by Pearson and Gallagher (1983), expanding on Vygotsky's concept of "zone of proximal development." This further becomes an important element to convey in the learner's *profile of modifiability*, relating both potential for change and ways of producing and sustaining that change.

From this point of view, we know that we must change the various mediational interventions and calibrate them in terms of the needed level of distance between the intervention of the examiner and the particular task, object, or event that we try to mediate to the individual, adjusted according to the learner's special needs.

For example, I can mediate the child by showing an object. I can mediate by requiring the imitation of a verbal instruction. On this level, the child is required only to reproduce a particular stimulus that is offered by the mediator and according to a specific goal. This represents the reproductive level, a very limited distance from the object. The child does not do anything but repeat. However, I can introduce the concept of retention. I repeat a number of stimuli, and the learner is encouraged to remember more than one element. At early stages in the process, at low levels of distance, we are working with Jensen's Level I type of intelligent behavior (see our description of Level I and Level II thinking in Chapter 7).

The mediational distance concept in MLE enables the mediator to become aware of the propensity of the individual to be changed by the interaction and to observe the changes that occur regarding the amount and nature of the needed mediation in order for the learner to reach a certain level of functioning. And from this point of view, making the individual able to use higher levels of mediation represents a goal in itself and guides the mediator in proceeding from stage to stage as the learner is ready.

Determinants of Mediational Distance

What determines the learner's readiness to increase the distance of mediation? The concept of distance basically describes the level of mediation that the individual needs in order to understand the instructions, the demands of the task, and certain operations.

> When I have to simply make the individual aware of a stimulus and I point out with my finger that this is a glass and from this glass we drink various liquids, the concept of glass is strongly linked to a very close and proximal function.

In this simple example, the operation with the particular stimulus is done in a very concrete way. However, it already requires or contains some potentially abstract elements. For instance, when I interpose myself between the child and the glass, and mediate the understanding that the glass has a function—to provide me with a liquid that I would like to drink, I am dealing with a concrete object and the distance of my mediation is very limited. When I do this and the child learns that drinking the liquid becomes possible by inclining the glass and bringing it to the mouth so that the liquid will flow, I am already describing physical characteristics of the liquid and the container. Even the word *container* makes a jump to a different distance of mediation—by creating a way to understand that many objects of different forms, materials, and sizes are containers, and as containers they have to be kept stable in order to have the element contained in the desired and efficient ways. The "concept" of container acquires increased distance from the simple presentation and reproducing of the object ("This is a glass") to containers of large volume, fulfilling different needs, and so on ("This container is a large ship that brings millions of liters of oil"). The learner represents an awareness—the arc widens to include the distance between these two objects. This extends the concept by bringing in the mental operation of categorization through comparison and contrasting, looking for common and differential elements—in this instance, taking the drinking glass together with a great number of other objects that also serve as containers. Some of the characteristics will be common to other very different objects that are experienced or conceptualized by the child.

Another example is that of a forest. It can be perceived as an aggregation of trees, albeit of different kinds—a pine forest, a rain forest, an orchard of fruit trees. There are many types of forests that share certain attributes but are also differentiated. Once conceptualized in this way, the "concept" of forest can be semantically broadened to include a close conjunction of ideas or other objects—a "forest" of people in a train station, or a "wealth of ideas proposed to solve a financial crisis."

The conceptual distance in learning will be achieved by applying progressively more superordinate concepts.

When I am teaching a child to "Look at this stimulus, look at this drawing," and I ask what the characteristics of the object are, the child may tell me the object is green. I ask, "What else do you see on the green field?" The child may say, "Sticks," responding at a very concrete level. The reference is only to the particular task that has "green" and "sticks." However, if I want to go to a different distance of my mediation, to a different level of cognitive functioning, the distance that I will impose will be characterized by the use of a concept that requires finding a common element between a variety of figures in terms of their color, shape, size, and so forth. "In what ways are they the same? In what ways are they different?" To this end, I have to teach the concept of *color*, and not only green, and to differentiate further between shape and color. The child must learn that white and black and green and red and rose and so on are all colors, and that the *form* is another attribute—that the sticks belong to the concept of form. The superordinate concept will include a great number of forms that have to be disassociated from the concept of color.

The use of *superordinate concepts* may become a goal of mediated learning experiences to promote cognitive modifiability; it is very important to enable moving (generalizing, elaborating) from simple, proximal interventions that have a close distance to the higher levels of mental operations that bring together a great diversity of objects and events. Another example is in helping children draw lines. We have observed many children who were not able to produce a required drawing, but when mediated to understand and use the terms *vertical* or *horizontal*, they were able to reproduce it. At low levels of distance, when the lines (and the descriptive terms verbalized) were done in front of them, they were able to imitate the mediator. At times, the mediator needs to take the learner's hand and orient it toward drawing a vertical or horizontal line, drawing the line for the learner, and holding the learner's hand. This is the lowest level of distance—a Level 0, where the behavior is produced and imposed upon the mediatee. If the same child, after having been offered MLE ("Let's draw five parallel horizontal lines and five parallel vertical lines," and these lines are drawn by the mediator and then imitated by holding the child's hand), indicates that this low distance of mediation is not needed, then the mediator can relax the controls and move to higher levels of distance, in a careful and systematic process.

I bring these examples because many teachers do not consider the level of mediation that they have to employ with their students in order to make them understand, produce, and enable them to vary and apply what is learned into situations that are more and more distant in terms of task demands and the kinds of mediation that can be offered to them.

MEDIATING FOR RESISTANCE

In our lexicon we have two different definitions for *resistance*. Somewhat unconventionally we consider it a *positive* aspect of the structuring of cognition: one of the indicators of structural cognitive change. However, from the more conventional perspective, another area to which mediation must be directed is the way it relates to the situations learners must face and their efforts to engage in the problem. The more unfamiliar, complex, or previously daunting the problem faced by the learner, the greater the effort the individual will have to make by using the previous mediation in order to go beyond the limitations imposed by previous experience. The more able the individual is to overcome the resistances imposed by the type of the task, the greater the capacity to adapt—showing plasticity and flexibility to new situations. This will be strongly related to the nature of mediation given to the individual at the beginning of the interaction, reflected in the capacity of the individual to apply the learned elements to a large variety of situations. Thus, the plasticity and flexibility in our behavior is a function of the nature of mediation received. Mediation does not only affect the level of behavior; it also affects the neural structure of the individual by creating the pathways that permit adaptive responding and higher-level mental operations.

GOING FURTHER

In the remainder of this book we have invited two close colleagues in the development and implementation of our work to offer their perspectives. They will elaborate much of what I have developed thus far, and add to the understanding of both the theory and practice of MLE. Dr. Shmuel Feuerstein will discuss the use of mediated questions in deepening the understanding of concepts as an important aspect of the provision of MLE, and Rabbi Refael Feuerstein will present aspects of MLE as they can be directed toward meeting the needs of individuals in contemporary digital environments.

These chapters will bring my observations regarding MLE to a full and satisfying conclusion.

CHAPTER 9

Questioning as a Basic Mechanism of Mediated Learning Experience

Shmuel Feuerstein

Mediation modifies the world of stimuli to render the learner more permeable to the wider sense of reality. One of the best ways to turn stimuli into a source of learning and an intellectual challenge is through reciprocal questioning. The interrogative form in itself elicits sharper attention from the person being questioned to the features and facts that may lead to the search for an answer. There is probably no better way of turning stimuli into reciprocal cognitive involvement than through questions. Questions have been used worldwide as a mediation of cultural transmission, expressed throughout human experience as a cross-cultural phenomenon.

This chapter explores systematic question paradigms and the ways they influence the learner. A question acts as a powerful mediator if it prompts the mediatee to search for an answer. A question creates a need in the individual as well as an orientation to focus on the world of data associated with the subject matter. Focusing on the question results in the selection of certain stimuli that can then be correlated and assessed in terms of their relevance. Thus, even the simplest question can trigger an orientation toward a specific search and the mobilization of specific mental processes. When a question is more sophisticated and involves complex units of information, more extensive elaboration processes are required. These processes require searching for and finding differences or relationships between sets of information. They lay the groundwork for more complex elaboration processes.

The way a question is formulated is of critical importance to the nature of the outcome of learning. Regardless of whether the set of answers is circumscribed or not, the learner needs to grasp the intent and the perception of the question. In this chapter, three paradigms for the process of questioning are briefly introduced and contrasted: the Socratic method, collaborative learning, and Talmudic study within the Judaic tradition of learning.

THE SOCRATIC DIALOGUE

Perhaps the best-known paradigm is the Socratic. It is considered the foundation of critical thinking. In this interaction, a question is formulated (open-ended or closed) to ensure a successful outcome of learning. Paul and Elder (2006) have identified six types of Socratic questions:

1. questions for clarification—"Why do you say that?";
2. questions that probe assumptions—"What
   could we assume instead?";
3. questions that probe for reasons and evidence—
   "What would be an example?";
4. questions about viewpoints and perspectives—
   "What is another way to look at it?";
5. questions that probe for implications and consequences; and
6. questions about the question—"Why do
   you think I asked the question?"

Paul and Elder's designations, to the extent that they are conveyed to the student, provide an *implicit* focus to the questions. Later in our discussion of the Talmudic paradigm, we will draw an important contrast to the issue of naming the questions.

Generally there are two types of structure to questions: Open-ended questions have many possible answers: "What would happen if . . . ? Is this true in all cases . . . ? Can you give me another problem with the same answer?" Closed questions do not necessarily have just one answer, but are more circumscribed: "Which row has the most fruit?" Both types of questions are appropriate depending on the circumstances. In both open and closed questions, the intention and perception of the questioner are extremely important. Teachers need to have questioning strategies that are clear and adapted to their students. According to Maimonides, the teacher needs to provoke questions to sharpen the students' minds (Hilchot Talmud Torah IV, par. 4–9). Students also need to ask questions. When students do not get satisfactory answers, they may not have sufficient knowledge to ask further questions or understand how to frame a question to obtain the information they need. However, when students are empowered to ask the right kind of questions, they will tend to ask more sophisticated questions.

Socratic teaching has been called "irony-based." It is characterized by feigned, ironic innocence that serves to undermine the fragile confidence of the teacher's dialogue partner. It breaks down the students' arguments, causing them to confess their lack of knowledge, eliciting short answers indicating agreement or disagreement, and shapes answers into teachers' conclusions.

The "Socratic" teacher may often be manifestly dissatisfied with the students' responses, not because the answer was incorrect, but because it was not the type of answer desired. The solution is "forced" out of the student. This disagreement tends to be ironic, designed to prove the students' lack of knowledge so that the teacher can lead students to accept the teacher's own opinion.

A metaphor for this process is the labyrinth: a maze that has one entrance and one exit, and many dead ends. For the modern "Socrates," the lesson is clear—the teacher has a predefined answer. Students are not encouraged to deviate from the path that leads to this answer. Socratic advocates would say that the method allows students to find their way on their own to correct answers, making the answer more meaningful to them. However, students' own opinions are initially acknowledged and then rejected (a stratagem?). They are not taught to think independently, resist, or criticize others' opinions. They are not given permission to make mistakes. Individuality is discounted, opinions ignored, to arrive at the predetermined conclusions. There is conflict in Socratic dialogue, but it has the closed quality described above. Our conclusion: When irony is used to produce conflict alone, it is not effective teaching!

In the classical literature, Plato creates a "dialogue" by way of offering criticism of this approach. He uses *Meno* to describe a reaction to this closed and arbitrary method of teaching (we quote it in part because it describes well our sense of the limitations):

> . . . yours was just a case of being in doubt yourself and making others doubt also; and so now I find you are merely bewitching me with your spells and incantations, which have reduced me to utter perplexity . . . for in truth I feel my soul and my tongue quite benumbed, and I am at a loss what answer to give you. . . . (Plato, *Protagoras* and *Meno*, quoted in S. Feuerstein, 2002, p. 124)

COLLABORATIVE LEARNING

This paradigm, whose description we take from Tomasello et al. (1993), focuses on the agent involved in the transmission of information, and offers three types of learning: (1) *imitative*, which requires reproducing an act or object; (2) *instructed*, where deliberate effort is directed toward transmission of given information; and (3) *collaborative,* in which both partners work together toward the acquisition of knowledge. They write:

> Imitative learning and instructed learning are means of cultural transmission: by modeling of instruction the adult passes on to the child valued elements of the culture. Collaborative learning is different. (It) takes place when neither interactant is an authority or expert; the inter-subjectivity is symmetrical. (p. 500)

MLE interaction is present in all these forms of learning; it mediates the learning into a collaborative experience, as is well described in earlier chapters of this book. We summarize here the intentionality and reciprocity of the interactive process. We can further summarize the distinctions between the three modes that Tomasello and his colleagues describes: imitative and instructed learning being a vertical relationship (teacher to student), and collaborative learning being horizontal (student and teacher on the same plane). For instance, in the latter, both teacher and student discuss a problem and search for solutions together. In collaborative interaction, there is a process of creative learning and not only the mere transfer of previously known information, and this creates various options for deeper understanding. The processes of questioning are framed by the dimensions of this interaction.

THE TALMUDIC STUDY PARADIGM

Questions are one of the main modalities of mediation in Judaic studies, that does not only involve the transmission of information to mediate higher mental processes needed to deepen the learner's experience. In so doing, questions shape the mediatee's mode of thinking and processing information and enrich the learner's repertoire. In particular, the search for an interpretation often leads to new, implicit questions. Each interpretation is based on given information in the text of the Bible or numerous related commentaries. Hence, one of the most important ways of guiding the mediatee to an autonomous search for answers is to facilitate the process of finding the underlying nature of the foundational question.

To offer some simple examples paraphrased from Bible stories with which most readers will be familiar: For Eve in the Garden of Eden, the serpent tempts Eve with a logical assessment of truth value: "Did God really say you shall not eat of any tree of the garden? Touch the tree and see what will happen." In another instance, when Moses is instructed to tell the people of Israel that God will free them from slavery in Egypt and lead them to a land of milk and honey, Moses doubts he will prevail and asks for a conditional solution for the people's lack of belief: "What if they do not believe me and do not listen to me but say 'the Lord did not appear to you'?" (Exodus IV: 1)

From this point of view, questions require the learner to analyze and organize the text, to identify its logical or historical consistency, and to make the connection between it and sources that have already been studied. The questions also introduce new terminology and evaluations and invite the student to explain certain terms or to base them on sources as well as analyze the advantages and shortcomings of each approach. Questions are also designed to elicit explanations for different events and their significance, and to relate them to other issues and circumstances. This leads the mediatee to build alternatives or possible reasons and discover the historical and theological underpinnings of the subject.

Talmudic study incorporates questioning in a formal way, even giving the questions special descriptive names that identify their purpose and guide the learner toward the kind of cognitive activity dictated by the form of the question. This can be considered an *explicit* mediation of intentionality. Further, the didactic created by the questions does not rely on immediate evidence but requires constructing (or reconstructing) from the past from multiple sources and previous learning. Here, we briefly describe the main types of questioning embedded in the processes of learning and offer brief examples: (1) questions designed to prompt the respondent to find differences between two approaches, viewpoints, or meanings (*maitaivi*)—finding the underlying differences in seemingly contradictory opinions; (2) questions that indicate a difference of opinion between two sources (*rami veriminu*)—finding balance through deductive reasoning and comparative analyses; (3) questions that reconstruct basic premises or clarify contradictory viewpoints, leading to understanding and analysis of abstract relationships (*mai taama*—literally, "What is the point?"); (4) questions that invoke logic to cope with multiple sources of information and find "hidden" meaning (*yud gimmel midot*—literally, the "13 attributes of mercy")—often through formulation of more precise questions; (5) questions that call for a mental act of elaboration, to formulate the problem underlying the contradiction—perhaps by reformulating the problem; (6) questions that search for the reason for the problem, leading to finding strategies to deal with the particular question through reconstruction of meaningful past events—(*ibye lei*—"What is the reason for the problem?"); (7) questions directed toward extension (*mai ka mashma lan*) "What does this teach us?"—a decoding of the meaning; and (8) questions that direct the learning toward (*mna annei milei and mna lan*) "Where does this information or ideation come from?" (*mai nafka mina*) "What do we learn from this?" "What can be deduced from it?"—such questions call for a wider sweep of information, invoking additional multiple sources.

SUMMARIZING THE CONTRIBUTIONS AND CONTRASTS

Mediated learning questions create awareness in the learner that not all answers are equally acceptable or applicable. Answers are based on rules, principles, and accepted interpretations. Questions thus play a role far in excess of plain pragmatic decisions.

For instance, when two opinions concur, why do we need two sources? Why is it not sufficient to rely on one source? Questions are exercises in higher mental processes and in particular in sharpening the need of the learner to use logical evidence as a way of interacting with the teacher, who frames the question and guides the learner through a process of internalization. The message becomes: Don't accept each answer at face value. Don't accept answers such as "because!" without giving a reason and searching for understanding. Make the answer understood, and don't accept simple, unsupported explanations or simple fantasy as sources of decisions.

With regard to the three paradigms we deal with in this chapter, we can say that all three paradigms evoke the need to continually explore the *what, how, when, where,* and *why* of both the past and the future, albeit with different emphases and implications for deepening cognitive processes.

CHAPTER 10

Mediated Learning Experience and "Generation Y"

Implications for Parents and Teachers

Refael S. Feuerstein

The MLE theory presented in this book was developed in the 1950s and 1960s. Since then, the world has undergone many changes: Man reached the moon; the PC was born; the brain sciences have taught us that the brain is flexible and developing. And the theory of mediated learning with its applications has not only survived, but the demand for it has grown increasingly. It seems to us that the question of how culture and technology have influenced the way in which the theory is regarded and applied has not yet been addressed in research. And with particular relevance for those of the current younger generation who are coming into influence and action in today's world—our "working definition" of *Generation Y*, a term that has been coined for those who were born into the electronic revolution of the last several decades. And it will certainly produce interesting insights regarding the manner in which the important concepts—such as "learning and thinking" in general, and "mediated learning" in particular—have been perceived. Such a broad analysis will not obviously come within the purview of this short chapter. Nevertheless, we feel that we cannot present the theory and its applications without at least discussing the significance of mediation to what we today call Generation Y.

MEDIATED LEARNING EXPERIENCE FOR GENERATION Y

Information, Knowledge, and Processing

A first question: Is information at the heart of the requirement for learning and mastery of content for the children of Generation Y? Is information the relative advantage of the teacher in our era? It seems to us that we already know the answer is "no." Furthermore, as we are all aware, at the touch of a button, the young pupil can discover a wealth of knowledge in every field. But what is the depth of "web" knowledge, its thoroughness, the degree of its accuracy or its validity? That poses an additional question. It seems that the sense of innovation that the pupil once experienced when the teacher imparted knowledge—the exciting feeling at the heart of the learning pleasure and the zeal for applying it—has already almost vanished from the world. Is "discovery" from the web a less intense experience than actual, hands-on, real-time exploration of the world? And even if pupils have not yet used the search engine to find the relevant material, they know that they have the power to do so and thus do not need to invest precious time listening to a teacher or lecturer, or even more so, going out into the world to gather data and feel/interpret it!

This means that even the sense of dependence on the teacher, this hierarchical sense between the source of the knowledge and the lack of knowledge, has also disappeared or has been significantly diluted! It is not necessarily bad news that the "academic podium/frontal teaching style" that teachers invoked when instructing pupils now must be replaced by a circular/collaborative formation in which the teacher sits with the students as an equal (albeit with a deeper knowledge base) among equals.

This, incidentally, does not characterize only teacher–pupil relations, but it also impacts on the expert's relations with his clients who sometimes are more up to date regarding innovations in the field, like doctors and their patients who come to consultations armed with very detailed knowledge (usually from the Internet). When doctors were students, they were given optimal conditions for studying: informed lecturers, library facilities, time to write papers and to receive reactions to them—in short, optimal conditions for studying. And then the student finished the course of studies in medicine and began to swim in the ocean of life. But the medical world continues to develop and advance, but our friend the doctor was increasingly occupied, running from patient to patient. When was there time to learn? How to keep up to date? Did the "optimal conditions," even over an extended period of time, teach *how to learn to learn*, with maximum efficiency when the optimal conditions for studying no longer exist and the necessity for learning is far more important and urgent?

If we return to the student or the pupil, we shall easily discern that a potential gap does not lie in lack of knowledge or lack of means to find it. The real problem is the surfeit of knowledge. Knowledge "attacks us" all the time; it does not wait for us to require it; it is so accessible that it seems to burst upon us. It seems, as it were, to possess life powers of its own that know how to locate our needs, our areas of interest. You ask for one article on the Internet, and hundreds, even thousands, jump into view that deal with the same subject or related ones. The wealth of knowledge redefines the term *ignorance* in a new light. A new variant of the "ignorant person" is the one who knows a lot but knows nothing. No wonder then that the important processes get lost. As the old saying goes, "One can't see the forest for the trees."

The Role of the Teacher in These Times

Therefore, what is the function of the teacher in this era? Today more than ever, the teacher must become a mediator. The essence of mediation in the generation of learners that we have described as within the *Generation Y* may well require imparting a variety of processing abilities and their application to the material being studied. This function is a double one. The first is to impart processing abilities, which will enable the pupil to be an independent learner. The second is to process with the student the material being studied by the conscious use of the relevant strategies. The teacher must continue to impart knowledge. Reliable and deep knowledge continues to be an important commodity, but it has to be transmitted in a dialogical and mediated fashion. The mediator/educator must create the knowledge together with the students. They (teacher and students together) must understand why knowledge has developed in the way it has. They should suggest alternative assumptions, other solutions that could be acceptable to valid and meaningful formulations of conclusions. The mediator has to lead the group to the core of the knowledge, to the processes that lead to it, and thereby obtain the knowledge that can be connected with other knowledge. In the eyes of the mediator, the open possibilities are made possible by the deep understanding of the processes that engendered the knowledge. These processes never end, because every theory leaves areas that have not been resolved. Dogmatic understanding of the knowledge does not involve the need to continue searching or inquiring, or even to test understandings and relevance. Bringing a learning process to the understanding of knowledge invites the learner to continue to search, analyze, criticize, and further to connect it to other knowledge networks that are found to be related to the original knowledge.

Such a mediator/teacher will exchange the hierarchical model of teaching for a dialogical model that gives the teacher superiority due to being equipped with strategies and processes that have engendered the knowledge that is imparted to pupils. Learning pleasure is also likely to increase among the pupils, because they feel the innovation in the teaching process. Here, the teacher/mediator meets students in a place (and modality) that they could not obtain in the web world. The web world is one of manufacturing, with rapid access and little interrelationship of content and implications, presented to the user already digested and pre-evaluated. The amount of patience required in discussion, and the "ramified thinking" characteristic of it, demands resources of time and attention that do not exist in the online world. Thus the knowledge gained is rendered superficial and essentially uncritical—without the processes we are describing throughout this chapter, and just above.

Professionals, like our aforementioned doctors—if they were subjected to an instructional modality and were the graduates of a *mediated* academy—will go out into the employment world equipped not only with content but also with a wealth of thinking and learning processes that will serve to garner efficient learning in spite of the constraints of the employment world.

WHAT ARE THE IMPLICATIONS FOR GENERATION Y?

If everything is in our cellphones, described as "smart phones" because they can do so much, what is missing? Where do we develop meaningful and deep friendships? Is electronic contact as meaningful and satisfying as face-to-face, hand-to-hand contact? Where do we develop our sense of morality and ethics, in the absence of direct human contact—when we cannot look someone in the eyes, observe the tensing or relaxing of the body, feel the mutuality of a jointly experienced event?

The Effects on *Attention*

I once gave a workshop to senior managers of a certain organization. One of the participants put a question to me: When I came to answer her, I immediately realized that she was no longer listening to me. She was busy writing a message on her smart phone, before I could answer. She was in her 40s, and we know that it is not just Generation Yers who are attached to their digital devices. But when we talk about *Generation Y*, we are talking about more than 1,000 SMS messages sent to children per day. Observe modern adolescents congregating during recess at school, or waiting to enter the building at the beginning of the day. They are often not talking to one another, but are texting on their cellphones, often about one another, but "electronically" behind their backs, so to speak! Another all too frequently observed phenomena is a couple dining in a restaurant not talking to one another but absorbed with their cellphones, or perhaps worst of all, a parent walking a child to school while talking on the phone instead of to the child!

The Consequences for Modern Life

All this does not take into account the films and sites and music available in the palm of the hand of each one of us. We hear about more and more interpersonal encounters where the participants are asked to place their cellphones in the center of the table until the end of the meeting. But is this sufficient? We read that the problem of attention has become strategic, and that it is not sufficient to impose external rules and limitations that will limit the use of the smart phones. One must fight to impart to the user of the new technologies those abilities that are within the range of abilities but are not fostered (and may in fact be interfering with) those that need to be developed.

However, it appears that the influence of the new technologies on attention lies not only in the competition with other factors (such as the teacher in class, friends, and so forth), but also in the change of our attention practices, even when our phones are turned off. The short messages characterizing the dialogue in the various social networks (Facebook, Twitter, etc.) have created a fragmented, abbreviated, shallow, and partial form of speech (and learning). The hunger for stimuli creates a situation in which a complex lecture that advances slowly to its goal causes the rapid disconnection of the young listeners from the lecturer. They are quite simply bored. Reading has diminished or almost been eliminated, because "it does not keep up with the tempo" of the supply of stimuli, relative to the alternatives. Incidentally, if you the reader have made it to this chapter, it means that you don't really belong to Generation Y, or have overcome its debilitating effects, but in some respects it means that you are a kind of dinosaur. But rather than be insulted, your achievement is to be saluted! And our goal is to find ways to help others to learn or recapture similar skills!

THE MEDIATED LEARNING EXPERIENCE RESPONSE TO THIS SITUATION

Given the situation described above, the provision of mediated learning experience is critical in the development of the learning of the child, and in fact for all of us. This is especially relevant to what we have described as mediation for the "regulation and control of behavior" at several earlier places in this book. Of course, we offer no judgmental stand against the new technologies because they constitute an existing and incontrovertible fact, and they undeniably add much to the qualities of our lives. Under the right circumstances—parental and education—they can offer benefits for the process of learning. We have seen many such instances, but teachers and parents must plan and strategize to bring this about!

However, the quality of mediation for behavior regulation has to begin at the stage of very early infancy. The parents must make sure to create eye contact with their babies when they take them in their arms. Whenever they tell their daughter a story, they must take special care that their daughter's attention will be focused on the pictures in the story and on their eyes when they talk to her. It is still more important that they use full and complex sentences as part of the dialogue with their children in order to create a cognitive and emotional infrastructure that will serve as an alternative to the bursting rivers of stimuli that the child will encounter as he or she grows up. The mediator has to ensure that the child will understand what the dominant stimulus is in a given context, in comparison with the totality of the many stimuli appearing in the environment. When the mediating parents go to choose a present for their children, it is best that they select an interactive game that requires dialogue, eye contact, talking together, planning, and sitting for a relatively long time. All this should be done in order to expand the child's attention span and to ensure that the child, when he or she grows up, will be able to focus attention on one continuing stimulus—for example, later in school classrooms, a 45-minute lesson during which the child (as pupil) must focus on the teacher.

In this connection, the "problem" in providing MLE directed toward focusing attention must be to recognize and strategize how to provide input to attend to what is likely to be the "pale" stimulus (the teacher's frontal and verbal presentation) compared with numerous other "strong" and seductive stimuli (such as a TV program, a computer game, and so forth) that the child is usually intensively exposed to. How do we attract the child's attention, how do we learn to divert from the distractors and maintain focus on the important but not so powerful stimuli in the learning environments? The challenge for MLE is to make both the gathering of information and the formulation of conclusions meaningful, and create differentiations, so that the "attention diverters" do not dominate the processes of learning. If we achieve this goal, the learner will come to encounters with the new media with a different and more cognitively "deep" point of view.

Regulating and Controlling Behavior

When we speak of mediation for the regulation of behavior, we must consider strategies for planning, associating, and limiting focus and differentiation. Many of these issues have been addressed in this book. The application of this principle is simply stated: "What do you want to see? What are you looking for?" If we are considering the new media modalities, additional issues include "For how long will we look?" In strategies for regulation and control of behavior, the clock—and an awareness of time—must be a prominent aspect of the interaction when the child enters the intoxicating world of the new media. Parents now face dilemmas with their children regarding regulating the amount of time spent with the new media, and balancing the other learning and developmental activities to which children should be exposed.

The regulation and control of behavior, in this context, must therefore work in two opposite directions: (1) to extend and prolong the child's attention capacity for the important but relatively "pale" stimuli from reading a story, doing homework, playing directly interactive games, and doing jigsaw puzzles, to name but a few of the many possibilities; and (2) there must be a limiting, controlling, and differentiating quality to the mediation when it is a matter of attractive and addictive stimuli. The importance of this second aspect is heightened by our knowledge that the game makers and the promotion of the new media have built in strategies to seduce more time and extended engagement with them—it is a matter of serious scientific inquiry and structure in the "industry."

The Consequences of Lack of Control

The limiting mediation toward the stimuli arising from the new media does not have to be negative in nature. We are not suggesting outright prohibiting or waging war against these stimuli. If so, we will lose! The behavioral regulatory mediation must lead to conscious and planned behavior of the child. I suppose that each parent knows from close observation the automatic behavior of the child toward the computer or other types of devices (the cellphone, tablet, and so on). If one becomes bored, the hand goes out to the redemptive machine. This can lead to aimless wandering in the Internet (otherwise called "surfing"), finding a computer game without limitations. The best metaphors are wandering, navigating, or the familiar surfing.

It is as if the learner, as a young or naïve child, would wander through the streets aimlessly for hours on end, with no definitive goal. It's not that it's forbidden to explore, but—to use a concrete example—if the child walks the streets of a city, or around a shopping center for hours each day without a goal or purpose, the average parent would feel uncomfortable with such aimless and uncontrolled behavior, especially when it represents an important component of the child's daily schedule and takes up many hours each day. This has become a major concern in cities where the school day is limited, and students have large portions of their day without structure or purpose—Singapore is one such place where this has become a major problem. And there are many other such places!

Browsing the Internet is no better, and potentially is much worse. The metaphor is close—the exploring is quite accessible. It doesn't require a physical effort, and is all based on tiny movements of a single finger. And the explorer is subject to the rich and powerful content that is readily available. It is said that the students who produced the Columbine High School in Colorado tragedy got most of their ideas and made their plans from the Internet. To emphasize this point and stay with our initial metaphor, the child who wanders the streets for hours per day would become tired, would feel hunger and thirst, would feel cold and get wet from the pouring rain. But sitting in front of the computer screen or holding the colorful (you choose your favorite color) cellphone does not exact any price; it is comfortable and easy. The low level of physical stress is likely to reinforce the automatic nature of the behavior. Sitting in one's comfortable chair in a familiar space, there is no physiological control liable to undermine the automatic tranquility accompanying the activity opposite the new media.

What to Do?

Therefore, the mediating parent and teacher must slow down the rate of activity of the child when it comes to "pressing the button." But we're not talking about slowdown for its own sake. We mean a slowdown that is liable to exploit the interval created in order to define the goal of the surfing and its extent by making the thought process *explicit*: "What site do I want to surf?" "For what purpose am I searching?" "What do I want to do with what I find there?" "For how long shall I search?" and many more such orienting questions. As a result of defining the surfing aim, there can be other more concrete means of control: a clock, a note pinned on the computer, a personal reminder. More advanced levels of mediation will try to understand with the child what was gained from the specific surfing. What was learned from it? What are the next steps in the search, and ultimately, the learning process?

The ultimate goal is to enhance the child's surfing consciousness and to build habits of planning, control, and criticism when new media modalities are utilized. Of course, these habits must be mediated at a very young age when the child is easy to influence and is open to receive mediation in this sweeping area.

CONSEQUENCES FOR THE DEVELOPMENT
OF LEARNING POTENTIAL

The Disappearance of Effort, and Educating for Laziness

For those of us who function within the age of computers, our reaction to our computers when they seem to work "slowly" is an apt metaphor for the point we make at this point in our discourse. There may be several reasons for the apparent delays, but what is important here is the *impatience* that affects us when we must wait! We count the seconds, rubbing our hands impatiently until the screen boots up. A simple calculation will reveal that it is all in all a matter of waiting just a few seconds. Why does it bother us so? Is it an expression of a kind of laziness? Is it because, as members of *Generation Y*, we are accustomed to having everything immediately available, coming easily to us, not having to struggle (or wait)? For earlier generations, without the benefit of our electronic cocoons, how much time and effort was required for producing responses, gathering and comparing information, and other such pursuits? How much time was required for handwriting a document or a university paper, and the thoughtful process of composing letters and sending them, waiting for their arrival and responses, or standing in long lines in order to carry out an action that today everyone carries out at home wearing slippers in almost immediate "real time"?

What we are describing, with its implication for the processes of learning, is the impact of the computer (and its electronic brethren) on life and the extent to which it has replaced the effort of human beings in the performance of complex and involved actions. Effort, which was once a value and a profound expression of human action, has been replaced by "the ease" of the action.

One significant expression of the human spirit was a person's readiness to "sacrifice" time for chosen actions to which significance was assigned. Today, an action has value the more it is efficient and quick. You will frequently hear members of the authors' generation (Generation X and above) express amazement at the saving of effort that the computer and the Internet provides, saving for them their precious time. Generation Y (our most current students and learners) has grown up in a world that is all Internet. They, of course, are not amazed—they take it for granted. Here is perhaps the source of their strength, but also of their weakness. The need for human effort has not departed from the world. We meet the need for effort in the world of employment, and in the world of studies and creativity. The need for effort is also found in blue-collar employment sectors.

Thus, when Generation Y enters the education system—from elementary levels through higher education—its threshold for frustration is low, its demand for quality is low, and it does not bring with it what Arthur Costa has labeled "the habits of mind." Analogously, life has become based on "fast food," the "fast food" of the Internet world. When a learning or intellectual effort is demanded, such as memorizing knowledge, the experience is often one of weakness and helplessness. This difficulty in making an effort impacts severely on students' ability "to scale the heights" in the field of studies.

One response to the situation we describe is to diagnose a "learning deficiency" that an increasing proportion of pupils suffer—they are not seen as lazy, but rather as "disabled." Recognizing that some students are truly disabled, we must be careful not to too readily remove from students the stigma of responsibility and demand. Saying, "They simply were born like that" removes from *them* the need to make a serious effort and to change. Many say and write: "Once we called them lazy and insulted them; today we know that they are suffering from some kind of learning deficiency." And the focus shifts to special educational interventions that take the onus away from the individual's responsibility and potential. And to some degree there is a kind of truth here: Does a child born into the world of computers need to know the multiplication tables by heart? Does the advanced research student need to know how to compute a test of statistical significance? Does the high school student need to know how to search for references? And closer to our point: Does the child who has the world of stimuli at easy and immediate access need to make an effort to read book-length texts? Thus, we realize this bitter truth, that although many students of the generation we have been describing are avid readers, many others read very little that does not appear on an electronic screen. By simply pressing a button, without any understanding and almost unconsciously, we activate systems that once required countless man hours. And further I believe that the process of reading print in text invokes a deeper, more reflective kind of learning—more mentally representational, with richly structured images.

The Need for Mediation

One of the most significant challenges of mediation is to restore the value of effort to its previously rightful and honored place. But how do we mediate for effort? How do we create the inner need of making an effort? The question we have posed here is answered by placing the emphasis on the creation of need, before that of creation of ability. Consequently, the major challenge confronting mediation is the creation of the inner need and urge to make an effort. Given the easy access we have described above, we have first of all to define where the effort is demanded. And after that, how is it possible to mediate the need to the child and the adolescent, to go beyond the superficiality and incompleteness of the "Internet" knowledge? The challenge becomes the need to expend effort, the meaningfulness of knowing deeply, of investing the requisite cognitive and emotional effort in order to close the gap between the body of knowledge students have acquired (albeit superficially) and that which is constantly developing that requires depth of meaning and insight.

We are not arguing for musty and staid learning environments. The need for effort can be created by means of sports lessons, as well as by means of high-level learning demands. The point is that there is a need for effort of a different kind, which is *a thinking effort*. We must create cognitive effort, and stress must be laid on mediation for curiosity and inquiry.

> Consider students who possess at their fingertips the best technology, in whose development thousands of man hours were invested. Should they not be amazed and ask themselves how this wonder is at all possible? How do the buttons that I press know how to find the cellphone number that I am dialing? And how does the phone know how to remain connected with its constant movement? These are, of course, only the opening questions. On no account must we remain only "passive consumers" of the technology; we must develop an active approach to the knowledge presented to us so easily, so ubiquitously.

In our view, we must ensure the investigative, processing tendency in two ways. The first and most basic one is by activating programs to encourage and develop thinking. These mediation-centered programs, such as, for example, the Feuerstein Instrumental Enrichment (FIE), constitute a systematic and structured experience for creating an intellectual effort whose goal is to solve other logical problems. However, in that program it is emphasized that it is not the answers to the tasks that are the primary objective, but rather *the way in which the solution was achieved.*

Mediating for consciousness and control of the thinking process is designed to overcome the effects that we have described above: to stop, plan, correct, to make assumptions about the continuation of the work process, and to assess what I have done while making a comparison with a model or instruction I have received. All these very partial examples require an effort, whose main objective is to interfere with the convenience of automatic thinking that does not require effort. All of these are the fruits of mediated learning. The mediating teacher builds the knowledge together with the pupil. It does not come in packages, in built-in tables. It is organized and processed with the students—together, they weave the fabric connecting the information, strategies, rules, and so on, creating a "theory of knowledge" that unites with other immediate or potential bodies of meaningful knowledge.

When the mediated didactic becomes the main dialogue in the classroom, it leads to a continuous intellectual effort, to situations in which students do not accept reality just as it is, to situations of curiosity and a constant search for solutions. A graduate of educational systems that not only teaches how to think but also implants the need to think will prepare students for a life of continuous change—a life in which the fact that you control the technology that you learned in school will not stop you from learning the new technology that you have never before encountered but will need in order to be adaptive.

The mediating dialogue makes the pupil active in the processes of acquiring knowledge. Through the mediating dialogue, the pupil delves deeply into the manner in which new knowledge has been and will continue to be mastered. The mediating dialogue turns the pupil into someone who knows how to locate the life lines that enable efficient mastery of new knowledge. But, above all, the graduate of mediating education is not afraid to make an effort. On the contrary, effort is welcomed and serves as a source of mastery and satisfaction.

SUMMING UP

It is impossible to ignore the fact that the digital media are dangerous for our children. More and more parent organizations, educators, and researchers call on parents to be active regarding the places in which their children are surfing and children's reliance upon and isolation with their "devices."

Although it is clear that all these "technical" means are an essential component of our modern lives, they alone cannot be sufficient. This is the role and necessity of mediated learning experience, for parents in the home and for teachers in the classroom. In this chapter we have outlined the problem and described its objective.

The aim of family mediation in this context is to create a focus of internal control in the child. The parent who protects and filters is at first the primary source of mediation, but cannot go on with this function indefinitely, as the child goes out into the world. The parent has only a few years in which to create "a little parent" in the child who is growing into adolescence. The "little parent" in our language is an internal mediator. The aim of the mediation in the final analysis is to turn our children into self-mediators as they are growing up. In our context, a self-mediator is someone who knows how to deal with the materials offered on our computers and the numerous social networks with wisdom and discretion. It is no secret that the murky subject matter circulating in the Internet appeals to our "primal needs," to our urges and most primitive instincts. It is no secret that the Internet is full of dishonest forces of temptation. If parents wish their children to be independent in the future in their ability to filter and select the contents of the social media, so easily and seductively accessible, it is not enough that the mediator filters, prevents, keeps track, limits. This seems to be the current advice that is given. Yet, as parents, we must mediate all these actions to our sons and daughters. This means that parents must confide in their children their innermost considerations and build with them together the filtering system that reduces exposure to noxious matter. In doing this, the steps taken by parents are procedural, filled with thought and discretion, and in the main are shared by both the parents and their children. Teachers in schools must reinforce the self-monitoring developed by parents and deepen it as they teach students to use the Internet and web tools in support of their research and learning. Parents and teachers can take the principles of the mediation that have been found to be effective in the education of children and adults to become independent and active learners, and apply them for renewed relevance to the educational challenges confronting the new generation.

Annotated Bibliography

These references will help the reader who would like to become more familiar with the theoretical and practical applications of the Feuerstein approach to cognitive modifiability and mediated learning experience.

Feuerstein, R., Feuerstein, R. S., & Falik, L. H. (2010). *Beyond smarter: mediated learning and the brain's capacity to change.* New York, NY: Teachers College Press.
> *The most up-to-date summary of the theory of structural cognitive modifiability, mediated learning, and the various methods of application, written in a way to bring the information regarding education and psychology to the general reader.*

Feuerstein, R., Feuerstein, R. S., Falik, L. H., & Rand, Y. (2006). *Creating and enhancing cognitive modifiability: The Feuerstein Instrumental Enrichment program.* Jerusalem, Israel: ICELP Publications.
> *This book offers the most detailed discussion of the operational concepts of the cognitive functions, the Cognitive Map, and the parameters of mediated learning experience. They are integrated into the structure and application of the Instrumental Standard and Basic programs. Brief descriptions of the instruments are included, as well as applications to various learning needs and situations.*

Feuerstein, R., Feuerstein, R. S., Falik, L. H., & Rand, Y. (2002). *The dynamic assessment of cognitive modifiability: The learning propensity assessment device, theory, instruments, and techniques.* Jerusalem, Israel: ICELP Press.
> *A detailed description of the Learning Propensity Assessment Device (LPAD) as a tool of dynamic assessment. A presentation of the background, theory, and applications of the assessment method. Presentation of both LPAD-Standard and LPAD-Basic (the instruments for the young child). Examples of interventions and the research support for the method.*

Feuerstein, R., Falik, L. H., Feuerstein, R. S., & Bohacs, K. (2013). *A think-aloud and talk-aloud approach to building language: Overcoming disability delay and deficiency.* New York, NY: Teachers College Press.
> *A description of a mediation-based approach to language stimulation and development. Presentation of the theoretical, developmental, and applicational*

elements of the approach. Case histories describing the ways in which the method is applied are presented.

Feuerstein, R., Rand, Y., & Feuerstein, R. A. (2006). *You love me . . . don't accept me as I am.* Jerusalem, Israel: The International Center for Enhancement of Learning Potential.

The classic book in the Feuerstein literature, first published in 1988 and since revised. The importance and description of mediated learning experience is emphasized. Lengthy case histories of individuals with special needs are presented that show how mediated learning experience helps overcome disabilities and move special-needs children and youth to more normalized experiences and lives. A final chapter on inclusion of special needs in normalized environments is an important feature of this more recent edition.

Lewin-Benham, A., & Feuerstein, R. (2012). *What learning looks like: Mediated learning in theory and practice.* New York, NY: Teachers College Press.

A book describing how mediated learning experience can be applied to the various learning experiences available to children. An emphasis is offered on how parents and teachers can mediate various learning experiences, in the classroom and in family interactions. The museum is identified as a readily accessible source of learning experience, with many illustrative examples.

References

Burt, C. (1940) *The factors of the mind*. London, UK: University of London Press.

Carbone, V. J., O'Brian, L., Sweeney-Kerwin, E. J., & Albert, K. M. (2013). Teaching eye contact to children with autism: A conceptual analysis and single case study. *Education and Treatment of Children, 36*(2), 139–159.

Davidson, R. J. (2004). Well-being and affective style: Neural substrates and biobehavioral correlates. *Philosophical Transactions Royal Society of London*, B, *359*, 1395–1411.

Diamond, J. (2012). *The world until yesterday: What can we learn from traditional societies?* New York, NY: Penguin Books.

Doidge, N. (2007). *The brain that changes itself*. New York, NY: Viking.

Exodus, IV: 1 (1988). Tanach. *The Holy Scriptures*. New York, NY: Jewish Publication Society.

Feuerstein, R., & Falik, L. H. (2010). Learning to think, thinking to learn: A comparative analysis of three approaches to instruction. *Journal of Cognitive Education and Psychology, 9*, 1, 4–20.

Feuerstein, R., Falik, L. H., Feuerstein, R. S., & Bohacs, K. (2013). *A think-aloud and talk-aloud approach to building language: Overcoming disability, delay, and deficiency*. New York, NY: Teachers College Press.

Feuerstein, R., Feuerstein, R. S., & Falik, L. H. (2010). *Beyond smarter: mediated learning and the brain's capacity to change*. New York, NY: Teachers College Press.

Feuerstein, R., Feuerstein, R. S., Falik, L. H., & Rand, Y. (2002). *The dynamic assessment of cognitive modifiability: The learning propensity assessment device, theory, instruments, and techniques*. Jerusalem, Israel: ICELP Press.

Feuerstein, R., & Lewin-Benham, A. (2012). *What learning looks like: mediated learning in theory and practice, K-6*. New York, NY: Teachers College Press.

Feuerstein, R., Rand, Y., & Feuerstein, R. A. (2006). *You love me . . . don't accept me as I am*. Jerusalem, Israel: The International Center for Enhancement of Learning Potential.

Feuerstein, R., Rand, Y., & Hoffman, M. B. (1979). *The dynamic assessment of retarded performers*. Baltimore, MD: University Park Press.

Feuerstein, R., Rand, Y., Hoffman, M. B., & Miller, R. B. (1980). *Instrumental enrichment*. Baltimore, MD: University Park Press.

Feuerstein, S. (2002). *Biblical and Talmudic antecedents of mediated learning experience theory: Educational and didactic implications for inter-generational cultural transmission*. Jerusalem, Israel: ICELP Publications.

Gallesse V. (2003). The manifold nature of interpersonal relations: From control to representation. *Philosophical Transactions of the Royal Society of London*, B, *358*, 517–528.

Gallesse, V. (2003). The roots of empathy: The shared manifold hypothesis and the neural basis of intersubjectivity. *Psychopathology*, *36*, 171–180.

Gallesse, V. (2005). "Being like me": Self-other identity, mirror neurons and empathy. In S. Hurley & N. Chater (Eds.), *Perspectives on imitation: From cognitive neuroscience to social science* (Vol. 1) (pp. 101–118). Cambridge, MA: MIT Press.

Gallesse, V. (2009). Mirror neurons, embodied simulation, and the neural basis of social identification. *Psychoanalytic Dialogues*, *19*, 519–536.

Gallesse, V., & Lakoff, G. (2005). The brain's concepts: The role of the sensory-motor system in conceptual knowledge. *Cognitive Neuropsychology, 22*(3/4), 455–479.

Gladwell, M. (2000). *The tipping point: How little things can make a big difference*. New York, NY: Little Brown.

Goleman, D. (2006). *Social intelligence*. New York, NY: Bantam.

Gould, S. J. (1996). *The mismeasure of man*. New York, NY: W. W. Norton.

Herrnstein, R. J., & Murray, C. (1994). *The bell curve: Intelligence and class structure in American life*. New York, NY: Free Press Paperback.

Herz-Piccioto, I., & Delwiche, L. (2009). The rise in autism and the role of age at diagnosis. *Epidemiology*, *20*(1), 84–90.

Hilchot Talmud Torah IV, par. 4–9. Talmud Bavli. Jerusalem, Israel: Meshorah Publications.

Jensen, A. R. (1969). How much can we boost IQ and scholastic achievement? *Harvard Educational Review*, *39*, 1–123.

Kamin, L. J. (1974). *The science and politics of IQ*. Potomac, MD: Lawrence Erlbaum.

Kandel, E. R. (2006). *In search of memory: The emergence of a new science of the mind*. New York, NY: W. W. Norton & Company.

Kleim , J. A., & Jones, T. A (2008). Principles of experience-dependent neural plasticity: Implications for rehabilitation after brain damage. [Supplement]. *Journal of Speech, Language, and Hearing Research*, *51*, 5225–5231.

Klein, P. (1996). *Early intervention: Cross-cultural experiences with a mediational approach*. London, England: Routledge.

Lewin-Benham, A., & Feuerstein, R. (2012). *What learning looks like: Mediated learning in theory and practice*. New York, NY: Teachers College Press.

Lifshitz, H. (1995). *Cognitive modifiability among elderly mentally retarded people* (Doctoral dissertation, School of Education, Bar-Ilan University).

Merzenech, M. (2004). Specialization of primary auditory cortex processing by sound exposure in the "critical period." *Proceedings of the National Academy of Sciences, 101*(18), 70–74.

Newshaffer, C. J., Croen, L. A., Daniels, J., et al. (2007). The epidemiology of autism spectrum disorders. *Annual Review of Public Health, 28*, 235–258.

Paul, R., & Elder, L. (2006). *The art of Socratic questioning*. Dillon Beach, CA: Foundation for Critical Thinking.

Pearson, P. D., & Gallagher, M. (1983). The instruction of reading comprehension. *Contemporary Educational Psychology, 4*(8), 317–344.

Pressinger, R. W. (1997). *Environmental circumstances that can damage the developing brain*. Special Education Department, University of South Florida. Retrieved from www. Tox/chem/pregnancy/learning disabilities.htm

Ramachandran, V. S. (1995). Mirror neurons and imitation learning as the driving force behind "the great leap forward" in human evolution. *Edge: The third culture*. Retrieved from www.edge.org/3rd_culture/

Rand, Y., Tannenbaum, A., Feuerstein, R., & Mintzker, Y. (1981). The Instrumental Enrichment program: Immediate and long-term effects. In. P. Mittler (Ed.), *Frontiers of knowledge in retardation*, Vol. 1 (pp. 141–152). Baltimore, MD: University Park Press.

Reik, M. (2007). Stability and flexibility of epigenetic regulation in mammalian development. *Nature, 447*, 425–432.

Rizzolatti, G., & Craighero, L. (2004). The mirror neuron system. *Annual Review of Neurosciences, 27*, 169–192.

Schwartz, J. M., & Begley, S. (2002). *The mind and the brain: Neuroplasticity and the power of mental force*. New York, NY: Regan Books/Harper Collins.

Siegel, D. J. (2010). *Mindsight: The new science of personal transformation*. New York, NY: Bantam.

Skodak, M. (1942). Intellectual growth of children in foster homes. In R. G. Barker, J. S. Kounin, & H. F. Wright (Eds.), *Child behavior and development* (pp. 259–278). New York, NY: McGraw-Hill.

Skodak, M., & Skeels, H. M. (1949). A final follow-up study of one hundred adopted children. *Journal of Genetic Psychology, 75*, 85–125.

Spector, T. (2012). *Identically different: Why you can change your genes*. London, England: Weidenfeld & Nicholson.

Tomasello, M. (1999). *The cultural origins of human cognition*. Cambridge, MA: MIT Press.

Tomasello, M., Kruger, A. C., & Ratner, H. H. (1993). Cultural learning. *Behavioral and Brain Sciences, 16*, 495–552.

Umlita, M. A., Kohler, E., Gallese, V., Fogassi, L., & Fadiga, L. (2001). "I know what you are doing": A neurological study. *Neuron, 32*, 91–101.

Index

About the Authors

Professor Falik is emeritus professor of counseling at San Francisco State University (USA) and a senior scholar focusing on training, research, and professional development at the international Feuerstein Institute (formerly, the International Center for the Enhancement of Learning Potential [ICELP]) in Jerusalem, Israel. He is author and coauthor of a number of books and research papers on dynamic assessment (LPAD), the Feuerstein Instrumental Enrichment (FIE) program, and mediated learning experience. He is a clinical and educational psychologist with extensive experience with the training and application of FIE and the LPAD in child, adolescent, and adult populations, focusing on both learning disabilities and academic performance and enhancement objectives.

Rabbi Refael S. Feuerstein is chairman of the Feuerstein Institute (formerly ICELP) in Jerusalem, Israel. He has furthered the work of Professor Reuven Feuerstein by extending the theoretical and practical applications of programs to materialize structural cognitive modifiability, bringing the practical benefits of this theory to an increasingly diverse range of populations and applications. He is also the primary developer of the Instrumental Enrichment—Basic and Learning Propensity Device—basic programs that are applied to young children and severely low-functioning older learners.

Professor Reuven Feuerstein formulated the theory of structural cognitive modifiability (SCM) and mediated learning experience (MLE) in the 1950s, as a response to the need to save the children who survived the Holocaust. Professor Feuerstein founded the Hadassah-WIZO-Canada Research Institute, which became the International Center for the Enhancement of Learning Potential (ICELP), and is now the Feuerstein Institute. He has fostered the development of programs for the assessment and intervention of learning and development, based on his theories, that have generated a new field of application—dynamic assessment and the improvement of cognitive functioning. These programs have been disseminated throughout the world, and have been translated into more than 17 languages. He continued to develop his concepts, to stimulate scholars and practitioners from all corners of the world, and to see and help children and families almost to the day he passed away at the end of May 2014, at the age of 92.